TROUBLEMAKERS

Troublemakers

Power, Representation, and the Fiction
of the Mass Worker

WILLIAM SCOTT

Rutgers University Press
NEW BRUNSWICK, NEW JERSEY, AND LONDON

Copyright © 2012 by William Scott. All rights reserved

No part of this book may be reproduced or utilized in any form or by any means, electronic or mechanical, or by any information storage and retrieval system, without written permission from the publisher. Please contact Rutgers University Press, 100 Joyce Kilmer Avenue, Piscataway, NJ 08854–8099. The only exception to this prohibition is "fair use" as defined by U.S. copyright law.

Visit our Web site: http://rutgerspress.rutgers.edu

Manufactured in the United States of America

LIBRARY OF CONGRESS CATALOGING-IN-PUBLICATION DATA

Scott, William.
  Troublemakers : power, representation, and the fiction of the mass worker / William Scott.
     p.   cm. — (American literatures initiative)
  Includes bibliographical references and index.
  ISBN 978-0-8135-5189-0 (hardcover : alk. paper)
  ISBN 978-0-8135-5190-6 (pbk. : alk. paper)
   1. Working class in literature.   2. American fiction—20th century—History and criticism.   3. Power (Social sciences) in literature.   4. Labor movement in literature.   5. Work in literature.   6. Social conflict in literature.   I. Title.   II. Title: Power, representation, and the fiction of the mass worker.
PS374.W64S36 2012
813'.5209352623—dc22

2011010861

A British Cataloging-in-Publication record for this book is available from the British Library.

A book in the American Literatures Initiative (ALI), a collaborative publishing project of NYU Press, Fordham University Press, Rutgers University Press, Temple University Press, and the University of Virginia Press. The Initiative is supported by The Andrew W. Mellon Foundation. For more information, please visit www.americanliteratures.org.

The objective limits of capitalism do not remain purely negative. That is to say that capitalism does not merely set "natural" laws in motion that provoke crises which it cannot comprehend. On the contrary, those limits acquire a historical embodiment with its own consciousness and its own actions: the proletariat.
—GEORG LUKÁCS, *HISTORY AND CLASS CONSCIOUSNESS*

In order to fight against capital, the working class—insofar as it, too, is capital—must fight against itself.
—MARIO TRONTI, *OPERAI E CAPITALE*

A factory is really the most absurd and disgusting thing that ever existed.
—NANNI BALESTRINI, *VOGLIAMO TUTTO*

and each of them was thinking
how with dialectical materialism, accidents happen:

how at any minute,
convenience can turn
        into a kind of trouble you never wanted.
—TONY HOAGLAND, "DIALECTICAL MATERIALISM"

Contents

Acknowledgments — ix

Introduction: Power—Representation—Fiction — 1

PART ONE. The Making of the Mass Worker — 23

1. The Powerless Worker and the Failure of Political Representation: "The lowest and most degraded of human beasts" — 33

2. The Empowered Worker and the Technological Representation of Capital: "Out of this furnace, this metal" — 65

PART TWO. Strategy and Structure at the Point of Production — 107

3. The Disempowering Worker and the Aesthetic Representation of Industrial Unionism: "I am the book that has no end!" — 121

4. The Powerful Worker and the Demand for Economic Representation: "They planned to use their flesh, their bones, as a barricade" — 183

Conclusion: Making Trouble on a Global Scale — 239

Notes — 259
Works Cited — 267
Index — 277

Acknowledgments

This work has benefited from the comments and thoughts of a number of individuals, and it is a pleasure to be able to thank them here. I owe the greatest thanks to three of my colleagues at the University of Pittsburgh—Jonathan Arac, Don Bialostosky, and Nancy Glazener—without whose generous support and feedback this project would never have been realized in its present form. I am especially grateful to Nancy Glazener, who read and commented on each part of the work at various stages of its preparation, improving it considerably. I would also like to extend my warmest thanks to the staff at Rutgers University Press, particularly Leslie Mitchner and Katie Keeran, for their help in seeing the book through to publication. The project has been significantly strengthened by the encouragement and expert advice I received from Nicholas Coles and David R. Roediger, as well as from ongoing conversations with Richard Purcell, Jimmy Souzas, and Stefan Wheelock. During the final stages of completing the book, I was fortunate to receive valuable input from James Kincaid.

I would like also to express my gratitude to the institutions with which I have been associated since I began working on this project. As a doctoral student in the Humanities Center at Johns Hopkins University, I benefited from the critical feedback and intellectual support I received from Giovanni Arrighi, Etienne Balibar, Sharon Cameron, Devora Carrier, Nahum D. Chandler, Peter Fenves, Paul Fleming, Doris Hachmeister, David Harvey, Neil Hertz, Eugene Holland, Philippe

Lacoue-Labarthe, Richard Macksey, Kadeshia Matthews, May Mergenthaler, Michael Moon, Alberto Moreiras, Fred Moten, Rainer Nägele, Christopher Powers, Robert Reid-Pharr, Eckhard Schumacher, Beverly Silver, SLAC, Cecil Taylor, Rochelle Tobias, and Arnd Wedemeyer. I am grateful as well for the support I received from Harriet Linkin, Brian Rourke, Elizabeth Schirmer, and Andrew Wiget while I was a member of the Department of English at New Mexico State University, Las Cruces. Finally, the Department of English at the University of Pittsburgh has offered me an intellectual and academic environment that is, in many respects, ideal. For their thoughts and suggestions—which in a number of different ways have helped to shape this project—I am especially grateful to Mark Lynn Anderson, Susan Andrade, David Bartholomae, Ken Boas, Troy Boone, David Brumble, CM Burroughs, Fiona Cheong, Eric Clarke, Jane Feuer, Marah Gubar, Ronald Judy, Katherine Kidd, James Knapp, Dan Kubis, Marcia Landy, Kimberly Latta, Ben Lerner, Adam Lowenstein, Neepa Majumdar, Daniel Morgan, Shalini Puri, Gayle Rogers, Philip and Susan Smith, Duane Walsh, and Alicia Williamson.

For inspiration, support, guidance, and timely suggestions along the way, I owe thanks to Jan Beatty, Elaine Bernard, Phillip Bonosky, Kah Kyung Cho, Susan Eisenberg, Percival Everett, Bruce Fink, Stefan Fleischer, Bill Fletcher Jr., Emanuel Fried, Newton Garver, Rodolphe Gasché, Oliver Gibson, Steven Gingerich, Barbara Hanavan, Terrance Hayes, Carol Jacobs, Charles Keller, Mary and Divakaran Masilamani, Charles McCollester, Aldon Lynn Nielsen, Andy Parker and Lien Truong, Paul N. Siegel, Hortense Spillers, Henry Sussman, James and Gabriela Walsh, and Lawrence and Nancy Wu. Thanks are due also to Elisabeth Magnus, who carefully copyedited the manuscript, and to Susan K. Cohen, who prepared the index.

Lastly, I owe a great deal to Rachel Masilamani, whose presence and support as a friend and critical interlocutor have helped me in innumerable ways to write and to think this project through to its completion.

Introduction: Power—Representation—Fiction

The emergence of mass production and monopoly enterprise in the United States in the early years of the twentieth century had a decisive impact on the way American novelists chose to represent industrial workers in fictional narratives. *Troublemakers* explores how the sudden appearance of a new form of mass working-class power, unlike anything U.S. workers had previously known, came to be reflected in a set of formal and aesthetic problems that attended the literary representation of the mass industrial worker.

As quickly as mass production industries were being established, the nature and forms of U.S. working-class power were undergoing dramatic changes. Since labor unions, political parties, and novelists each claimed the right to represent these workers (albeit for different purposes), the widespread labor unrest in mass production industries during the period from 1900 to 1940 led not only to crises in the political and economic representation of the working class but also to a profound artistic crisis for novelists attempting to represent these new mass workers—workers who either could not be, or did not want to be, represented by others.

With the rapid growth of mechanized and assembly-line labor processes in the first decades of the twentieth century, U.S. industrial workers found that they had been transformed into a class of "mass" workers. Mario Tronti, a theoretician of Italian labor movements, proposed the term *massification* to describe the process through which a new type of working class was created at the point of production in the factory. This process involved a systematic deskilling of craft-oriented workers, combined with a series of bold technological innovations (308–309). Those who worked tending machines in mass production industries (such as auto, rubber, and steel) seldom required any traditional skills. The notion of "mass" labor power—both homogeneous and abstract—thus came to be associated with a workforce that was composed mainly of unskilled laborers, or skilled laborers whose skills had recently been made obsolete by machinery. Whatever skills mass workers had once possessed now became relatively simplified and homogenized by standardized labor processes. In addition, because of the high level of technical coordination demanded by mass production in factories, they came to be seen not as an aggregate of individual workers but as an undifferentiated and collective force of industrial labor power.

Mass workers as such were therefore initially produced in a variety of factory settings over three decades, from 1890 to 1920, to meet the ever-changing and expanding needs of large-scale industrial production (Veblen 146). However, as soon as these workers realized that the value of their labor had been reduced to a function of the material location and actions of their bodies in the workplace, they discovered two important consequences of this fact. First, they realized that traditional craft-oriented trade unions and mainstream political parties, whose ties to such workers had become severely restricted, were not in a position adequately to represent and fight on behalf of their interests. Second, they learned that by interfering with the elaborate system of technical controls that was established in the mass industrial workplace (including machinery, assembly lines, and the various techniques of scientific management) they could independently obtain their own leverage and bargaining power without relying on the mediation of representative organizations or institutions.

Mass workers thus acquired a new form of power that was directly linked to the environment of the modern industrial workplace. Yet for this very reason it was a form of power that could not be expressed through the various modes and practices of political power (electoral, representational, and parliamentarian) that working-class organizations had inherited from the nineteenth century. This new form of power was structural—a material force associated with the worker's body at the point of production—instead of a discursive or ideological articulation of workers' interests, originating in representative institutions located outside the workplace. Sitdown strikes, sabotage, and other spontaneous acts of rank-and-file "troublemaking" on the job, often carried out independently of union leadership, were its principal means of expression.

As a result of this twofold change—the massification of the modern worker and the appearance of a new form of workers' agency in a setting where it was presumed that they had none—novelists who wrote about mass industrial workers, such as Clara Weatherwax, Ernest Poole, Ruth McKenney, and Paul Gallico, were led to imagine new techniques for representing human agency in their fictional narratives. They did this by locating the source of the agency of their working-class characters not primarily in their abstract consciousnesses or shared political ideology but in the material environment of the modern workplace, including workers' actual bodies.

For example, a comparison of Upton Sinclair's 1906 novel about the meatpacking industry, *The Jungle*, to Ruth McKenney's 1939 novel about the sitdown strikes in the rubber industry, *Industrial Valley*, reveals that a dramatic shift in the nature of working-class power—as well as in the value attributed to different aesthetic, social, and political forms of representation—took place over this thirty-three-year period. While both narratives emphasize the materially degraded and oppressed condition of the modern workforce, they have diametrically opposed views regarding the capacity of trade unions and political parties to represent industrial workers effectively. Not only do these novels stake out different political positions; their forms of characterization and their narrative structures differ in significant ways. Sinclair's novel is organized around its protagonist's conversion and subsequent loyalty to the Socialist Party, while McKenney's novel, having no protagonist, depicts workers' empowerment through their collective acts of resistance in the workplace. For Sinclair, then, workers' power depends on their representation by external political parties, while for McKenney the material environment of the workplace enables workers to represent themselves directly. The differences between these two texts mark a change in the conception and practice of representation itself—a change that extends to the representational form of the novel, the various kinds of representative working-class organizations, and the abstract, technical character of managerial control that underlies the logistics of modern capitalist firms. The novel of the mass industrial worker thus invites us to rethink our understanding of modern forms of representation through its attempts to imagine and depict workers' agency in an environment where it appears to be completely suppressed.

Critics often study these novels in isolation from historical labor struggles to cast judgment on the relative value of their politics for contemporary readers. To various degrees, then, previous studies of this literature suffer from paying little attention to the historical relations, the concrete points of intersection, between the formal aspects of novels from this period, on the one hand, and workers' movements, economic forces, and the rise of mass industrial enterprise in the United States, on the other. While critical surveys of this literature have tended to focus on narrowly defined political topics—such as the "proletarian" literary movement of the 1930s Left—*Troublemakers* instead examines how novelists during this period sought to lend support to actual movements for industrial unionism (those of the Industrial Workers of the World [IWW] and Congress of Industrial Organizations [CIO]) through specifically aesthetic forms of representation, which articulated the ideals of real workers rather than party ideologues. Likewise, through its focus on the internal culture and power dynamics of the modern workplace, its principal aim is to explore (rather than presume) the degree to which the experience of the mass industrial worker can or cannot be adequately represented in the form of a fictional narrative.

Certainly, a number of prior studies of U.S. working-class fiction from this period have been extremely valuable as recovery projects—bringing overdue attention to neglected working-class authors—and as starting points for thinking through the complex relation between literary and political practices of representation. Yet instead of considering such novels in the material contexts in which they were written and published, the authors of these studies have more often pursued a thematic analysis of the novels' various political and trade union ideologies. While such studies may be useful for their wide coverage and recovery of forgotten novels, they frequently interpret these novels through narrow political and ideological grids. For example, their analyses often begin and end with questions such as "Is this truly a communist novel, or is it reformist?" They tend, therefore, to ignore a host of questions about how different modes and practices of representation (aesthetic, economic, and political) relate to one another—questions that are repeatedly raised by the novels themselves.

To some degree, *Troublemakers* is also a recovery project, closely examining several novels that have so far received little or no critical attention, such as Leroy Scott's *The Walking Delegate* (1905), Arthur Bullard's *Comrade Yetta* (1913), Ernest Poole's *The Harbor* (1915), Lawrence H. Conrad's *Temper* (1924), and Paul Gallico's *Sit-Down Strike* (1938). However, it distinguishes itself from prior studies of this literature in three significant ways. First, unlike them, it focuses exclusively on the figure of the mass worker that accompanied the growth of mass production industries during the first half of the twentieth century. Because this figure is most often associated with what labor historian Michael Torigian calls the "Fordist-Taylorist factory system"—particularly the U.S. automobile industry in the 1920s and 1930s—the arguments and literary interpretations of the book center on novels about modern factory and assembly-line workers (324n1).

Second, also unlike previous studies, *Troublemakers* examines a broad range of literary representations of the mass worker in close proximity to the real historical forces and events that marked the growth of U.S. industrial capitalism from 1900 to 1940. In this regard, it pays special attention to the rise of big business, the technical and economic conditions of mass production, and the dynamics of the U.S. labor movement. Instead of studying these novels as more or less successful expressions of leftist political programs, its aim is to reveal how their formal and aesthetic features were closely tied to the actual ebb and flow of rank-and-file workers' movements during this period. The questions it poses about representation, then, refer not only to the ideological themes or political tendencies that these novels exhibit but also to the relations of power embedded in the material structures of the modern industrial workplace.

Finally, and most importantly, *Troublemakers* differs from earlier studies of U.S. working-class fiction through its focus on acts of workplace resistance. Prior accounts of this literature generally overlook (or take for granted) the phenomenon of workers exercising power in the workplace. Even the attention that has been paid in recent years to radical, leftist, and working-class writers from the Great Depression—exemplified by the groundbreaking work of critics such as Constance Coiner, Michael Denning, Barbara Foley, Paula Rabinowitz, and Alan Wald—frequently disregards what, from the 1910s to the 1940s, had become a common, everyday occurrence: workers exercising power on the job by refusing to work, slowing down, sitting down, talking back, or otherwise "acting up." Similarly, other studies devoted to the broader history of U.S. working-class fiction have sought to provide an overview of various narrative accounts of the day-to-day experience of work. Such projects (the work of Janet Zandy and Laura Hapke, for example) treat working-class fiction as mainly a documentary record of different types of work. However, when it comes to narratives about workers who *refuse* to work—by exercising power on the job in a number of ways that are unrelated, and often in direct opposition, to their productivity as workers—these studies have had relatively little to say. What challenges, then, might such refusals to work pose for the novelist who wants to represent workers? How should one represent workers who are in the act of resisting the category of work itself?

The Fictitious Commodity of Labor

Troublemakers is a book about fiction, in two different senses of the term: the fictitious commodity that is bought and sold every day under the heading of "labor power," as well as fictional representations of this commodity in the form of literary narratives. Because novels about mass industrial workers in the twentieth century are self-consciously fictional representations of the modern workplace, they offer an especially fruitful means to study and question the fictitious nature of the commodity of human labor power. Much of *Troublemakers* is therefore devoted to exploring the formal, thematic, and conceptual relations between these two types of fiction.

Throughout this book, the commodity of labor power in capitalist society is taken to be uniquely fictitious because it is embodied in living human beings. Beverly Silver, a contemporary sociologist of world labor movements, reminds us how, for Karl Marx, "the fictitious nature of the commodity of labor power reveals itself in the 'hidden abode of production' [where] the purchaser of labor power soon finds out that it is not a commodity like any other. Rather, it is embodied in human beings who complain and resist if they are driven too long, too hard, or too fast. Struggle thus becomes endemic to, and in theory defines, the labor-capital relation at the point of production" (16–17). Because labor power is always embodied in people, the modern industrial workplace should be understood first and foremost as an environment made up of individuals "who have their own interests and needs and who retain their power to resist being treated like a commodity. . . . The workplace becomes a battleground, as employers attempt to extract the maximum effort from workers and workers necessarily resist their bosses' impositions" (Edwards 12–13). Likewise, the radical political and cultural theorist C.L.R. James explained in 1950 that we must never forget to situate "the theory of class struggle in the process of production itself" (34). Over twenty years later, Mario Tronti reaffirmed James's point, noting how "the production process, the act of the production of capital, is simultaneously the moment of workers' struggles *against* capital" (215).[1] Just as Roland Barthes defined modern literary style as a "recollection locked within the body of the writer" (12), so the analyses of *Troublemakers* assume that the industrial worker's bodily experience of working—in the actual workplace, at the point of production—is an originary instance of the fictitious representation, or commodification, of human labor power. The worker's body at the point of production is thus the primary site at which this fiction is enforced, challenged, and revealed in its various dimensions.[2]

From a broader historical perspective, Karl Polanyi based his account of the emergence of modern capitalist society on the role played by three such fictitious commodities: labor, land, and money. All three of these are required for the ideal of a self-regulating market to function efficiently. Since labor, land, and money are all "essential elements of industry," Polanyi argues, they "also must be organized in markets. But labor, land, and money are obviously not commodities" (72). This is because, even though labor, land, and money are all bought and sold every day in market societies, none of these was originally produced to be sold on the market. "Labor and land," he points out, "are no other than the human beings themselves of which every society consists and the natural surroundings in which it exists. To include them in the market mechanism means to subordinate the substance of society itself to the laws of the market." Labor, for example, is "only another name for a human activity which goes with life itself, which in its turn is not produced for sale but for entirely different reasons, nor can that activity be detached from the rest of life, be stored or mobilized."[3] Nevertheless, Polanyi adds, "The fiction of [its] being so produced became the organizing principle of society" (71).

Around 1850—first in England, but spreading quickly to other industrializing regions—human labor power was economically, politically, legally, and juridically defined as a commodity. Henceforth, as a raw material that was necessary for industrial production, the commodity known as "labor power" was ideally to be made available in sufficient quantity for sale on the market, with a price that was ideally to be determined only by the activity of buying and selling (Polanyi 73–75). For the first time in human history, Polanyi claims, society as a whole came to be run as though it were a mere adjunct to the market. The principle of freedom of contract now provided the surest way to separate human labor from the other activities with which it had been traditionally associated, subjecting it entirely to the force of market mechanisms (57, 71, 163). In addition, to safeguard the functioning of a supposedly self-regulated market, society itself had to be strictly divided into separate economic and political institutions, a separation of powers that "was now used to separate the people from power over their own economic life" (225).

Struggle at the Point of Production

Human labor power thus began (and continues) to be bought and sold every day as a commodity. Yet, as Richard Edwards explains, there will always be a "discrepancy between what the capitalist can buy in the market and what he needs for production" (12). This is why it is imperative for capitalists to control workers' activities at all times (16–17). Throughout the first decades of the twentieth century, workers' daily acts of resistance on the job reflected a more basic struggle over control that had come to characterize every capitalist workplace. Underlying all of their acts of resistance was the fact that workers were attempting "to wrest at least a part of the power over their lives away from their employers and exercise it themselves" (Brecher 282). While modern forms of industrial capitalism were first being created in the late nineteenth century, the workplace increasingly became a site where workers were expected to adapt their "habits of life ... to the exigencies of the machine process" (Veblen 191n9). This process of adaptation, in Thorstein Veblen's view, aimed to yoke even the "ideals and aspirations" of workers to the needs of production (191n9); it was only a matter of time, therefore, before industrial workers started to carry out both small- and large-scale acts of resistance against such "subordination to the machine" (Giedion 126).

According to Polanyi, while labor and land were being redefined and fictionalized as commodities, workers and farmers were struggling to establish a variety of protective measures either to improve and secure their livelihood or to defend their basic means of survival as human beings. "The commodity fiction," Polanyi notes, "disregarded the fact that leaving the fate of soil and people to the market would be tantamount to annihilating them. Accordingly, the countermove consisted in checking the action of the market in respect to the factors of production, labor, and land. This was the main function of interventionism" (131). The particular countermoves Polanyi has in mind here—including various kinds of strike activity, union organizing, political activism, and legislative reforms—attended, and in some cases severely checked or thwarted, the attempts of free-market advocates to subordinate society to the mechanisms of the self-regulating market (cf. Adamic, *Dynamite* 416–417).

The commodification of human labor power was thus everywhere met with efforts to decommodify, or rescue, the lives of actual human workers. The historical dynamics of market society, Polanyi claims, therefore reveal a to-and-fro pattern whereby "the extension of the market organization in respect to genuine commodities was accompanied by its restriction in respect to fictitious ones" (76). In other words, the push toward commodification and the spread of markets produced a reverse push toward decommodification—society's self-protective measures to ensure its survival—which was met by another wave of market expansion, and so on (Silver 17–18). Market-oriented (industrial capitalist) societies, as Polanyi sees them, are thus constantly torn between preserving the basic social conditions of human life and reinforcing the fictitious ideals of a self-regulating market.

The Irony of the Mass Worker

Troublemakers in no way claims to offer a comprehensive survey of U.S. working-class fiction from the first half of the twentieth century. Rather, it is focused exclusively on novels about mass industrial workers, with a particular emphasis on the automobile industry. One reason for the relatively narrow scope of its concerns is that, as Charles Reitell, an American industrial sociologist, pointed out in the early 1920s, "in no industry has mechanical development been so rapid or so far reaching in its effects upon workers as in the automobile industry" (182). According to Reitell, because U.S. autoworkers were "being shaped physically and mentally by these machines" that they operated day in and day out, they afforded a privileged view of an entirely new type of working class, one that was just beginning to appear in a variety of mass industrial factory settings (187). Novels from this period that are specifically about mass industrial workers therefore provide a unique sense of what sociologists like Reitell (and other curious onlookers) imagined was in store for such workers. In addition, it was within this growing class of mass industrial workers that the two most significant twentieth-century campaigns for industrial unionism in the United States—the organizing drives of the IWW and the CIO, which lasted from 1905 to 1920 and from 1935 to 1941, respectively—received their strongest support. Only because of the success of the second of these campaigns did industrial unionism finally become a reality throughout much of the U.S. economy. The CIO's effectiveness stemmed directly from the fact that the idea of industrial unionism "manifested itself first where mass pressure was strongest—in the automobile industry" (Levinson 222).

In general, from the point of view of existing trade unions, it was widely known that mass production industries such as automobiles, rubber, steel, and glass were the most difficult to unionize. This was because all of these industries had recently been developed and expanded on the basis of the Fordist-Taylorist system of production. Workers in them were accordingly "subject to high rates of turnover, divided by various ascriptive differences (especially related to ethnicity) and isolated by an awesome array of fragmenting and alienating technologies" (Torigian 336). When these industries were eventually unionized in the successful series of organizing drives under the auspices of the CIO in the late 1930s, it seemed to many as though the "highest stage" in the history of the U.S. labor movement had finally been attained (324).

The great irony in all of this, of course, is that the Fordist-Taylorist system of production—a system that had been created to prevent the unionization of mass production industries—was itself the primary reason for the success of the various campaigns to organize mass industrial workers in the United States during this period. That is, the system of mass production created by Frederick Winslow Taylor and Henry Ford, which was explicitly designed to increase output, lower production costs, and protect employers from the threat of unionization, ended up strengthening the power of mass industrial workers and leading to a string of victories among the industrial union campaigns of the late 1930s. "It was only post facto—with the success of mass production unionization," notes Beverly Silver, "that Fordism came to be seen as inherently labor strengthening rather than inherently labor weakening" (6). Strange as it may seem, then, a system that was based on the goal of progressively weakening the bargaining power of skilled workers in the labor market (through automation and deskilling) only served to enhance the bargaining power of unskilled workers at the point of production inside the factory.

Power and Representation

To understand how the Fordist-Taylorist system of production could have strengthened the bargaining power of those very same workers it was originally meant to control, it is necessary to distinguish clearly between a few different types of power that mass industrial workers may be said to possess. The sociologist Erik Olin Wright draws a useful distinction between what he calls *associational* power, or "the various forms of power that result from the formation of collective organizations of workers," and *structural* power, or the "power that results simply from the location of workers within the economic system"—which includes, for example, "the strategic location of a particular group of workers within a key industrial sector" (962). Of the second, structural type of power, Beverly Silver further distinguishes between two varieties, "marketplace" bargaining power and "workplace" bargaining power:

> Marketplace bargaining power can take several forms including (1) the possession of scarce skills that are in demand by employers, (2) low levels of general unemployment, and (3) the ability of workers to pull out of the labor market entirely and survive on nonwage sources of income. Workplace bargaining power, on the other hand, accrues to workers who are enmeshed in tightly integrated production processes, where a localized work stoppage in a key node can cause disruptions on a much wider scale than the stoppage itself. Such bargaining power has been in evidence when entire assembly lines have been shut down by a stoppage in one segment of the line, and when entire corporations relying on the just-in-time delivery of parts have been brought to a standstill by railway workers' strikes. (13)

The second type of structural power Silver describes here—the "workplace" bargaining power that workers on Fordist assembly lines are able to exercise—was responsible for the victories of most of the major unionizing drives in U.S. mass production industries during the final years of the Great Depression (Silver 92–93). For example, the famous sitdown strikes carried out by GM workers in Flint, Cleveland, and Detroit in early 1937 provide some of the clearest illustrations of the effects of workplace bargaining power. In the case of these strikes, Silver observes, "Just as a militant minority could stop production in an entire plant, so if the plant was a key link in an integrated corporate empire, its occupation could paralyze the corporation." Moreover, she goes on to explain, because the "complex technical division of labor characteristic of mass production in the automobile industry increases the vulnerability of capital to workers' direct action at the point of production," the very same industrial environment that effectively deprives workers of associational forms of power (unions) can simultaneously increase the structural forms of power they possess. The truth of this observation is evident in the enormous amount of damage that can result from even a small work stoppage in a strategic location within a vertically integrated firm (46–47).

It was only because U.S. mass workers possessed this second form of structural power—*workplace* bargaining power—that they were able to claim so many victories in the industrial unionization campaigns of the late 1930s. Yet it was precisely this kind of power that they could not have exercised prior to the growth of vertically integrated industrial firms beginning around 1900 and prior to the widespread application of Taylor's and Ford's techniques of mass production. It must also be recalled that this new kind of structural power was entirely distinct from the associational forms of power that had characterized the strategy and goals of the mainstream labor movement up till then. Ever since their creation in the early nineteenth century, trade unions, like political parties, had promised to provide workers with bargaining power by way of the procedures, conventions, and institutions of electoral representation. However, by the 1930s, industrial workers had come to realize that they possessed a quite different—nonrepresentational and nondiscursive—source of power, one that derived from the technical integration of the production process itself. Significantly, this unique type of bargaining power that mass workers acquired in modern factories did not come to them from labor unions, working-class organizations, or political parties (mainstream or otherwise) that were located outside the workplace. Moreover, it was a type of power that was only contingently linked to various forms of class consciousness, ideological perspective, or political "persuasion."

Strikes that rely for their effectiveness on a strategic use of workplace bargaining power play out entirely at the point of production inside the factory, apart from the decisions handed down by the executive committees of trade unions and political parties. Workers who carry out such strikes are thus striking not merely against their employer but also indirectly against a certain notion of representational power: the notion, that is to say, that power must always stem from symbolic or discursive modes and practices of representation. On the contrary, the critical role played by workplace bargaining power in the industrial labor struggles of the late 1930s proved that workers' power could emanate from the material and technological environment of the industrial workplace. To a large extent, then, major strikes in mass production industries can be initiated and won on the basis of the technical and logistical organization of production in those particular industries, without being determined in the last instance by the political affiliations, ideological tendencies, or level of working-class consciousness that workers may possess at a given time.

Overview

Most of the strikes depicted in the novels *Troublemakers* examines are strikes of this sort. That is, they are strikes that resist a number of different practices of representation, including, at times, those aesthetic practices of narrative fiction through which they are themselves represented.[4] Indeed, the analyses of *Troublemakers* focus on strike novels in particular because in fictional representations of strikes—no less so than during actual strikes—the distinction between economic and political forms of struggle "breaks down," according to Jeremy Brecher. "Strikes," Brecher argues, "aim not just to win concessions but to increase the power of workers within the economy; this is a quintessentially political objective, for the economy itself is a system of political power—indeed, in our society, a central one" (285; see also Luxemburg 241, 243). Because mass industrial strikes have the potential to blur the distinctions between different types of power (political/economic), they may be overdetermined, in a critically productive sense, insofar as they are sites of general confusion and negotiation among forms of representation. A species of "ground-zero" event, as it were, mass industrial strikes—including those depicted in fictional narratives—invite us to reflect critically on the boundaries, relations, and points of intersection between a range of different representational practices. These can include not only political and economic practices of representation but aesthetic, technological, and scientific practices as well.

The first part of *Troublemakers*, "The Making of the Mass Worker," examines a series of novels that stress the degrading conditions of the mass industrial workplace. These novels—all published between 1906 and 1941—detail the modern factory's high degree of technological integration, as well as changes in the meaning of work itself after the introduction of Taylorist and Fordist production methods between 1900 and 1920. They also depict the shifting function of human labor in the context of monopoly capitalist firms and the value that modern corporate enterprise had assigned to the body of the worker in the production process. According to this group of writers, the productive power of modern industry not only was founded upon the material bodies of workers but also reduced those workers as much as possible to their physical, bodily functions. Chapters 1 and 2 therefore aim to explore how, exactly, these novels represented the various efforts of employers to commodify the bodies of workers in mass production industries, treating them as though they were mere machines.

All the novels examined in this first part of the study share a focus on the variety of dehumanizing modern labor processes and techniques of mass production. They differ, however, with respect to the conclusions they draw concerning the effects that these labor processes had on the experience of mass industrial workers. So, whereas chapter 1 studies a selection of texts by novelists who viewed mass production techniques as essentially degrading to workers, chapter 2 considers texts by a second group of novelists from the same period who saw these same production techniques as ennobling and strengthening workers in mass production factories.

The second part of *Troublemakers*, "Strategy and Structure at the Point of Production," takes for its guide Karl Polanyi's insight that workers will always find ways to resist the commodification of their labor. This second part of the book explores a different set of novels about workers' efforts to decommodify themselves through various forms of direct action that occurred inside the factory at the point of production. The novels it discusses highlight acts of rank-and-file resistance toward being treated as mere machines, focusing particularly on the use of the sitdown strike. In resorting to the sitdown—a bodily means of resisting the commodification of their labor by revealing its fictitious nature—industrial workers not only deployed a tactic that was highly effective in its own right but also discovered and learned how to exercise a kind of power that was at odds with the representational (and, for Polanyi, similarly fictitious) basis of modern capitalist production. Novels about such workers likewise sought to portray a materially embodied workforce that needed its own kind of union, its own peculiarly "mass" forms of representation, to realize itself as an agent of social power. Chapters 3 and 4 of *Troublemakers* therefore analyze how these novels self-consciously reflect the technical and theoretical difficulties encountered by their authors in the process of writing them. These novelists, after all, were trying to represent in aesthetic terms an industrial workforce that otherwise refused to be represented by contemporary labor leaders and politicians. Finally, the narratives examined in this second part of *Troublemakers*, much like those in the first part, are fixated on a range of bodily motifs. The literary analyses of chapters 3 and 4 consequently explore the ways in which these writers were invoking the authenticity of workers' corporeal experience to support a critique of modern industrial capitalism.

In contrast to the novels discussed in the first part of *Troublemakers*, all the novels examined in the second part share a focus on workers' acts of resistance at the point of production. They differ from one another only in chronological terms. Chapter 3 examines novels written and published between 1905 and 1915 that were associated with the strikes and organizing drives of the IWW; chapter 4 examines a group of novels from between 1934 and 1941 that were associated with various aspects of the campaigns of the CIO.

In the field of U.S. working-class literary and cultural criticism, few studies squarely confront the theoretical problems of representation posed by novels about workers in modern, mass industrial settings. In part, this oversight could reflect the fact that the thematic and political concerns that inform much of the scholarship in this field have seldom been combined with a more philosophically oriented critique of representation. Thus, in its analyses of novels such as Clara Weatherwax's *Marching! Marching!*, Jack London's *The Iron Heel*, and Thomas Bell's *Out of This Furnace*, the present study strives to bring several sets of related concerns—political, formal, and theoretical—into a fresh intellectual exchange.

Departing, then, from the strictly thematic approach taken by previous critics, *Troublemakers* instead explores how these novels' various techniques of fictional representation are closely tied to political, economic, and institutional practices of representation. For instance, it considers the problems of fictional representation that arise in these texts in relation to the logistical plans that served to manage, discipline, and control the workforce of large-scale U.S. capitalist firms. These include innovations such as Taylor's time and motion studies and Ford's development of assembly lines. Throughout *Troublemakers*, the literary analyses that form the core of its chapters share one basic assumption: that aesthetic practices of representation can be fruitfully examined in relation to economic and political practices of representation, and vice versa. Accordingly, the book assumes that the kinds of organizations that were held to represent the interests of working people, such as unions and political parties (economic and political representation), could potentially have both formal and conceptual ties to the narrative devices through which novelists chose to represent workers in fictional terms (aesthetic representation).

For analytic purposes, therefore, it is useful to distinguish initially among four different fields of representational practices: political, technological, aesthetic, and economic. These four terms designate general categories of representational practices, which may—and often do—overlap and intersect with one another. The field of *political* representation includes mainly parliamentary and electoral institutions, as well as political parties, labor unions, and any other form of social organization based upon the accountability of elected representatives. The field of *technological* representation, in contrast, refers to the mechanical, logistical, and calculating discourses that underlie and make possible the technical organization of mass production. This field includes the practices of scientific managers, industrial engineers, and social planners, as well as the disciplinary discourses of factory and assembly-line supervisors. The field of *aesthetic* representation consists of self-consciously artistic, performative, or dramatic objects and practices. These would include anything from novels to songs, plays, parades, rallies, demonstrations, banners, slogans, cartoons, and (most broadly) imaginary identifications among individuals. Finally, the field of *economic* representation encompasses the conceptual discourses and categories that provide the basis for modern, monopoly capitalist forms of production. This field may include everything from the representational practices of accountants and bookkeepers to the language of contracts negotiated between labor and management. It also refers to the various types of "business philosophy" pronouncements that are occasionally made by leading industrialists such as Henry Ford (or, more recently, by figures such as Lee Iacocca, Michael Eisner, Warren Buffett, and Bill Gates).

Furthermore, representational practices may operate in one of several different modes: they may be iconic, symbolic, or indexical.[5] In the *iconic* mode of representation, the object of the representation is identical with the form of the representational practice itself. Simply put, that which is represented is the same thing as that which is doing the job of representing (for example, a statue of Christ on a crucifix). The icon thus amounts to an embodied sign, as it were: both signifier and signified are combined in the same object. In the *symbolic* mode of representation, something or someone "stands for" or "speaks for" something or someone else. Figurative acts of language such as metaphors, for example, generally operate symbolically. In social terms, this mode of representation is most often associated with the political field of electoral practices and institutions. In the *indexical* mode of representation, a part may stand for, or be interchangeable with, the whole. Likewise, a particular may stand for, or be interchangeable with, a universal. In contrast to metaphors, linguistic figures such as metonyms and synecdoches operate indexically; that is, they point toward and indicate the existence of some whole or part.

Within each of these four fields of representation—political, technological, aesthetic, and economic—one may frequently find iconic, symbolic, and indexical modes of representational practice, as well as practices that combine two (or all three) of these modes. Obviously, then, these four fields and three modes of representation will often intersect and overlap with one another, depending on the circumstances. The strategies and practices of representation unique to each of them can appear and function alongside, or in conjunction with, any of the others. For instance, political and aesthetic fields of representation are often combined or used to support one another in social contexts, just as economic and technological fields of representation often appear together in the context of capitalist enterprises.

However, for the purpose of analysis and comparative study, it is not only useful but necessary to distinguish these fields and modes of representation from one another, if only in a provisional manner. Each of the four individual chapters of *Troublemakers* thus focuses on a particular configuration of representation and power. In turn, each of these configurations ends up privileging a specific figure of the mass worker that is represented, in more or less similar ways, by a certain group of novels. Accordingly, the four different figures of the mass worker that are analyzed by the book's four chapters—the "powerless," "empowered," "disempowering," and "powerful" worker—are distinguished from each other by their capacity to exercise power in the industrial workplace.

The first chapter of *Troublemakers*, "The Powerless Worker and the Failure of Political Representation," explores how one group of novelists portrayed the figure of the mass worker as generally powerless and in need of symbolic social forms of representation. The politicians and political parties that appear in these novels, published between 1905 and 1941, thus take it upon themselves to "speak for" and in the place of a mute, abject working class. The second chapter, "The Empowered Worker and the Technological Representation of Capital," examines a separate group of writers from the same period. Unlike many of their contemporaries, this second group of writers was convinced that mass workers could indeed be represented, but in iconic terms—namely, as representations of capital itself. For these writers, the mass worker was above all a technological phenomenon. Their novels therefore present an image of the "empowered" worker, one that was filled with the superhuman forces of the machine technology of the modern factory and that appeared to be produced as the quasi-natural offspring of modern industrial capitalism.

The novelists examined in the third chapter, "The Disempowering Worker and the Aesthetic Representation of Industrial Unionism," contrast sharply with both of these first two groups of writers. Their representations of industrial unionism depict mass workers for the first time as subjects of their own labor power, rather than as objects to be consumed in the process of capitalist production. Published during a brief period between 1905 and 1915, the fictional images of mass workers in this third group of novels were shown struggling to decommodify themselves. They aimed to do this by rejecting both the political (symbolic) and technological (iconic) strategies of representation that—as the novels considered in the first two chapters made clear—would have typically been used to commodify them. The writers and artists affiliated with the IWW, or Wobblies, instead portrayed mass workers as actively disempowering anyone—politicians, capitalists, or labor leaders—who sought to gain power over them by representing them for their own purposes. By promoting direct action and sabotage at the point of production in the workplace, and by insisting that workers avoid signing labor contracts with their employers, the IWW encouraged these workers to develop the means to represent themselves. Indeed, through their own direct action in the workplace, mass workers discovered a way to speak *for themselves,* in order to say that they refused to be representations *of capital.*

However, the IWW principles of solidarity could not be articulated through the existing categories of economic and political discourse without at the same time being constrained by the conceptual and ideological limits of these categories. Their principles could therefore be faithfully represented only in aesthetic terms, as the index of a political, social, and economic ideal to be realized sometime in the future. Through its aesthetic representation in songs, literature, and art, the abstract ideal of "One Big Union," for example, was made to appear concrete. That is, its potential effects could be indexed, and it could be made to seem tangibly present, in the eyes of workers who only rarely encountered actual solidarity among the various members of their class.

For this very reason, however, the figure of the "disempowering" worker was especially ambiguous. A creature of the material conditions of mass industrial production, but organized and valorized by the IWW, such a figure relied upon aesthetic forms of representation to express its ideals. However, these aesthetic representations were also used to express the significance of its rejection of political, economic, and technological forms of representation. Hence, the act of refusing to be represented in one sense led Wobblies to demand to be represented in another, opposing sense. But their demand for aesthetic forms of representation could never fully compensate for the political and economic forms of representation it was intended to replace. That is to say, since the One Big Union was an ideal, by definition it could never fulfill the practical need for the political and economic representation of the mass worker. Consequently, although the aim of aesthetic representations of the One Big Union was to provide a concrete illustration of the ideal of universal working-class solidarity and self-representation, such a sublime ideal could only ever be intimated, or hinted at. Its full meaning could only be partially indexed by way of actual, individual (and thus relatively limited) occurrences of direct action and solidarity.

The novels examined in the fourth chapter, "The Powerful Worker and the Demand for Economic Representation," explain how the IWW's demand for the aesthetic representation of the industrial workforce was transformed into the CIO's demand for its economic representation. In these novels, published between 1934 and 1941, mass workers are even more prominently shown using tactics of direct action—most evident in the form of the sitdown strike—to challenge the existing political and technological regimes of working-class representation. In contrast to the earlier IWW novels, however, these Depression-era narratives show the figure of the mass worker exercising a power that is rooted, not primarily in an aesthetic ideal, but in the material environment of the actual workplace.

Taken together, these four different figures of the worker will perhaps inevitably be read as detailing a series of successive stages in the development of the mass worker's class consciousness. Yet this should not be taken to imply, for instance, that "powerless" workers will someday become "powerful" workers once they have first spent an appropriate amount of time as "empowered" and "disempowering" workers. Though the book is organized according to a set of worker types that follow one another in roughly chronological order, it deliberately avoids theorizing about the developmental stages of mass workers' class consciousness. If there is a single, coherent line of argument in this study that resembles a "phenomenology" of the mass worker, then, it is centered primarily on the relationship between power and representation in the industrial workplace. The shifting states of consciousness of the general class of mass industrial workers are only, at best, a secondary and implicit concern of the analyses that follow.

Likewise, these four fictional figures cannot be strictly identified with the historical periods in which their respective novels were published. Generally, novels depicting "powerful" workers were more common in the 1930s and 1940s—after Fordist methods had come to dominate mass production industries in the United States—while novels depicting "powerless" workers were far more common earlier in the century. Nevertheless, one may also find novels depicting "powerful" workers that were published around 1900, such as Leroy Scott's *The Walking Delegate* (1905). Likewise, one may find novels about "powerless" workers that were published in the late 1930s, such as Dalton Trumbo's *Johnny Got His Gun* (1939). Indeed, one can usually find examples of all four of these literary figures in every one of the novels examined in *Troublemakers*. As a rule, though, each of these novels tends to emphasize one figure of the mass worker over the others. For instance, while Ruth McKenney's 1939 novel *Industrial Valley* highlights "powerful" figures of mass workers more than any of the others, it still contains depictions of powerless, empowered, and disempowering mass workers. Similarly, while Thomas Bell's 1941 novel *Out of This Furnace* emphasizes the "empowered" figure of the mass worker, it also contains noteworthy examples of powerless and powerful workers. The book's chapters are therefore organized according to whichever figure of the mass worker is most prominently featured in a particular group of novels.

Further, the division of *Troublemakers* into two parts is designed to reflect the book's overarching thesis. Simply stated, the argument is that workers in mass production industries are able to acquire and use structural forms of power in the degree to which they are reduced to a mere mass of laboring bodies on an assembly line. As mass industrial workers experience their commodification on the job in ever more extreme forms (Part One), they come to realize that traditional labor organizations are increasingly unable to represent them and lend support to their struggles. At the same time, they learn that they can act themselves to challenge the dictates of capitalist accumulation (Part Two). Although both of these experiences or realizations may occur simultaneously—for real-life as well as fictitious workers—the present study has divided them into two parts to better analyze the two basic tendencies of novelists' representations of the mass worker. Accordingly, the analyses of Part One center on novels that emphasize the degrading or dehumanizing characteristics of mass workers' treatment in the industrial workplace. Part Two instead focuses on novels that highlight the multitude of ways these same workers—often at the same time—learn to resist such treatment. The shift from Part One to Part Two of *Troublemakers* is therefore a shift from an examination of novels that treat the mass worker primarily as an *object* to an examination of novels that treat the mass worker primarily as a *subject*.

Finally, while a certain figure of the mass worker tends to be manifested in a particular field of representational practices, it also tends, within a given field, to be articulated through a particular mode of representation. Yet these associations between literary figures of mass workers and their respective fields and modes of representation are by no means to be taken as fixed once and for all. In chronological terms, the apparent tendencies of mass workers (either to suffer exploitation or to turn to direct action), like those of social classes more generally, cannot be rigorously identified with particular historical periods. The chapter organization of *Troublemakers* suggests, for example, that "disempowering" workers are synonymous with Wobblies and that "powerful" workers are synonymous with members of CIO-affiliated unions. But to view them in this manner would be to impose too rigid a conceptual schema over the analyses contained within the individual chapters. Moreover, to make such a direct association would be to equate, naively, a certain figure of the mass worker represented in a fictional literary narrative with a particular, historically determinate political party or trade union ideology.

As Mario Tronti warns us, "Not only is it an error to try to formalize a concept of 'class' valid for all epochs of human history. It is also an error to want to define a class once and for all within the development of capitalist society. Workers and capital are not only classes contraposed to each other but always changing economic realities, social formations, and political organizations" (309). Similarly, in what follows, one should bear in mind that the figures of mass workers, working classes, capitalists, and material forms of capital depicted in these novels are constantly subject to change from one historical period to the next. In some cases, as we will see, they may even undergo dramatic changes within the confines of a single novel.

PART ONE

The Making of the Mass Worker

Between 1900 and 1920 a new type of worker appeared in mass production industries in the United States. In the eyes of sociologists, business executives, trade union leaders, and other curious onlookers who noted the phenomenon, such workers were routinely identified with the complex and imposing machines that they operated. Moreover, as if they, too, were machines, the new breed of industrial workers was considered an inevitable product of the highly mechanized environments in which they worked. As a group, mass workers were thus distinguished from other workers of the era through the specific process of adaptation they underwent with respect to a variety of recently mechanized methods of production.

This process of adaptation occurred in two phases. The first phase, which lasted from roughly 1890 to 1915, involved the transfer of industrial workers' skills, intuitions, and general know-how to a small group of "expert" managers and engineers, as well as the transfer of the physical force of their laboring bodies to the force of the machines they operated. The changes to the labor process that occurred during this period are today most often associated with the name of Frederick W. Taylor and referred to by the labels of *Taylorism* and *scientific management*. The second phase of adaptation, which lasted from roughly 1915 to 1930, involved the transfer of workers' bodily movements and a transfer of the personal forms of authority exercised by foremen and supervisors to the new types of machinery that were required for continuous-flow, assembly-line methods of manufacture. The system of production that resulted from this second wave of changes to the labor process is most commonly identified with the term *Fordism*.

While this fourfold transfer from workers to machines (of skills, force, motion, and authority) was taking place, those who made up the bulk of the workforce in large industrial enterprises seemed more and more to become a homogeneous mass, composed of undifferentiated and unskilled units of anonymous labor power. For instance, to early observers of workers on Ford's continuously moving assembly lines, "The chain drive proved to be a very great improvement, hurrying the slow men, holding the fast men back from pushing work on to those in advance, and acting as an all-round adjuster and equalizer" (Arnold and Faurote 114). These machines were "adjusting" and "equalizing" nothing less than the sum of the distinguishing features of the individual workers, making the labor of one resemble that of all the others in an "all-round" way. By the mid-1920s, then, autoworkers were being singled out by industrial sociologists for best illustrating the new type of mass, homogenized labor power that was employed in mass production industries (Reitell 184).

The process of making mass workers, however, was already under way by the mid-1890s, well before the auto industry emerged as a major force in the U.S. economy. In the last quarter of the nineteenth century—mainly because of the swift construction of railroads in the 1850s—large U.S. business enterprises were being created, expanded, and reorganized through a process known as "vertical integration." In its most basic sense, *vertical integration* denotes a type of expansion by means of which a business firm includes more stages of production in its total field of operations. Normally, this involves a company's gaining control over the means of distribution and retailing or over its sources of raw materials. By expanding its operations in one or both of these directions—"upstream" to control sources of supply or "downstream" to control the means of distribution—a firm achieved much more control over its overall rate of production than it initially had, for it could now reliably time each of its different operations to coincide with all the others.[1]

The Works Management Movement

By the 1890s, as a result of the expansions they were rapidly undertaking, large U.S. business enterprises were faced with a host of new challenges, mainly involving three areas of their operations: finance and accounting, administration and coordination, and the management of their workforces. For the first time, large corporations were forced to hire top-level executives, as well as full-time staffs of expert advisors and organizational engineers, to coordinate and manage their various activities. In short, a wholly new type of executive manager was needed to manage the work of all the other managers at different strata within the expanded firm (Edwards 87). With regard to their rank-and-file workers, however, the problems these huge multidivisional companies faced were matters not simply of logistics but of dictating the precise use to which human labor power would be put from one moment to the next. That is, the management of a large and diverse workforce involves basic problems not only of coordination but of control (Aitken 37; Edwards 16–17). For the firm to calculate its rate of production as a stable factor in its overall plans, it needed to be able to regulate the rate of output of its workers on a day-to-day basis. Production-level managers therefore needed to gain as much control as possible over their workers' various labor processes.

To this end, many large firms sought assistance from a new school of managerial expertise that had recently emerged, centered primarily in the machine-making industry, which dubbed itself the "works management movement." "A new order of managers is needed for the new order of agencies," proclaimed the representatives of this school in the pages of its most popular organ, *Engineering Magazine*, founded in 1891 by John R. Dunlap ("Editorial Comment" [1900] 433; see also Jenks 427n15). Throughout the nineteenth century, industrial engineers had been haphazardly experimenting with designs for the systematic organization of production in single factories in the steel, meatpacking, and electrical manufacturing industries. But with the founding of the American Society of Mechanical Engineers (ASME) in 1880—particularly the papers that were presented at the society's 1886 convention, which included Henry R. Towne's influential contribution "The Engineer as Economist" (Aitken 35)—a new generation of industrialists began to adopt a self-consciously methodical and systematic approach to dealing with the problem of the organization of production. Consisting of far more than a set of techniques for managing workers, the new movement claimed the honor of being the first to stress "the self-conscious and deliberate extension of rationalism to the analysis of industrial work" (Aitken 15; see also Chandler, *Strategy* 24, 318; Jenks 429).

Generally speaking, the members of the works management movement shared a commitment to the following goals: to increase a plant's or firm's productivity, lower its unit costs, eliminate so-called "waste" (of labor, energy, resources, time, and space), provide a certain degree of harmony between workers and managers in the shop, and, finally, improve the physical, cultural, and moral environment of the plants themselves (Jenks 432). Their bottom-line concern, however, was to develop a repertoire of managerial methods that would ensure the realization of the first two of these goals—the constant increase of productivity, accompanied by a constant lowering of costs (443; see also "Editorial Comment" [1899]).

If this was the movement's primary aim—intensified production at lower cost—the methods its members devised to achieve it also shared several principles and working assumptions. First, Leland Jenks tells us, there was "emphatic unanimity about the replacement of oral by written instructions," a change that demanded "the complete separation of drafting from execution" (441). Related to this principle of abstraction was the collective adherence of the various members of the movement to J. Slater Lewis's 1899 claim that "it was no longer enough to approach the elements of production by instinctive perception; they must be 'placed artificially in juxtaposition'" (qtd. in Jenks 434–435). In other words, the members of the movement assumed that the worker's intuitive knowledge of a task was not a sufficient basis for drawing scientific conclusions as to the proper method of carrying out that task. Instead, to arrive at a reliable estimate of the efficiency of a given labor process, one had to first subject the worker's actions to analysis according to a new set of rules—rules that were designed and enforced exclusively by a staff of neutral (apparently disinterested) observers (Aitken 16).

To the spokespeople of the works management movement, the biggest obstacle to achieving total control over the production process was the role played by the individual worker's own skills, ideas, and initiative in the performance of any given task. Frederick Taylor, for instance, was certain that, given the opportunity, all workers would prefer to work according to their own personal methods and pace. The easiest way to overcome this obstacle was therefore to replace the worker's own initiative and ideas with commands that emanated from a detached point of view—a supervisory position located apart from the actual labor process but still close enough to allow for its methodical, scientific observation. "Thus under scientific management," Taylor proclaimed, "exact scientific knowledge and methods are everywhere, sooner or later, sure to replace rule of thumb" (104). In time, these managers imagined, the very idea of "skilled" labor would be made obsolete by the exact scientific knowledge of the trained observer.[2]

The Mechanized Worker

The members of the works management movement were not the first to explore different forms of factory organization for raising productivity and lowering costs. Throughout the previous century, a variety of automated and mechanized labor processes had been developed in the grain, biscuit-making, machine shop, and meatpacking industries (Giedion 77–96). But around 1885, before any of the production methods in these industries had become fully mechanized, several industrialists and engineers, including Frederick Taylor, Henry R. Towne, Frederick A. Halsey, and Henry L. Gannt, were experimenting with different kinds of wage-incentive schemes to persuade (or coerce) workers to increase their rates of output (Aitken 46, 247n19; Jenks 435).

The theory behind wage incentives was simple: the more workers earn, the more contented they will be, and, consequently, the more work they will be likely to perform in a given period of time. Hence, the payment of higher wages in the short term would lower the overall labor costs per unit of production in the long term. Simply put, this was because, according to Horace Arnold, the healthy and contented worker would perform work in a more predictable, machinelike fashion ("Modern Machine-Shop" 65). As Arnold explained, in his customary matter-of-fact style, "While the workman is, commercially, a tool, he is also a living animal, and must have a suitable vital environment to make his greatest earning. This living tool has also the power of thought, which leads to content or discontent from either real or fancied causes and again the greatest earning of this living, thinking tool can be made only when his mind is at ease" (1090). Therefore, "The first requirement for low labor cost production is a healthy, contented worker, capable of continued efficient exertion, and not only willing, but eager, to give his utmost effort to advance the designs of the employer" (65, cf. 477, 692). While a variety of different piece-rate wage incentives were designed and implemented around the turn of the century (in the hope that they would function as virtual conveyor belts), the use of a real conveyor belt in continuous-flow methods of production—starting in 1913, at the Ford Motor Company—would eventually eliminate the need for piecerate systems altogether (Thompson; Arnold, "Six Examples" 831; Arnold and Faurote 114). In the end, what all these different methods for regulating workers' productivity had in common was the implicit goal of total mechanization: a completely automated system of mass production, in which human workers were to play as minimal a role as possible (Giedion 77, 99; Jenks 439).[3]

Ford, Fordism, and the Mass Autoworker

The specific figure of the "mass" worker that so fascinated novelists, sociologists, and interested observers of large-scale industrialism in the United States during the first half of the twentieth century was most commonly associated with the highly mechanized environment of the automobile industry. The U.S. auto industry, in addition to having a dramatic impact on the U.S. economy, was more able than any other branch of mass production to fully realize many of the core goals of the works management movement.

The U.S. auto industry expanded the nation's general economy by roughly 500 percent in the first three decades of the century, increasing national income from twenty billion to one hundred billion dollars. The Ford Motor Company played a key role in this development, constantly setting a standard that the other leaders in the industry had no choice but to follow (Chandler, "New Type" 179). As Ford himself saw it, the term *mass production* referred to a method of manufacture that combined three basic elements: (1) fully standardized and interchangeable parts; (2) efficient handling of materials, with a minimum of "lost" time and space; and (3) continuously flowing assembly, made possible through an elaborate network of conveyors, slides, and rollways.

Following the views of Taylor, Arnold, and the majority of scientific managers of the time, Ford preferred to employ unskilled workers and to treat them as just so many units of the fixed costs of production, exactly like the machines in the plant. "As the necessity for production increased it became apparent," according to Ford, "that skilled men were not necessary in production" (*My Life* 77). Almost flippantly, he goes on to explain: "The rank and file of men come to us unskilled; they learn their jobs within a few hours or a few days. If they do not learn within that time they will never be of any use to us. These men are, many of them, foreigners, and all that is required before they are taken on is that they should be potentially able to do enough work to pay the overhead charges on the floor space they occupy" (79; see also Reitell 186).

Because Ford insisted that "pressing always to do work better and faster solves nearly every factory problem," the rate of production in his plants seemed to grow perpetually faster (*My Life* 98). The speedup, therefore, was not an ephemeral or secondary phenomenon but an essential element of Ford's program of mass production. Moreover, the relation Ford assumed between high-volume output and a steadily lower cost per unit was in fact created as a result of the speedup policies Ford instituted in his plants (Ford, *My Life* 146–147; Gartman 114–124). While the origins of this policy are often traced back to Ford's innovative use of moving assembly lines, in this case, too, his thinking is consonant with the principles of members of the works management movement (Arnold, "Production"). In addition, the Ford Motor Company's so-called high-wage policy (the famous "five-dollar day"), while often cited as one of Ford's chief innovations—and a key element of Fordist-style production more generally—was also a direct application of strategies that had been thoroughly hammered out by leaders of the works management movement, beginning in the early 1890s.[4] Once his workers had grown dependent upon a relatively high wage, Ford was certain that this alone would make them docile, obedient, and less prone to limit production in any manner, particularly by trying to unionize (Ford, *My Life* 114–115, 147, 256–257).

The one feature of mass production most closely identified with the term *Fordism* is the use of moving assembly lines, which were fully implemented in Ford's Highland Park plant beginning in 1914.[5] Surveying his accomplishments, Ford recalled how "this was the first moving line ever installed. The idea came in a general way from the overhead trolley that the Chicago packers use in dressing beef" (*My Life* 81). Once the moving line was fully operational, its impact on the different processes of automobile production was both immediate and significant (Chandler, "Ford Expansion" 26; Gartman 83–101).

With the introduction of moving assembly lines at Highland Park, Ford had finally discovered a method to transfer the physical stress demanded by high-volume levels of production from workers to machines (Federal Trade Commission 30). The use of moving assembly lines also allowed for the transfer of control over workers' individual motions—from the workers themselves to their machines. This apparently minor change in production methods in fact signaled a paradigm shift in the overall conception of industrial labor power. For now, instead of the worker being seen as the dynamic element of production, the work itself—the impersonal job or set of tasks that needed to be performed—embodied the dynamic principle of the factory. In opposition to the work, the worker now occupied a stationary and fixed position in the general system of production. The work alone moved, and it moved past a series of individual workers who were fixed in their places (Ford, *My Life* 83). Recalling the days before this shift occurred, Ford explains how, at first, "we simply started to put a car together at a spot on the floor and workmen brought to it the parts as they were needed in exactly the same way that one builds a house.... The first step forward in assembly came when we began taking the work to the men instead of the men to the work" (*My Life* 79–80). Since the primary aim here was to keep the various "jobs" in a state of constant motion, the workers, in the eyes of management, came to be seen as merely "fixed points of component supply" stationed along the endless conveyor belt (Arnold and Faurote 129). Oddly enough, in spite of these measures to achieve the maximum degree of control over workers' bodily movements, Ford continued to maintain that his workers were not "mere machines," as he put it (*My Life* 279).

A New Boss: Technical Control

From 1915 to 1935, the Ford Motor Company served as a model of mass production techniques, demonstrating to other large industrialists in these years how, in a plant where "the work moves and the men stand still," rates of productivity can be increased tenfold in a very short time (Nevins and Hill, *Ford: Expansion* 288). From the workers' perspective, however, Ford's brand of continuous-flow production meant a completely different shop-floor environment, one in which they were no longer expected to move around, think, or speak to one another while performing their tasks. As Ford saw it, this was undoubtedly a positive development, for it eliminated every type of soldiering on the job—a change that would supposedly benefit workers and management alike (Ford, *My Life* 80). Yet, for Ford workers at the point of production, the environment of the shop floor had turned into a virtual nightmare of automated, never-ending processes, which seemed to be moving faster and faster all the time.

Although continuous-flow assembly and its characteristic forms of speedup originated at Ford, they quickly became common features of auto manufacturing plants throughout the industry (Adamic, *Dynamite* 402). In contrast to earlier schemes to intensify rates of production, what was distinctly new about this type of speedup was that it seemed to rely exclusively on the technology of the conveyor belt. That is, it appeared to transfer control over the whole process of production, taking it out of the hands of the plant's various supervisors, foremen, and straw bosses and relocating it in the impersonal operations of the plant's machinery.

The industrial labor historian Richard Edwards has argued that this new form of factory-level authority should be understood as an example of what he calls "technical control": a method for controlling the labor process at the point of production through impersonal technological means instead of personal directives and supervision (110, 116–120). "It was the Ford assembly line," according to Edwards, "that brought the technical direction of work to its fullest potential" (117). Likewise, in any plant that has been organized according to Fordist principles, the power exercised by the firm's management gets translated, literally and figuratively, into the power of the moving conveyor lines. This means that the abstract control exercised by management over the rate of production is now seemingly embodied in the form of the physical structures of the plant itself. Hence, "whatever the sequence of tasks" chosen by the production managers, the continuously moving assembly line, Edwards notes, "transformed that order into a technological necessity. Even if many assembly sequences were physically possible, the line left the workers no choice about how to do their jobs" (118).

One result of this transfer of control was that workers and entrepreneurs alike were led to believe that large-scale, mass industrial production was an impersonal, superhuman process. Their involvement in this process at any level therefore implied submission to a power that not only was outside themselves but transcended the limits of every form of human agency (Ford, *My Life* 73, 263–264; Ford, *My Philosophy* 40, 45, 65). Such an awe-inspired perspective left mass industrial workers few, if any, opportunities to "do things" in their own right. Instead, they all seemed to be just so many cogs in a larger mechanism, one that moved according to the dictates of its own momentum, obeying only its own commands.

However, as we will see in Part Two of this study ("Strategy and Structure at the Point of Production"), neither Ford nor any of the other major industrialists during this period were able to safeguard such a system of production against the possibility of workers' acts of resistance. The seeds of a large wave of labor unrest in Fordist mass production industries during the 1930s had already been planted, ironically, by the very same devices (namely, technical control) that Ford had implemented specifically to protect his interests against the threat of recalcitrant workers. Large vertically integrated manufacturing concerns such as Ford and GM discovered that they were structurally vulnerable to even the smallest acts of resistance at the point of production.

In addition to this structural vulnerability, the ongoing efforts of large firms to mechanize and automate their systems of production—replacing skilled with unskilled and semiskilled labor processes—consistently generated spontaneous acts of retaliation from workers, who resented being treated as if they were elements of the fixed capital (machinery) of the plant in which they worked. Local disputes over speedups, centered at the point of production in the plant, were therefore the most common form of labor unrest in mass production industries in the United States throughout the 1920s and 1930s. Added to this was the fact that workers who were incessantly driven to produce more, at faster rates, lost whatever sense of satisfaction they might have gained from their job. Since such workers felt they had no real personal stake in the overall health of the company that employed them, it became that much easier for them to justify their own random acts of sabotage (slowdowns, work-to-rules, and so forth).

Finally, and most importantly, because mass workers on continuously moving assembly lines were regularly admonished by foremen for working either too fast or too slow, they very quickly realized, collectively, how important each individual worker was for maintaining the overall smooth operation of the plant. Although they were viewed by management as a mere mass of unskilled "line" workers—or, at best, as a collection of semiskilled, interchangeable machine tenders—these same workers came to see that even a small minority of them possessed the power to block the flow of production throughout the entire plant (and, potentially, throughout the entire company).

For all of these reasons, Richard Edwards reminds us, the "struggle between workers and bosses over the transformation of labor power into labor" changed qualitatively once Ford's continuous-flow methods of production came to dominate the operations of large industrial firms in the first decades of the twentieth century. In the context of huge, highly integrated, multidivisional plants, any conflict between labor and management was therefore "no longer a simple and direct *personal* confrontation," as it had been in the previous century. "Now the conflict was mediated by the production technology itself. Workers had to oppose the pace of the *line*, not the (direct) tyranny of their bosses" (118). How mass workers found ways to do this—and how novelists chose to represent it, exactly—will be the concern of the second part of this study.

For now, our attention will focus on two thematically different, but logically related, ways in which certain novelists chose to portray mass workers in this period. The figures of mass workers one encounters in their novels have either submitted themselves to or been absorbed by the overwhelming and inhuman power of modern industry. In such fictional portraits mass workers therefore appear either as the degraded and powerless victims of mass production or as heroic, empowered icons—embodiments of the technological wonders of modern industrial capitalism.

1 / The Powerless Worker and the Failure of Political Representation: "The lowest and most degraded of human beasts"

Upton Sinclair reserves this designation—"the lowest and most degraded of human beasts"—to describe what he considered to be the ethnically and racially inferior "scab" workers during a meatpackers' strike in Chicago (*Jungle* 255). From another angle, though, this phrase could also be taken as conveying one of the more common images of mass industrial workers that novelists invoked during the first two decades of the twentieth century. However, because Sinclair goes to such great lengths to portray the horrific effects of the mechanized meatpacking industry on its workforce, by the end of his novel there is practically no way to distinguish legitimate workers from their scab counterparts. In Sinclair's view, all of the workers he describes sooner or later become transformed into "human beasts" by the processes of mass production. Indeed, their degradation in the environment of the industrial workplace is so profound that it finally escapes the descriptive and representational resources of Sinclair's language. Hence, Sinclair must frequently have recourse to the metaphor of the "worker-as-beast": his fictitious workers enter the realm of mass production only to become slaughtered, victims of the very labor processes they are forced to perform.

This first chapter examines how the mass worker was portrayed in certain fictional narratives as powerless and in need of symbolic social forms of representation. The politicians and political parties that appear in these novels see it as their duty to "speak for" and in the place of a working class that has no voice of its own. Guided by the assumption that mass workers lack social agency, the authors of these novels tend to imagine them as a brute, intractable force. They describe such workers as nothing more than mute, suffering, helpless bodies—masses of flesh that simultaneously require representation and resist being represented in symbolic terms. According to the contradictory logic of these narratives, mass workers need to be symbolically represented—that is, politically spoken for—to better their condition, yet the horrific nature of their condition implies that they can never be symbolized as such.

The figure of the degraded and powerless mass worker began to appear in fictional narratives during the first years of the twentieth century, and it continued to surface in U.S. working-class novels up through the 1940s. This chapter examines a series of novels in which an especially degraded figure of the mass worker, present in a variety of different industrial settings, plays a central role. It begins by exploring some general questions about the relationship between degradation and representation in the industrial workplace, through studying the example of Frederick Taylor's racialized brand of scientific management. It then analyzes a short section of Thomas Bell's CIO-era novel *Out of This Furnace* (1941), about Pittsburgh steelworkers who find themselves struggling for the most elementary forms of respect against both managerial and trade union bureaucracies. Next, it considers the ways in which Upton Sinclair's novel about the experience of Chicago meatpackers, *The Jungle* (1906), differs radically from another famous novel by one of Sinclair's socialist contemporaries, Jack London's *The Iron Heel* (1907). While Sinclair's novel focuses almost exclusively on meatpackers, London's novel details the recent emergence of a general—and, for London, horrific—mass industrial working class, not tied to any specific industry. Finally, the chapter concludes by juxtaposing two novels that pushed the degraded, dehumanized image of the mass worker to its logical limits. Dalton Trumbo's *Johnny Got His Gun* (1939) emphasizes the universally degrading effects of having to work in a society defined by mass production, where humans are used and disposed of as nothing more than pieces of flesh. As Trumbo's novel shows, such extreme forms of degradation are difficult (perhaps impossible) to represent through the medium of fictional narrative. Clara Weatherwax's *Marching! Marching!* (1935), on the other hand, is about lumber mill workers in the Pacific Northwest whose bodies become dismembered by mechanized saws, to be literally fused into the material of the lumber products they make. Weatherwax's excessively gruesome depictions of workers who die or become dismembered in the lumber mill imply that the class-conscious solidarity of the industrial workforce does not emanate from the U.S.

Communist Party's ideological doctrine (as the novel is usually interpreted). Rather, the novel demonstrates how solidarity among industrial workers is a concrete, nondiscursive effect of their shared experience of mechanized degradation.

All of these novels share a focus on the image of the mass worker as a helpless, degraded, and abject victim of the processes of mechanized mass production. It is important to examine them together as a group, not only for their own sake, but as a point of departure for the rest of the novels we will be considering in later chapters. For, as a whole, this particular group of novels provides an overview of the extreme forms of abject suffering that many writers in the first half of the century associated with the new methods of mass production in factories. They serve as a sort of barometer, then, of the state of shock that many writers and intellectuals experienced upon first realizing what actually took place in the modern factory. The aim of the following analyses is thus to gain a sense of the specific reasons why certain novelists during this period (1905–1941) were apt to dismiss the notion that mass workers could benefit from traditional political forms of representation.

The Taylor System

Although Frederick Taylor was only one of many industrial engineers who proposed rationalized production methods in the first years of the twentieth century, his contributions are significant for having formulated and synthesized much of the thinking of the works management movement. Taylor's idealized vision of a society organized by "experts" was shared by many industrial and civil engineers of the period, as well as by bourgeois (reform) socialists, such as Upton Sinclair. It is therefore appropriate to begin by examining in somewhat greater detail how Taylor defined the terms of his own system, in order better to discern the specific impact this system had on the conception of the modern mass worker.

The basic aim not only of Taylor's brand of management but of the works management movement as a whole was to produce a maximum of industrial output in the shortest period of time, at a minimum cost, through achieving complete control over each element of the labor process. This control was gained, first, through the close analysis of workers while they were performing their tasks. The results of such an analysis were then carefully studied, by self-professed "experts," to find the most efficient ways to perform these tasks. Finally, their analysis culminated in the systematic rearrangement of the entire labor process, with specifically and narrowly defined tasks assigned to individual workers.

Throughout his writings, Taylor makes emphatic claims for the scientific nature of his method. However, by taking away the right of workers to decide how they would perform their work, the program of rationalization, in the name of scientific "efficiency," actually sought to make collective bargaining irrelevant to the whole process of production. Hence, Richard Edwards reminds us, "In order to impose the new Taylorized standards, management had to break the workers' power to resist" (102).

One way Taylor and his colleagues sought to break the power of workers to resist the reorganization of the workplace was to posit an imaginary relationship of cooperation between workers and management, which was then prescribed to the managers of industrial firms as an ideal to be realized at the point of production. The logical corollary to this ideal of a quasi-natural harmony between workers and employers was that any form of labor strife was to be regarded as an irrational outburst, "senseless folly" (Arnold, "Modern Machine-Shop" 1095), an instance of "that war of self on self . . . which is now the bitter disgrace of civilization in its highest form" (1096, cf. 1091–1092; Arnold, "Six Examples" 80, 276).

In a lecture Taylor delivered in 1909, entitled "Why Manufacturers Dislike College Students," he defined the notion of "cooperation," with respect to workers, to mean simply "to do what they are told to do promptly and without asking questions or making suggestions" (qtd. in Aitken 46). In the same spirit, Horace Arnold—an engineering journalist who was one of Taylor's supporters and a well-informed advocate of rationalized production methods—claimed that geographically isolated factories were ideally suited to foster this sort of cooperation, since they "favor the growth and education of successive generations [of workers] inclined by heredity to become efficient and docile operatives" ("Six Examples" 285). To Taylor, Arnold, and the other representatives of the works management movement, it was a commonly accepted fact that efficient workers would have to be docile as well. Because the machinery of modern industrial production embodied, in their eyes, the perfect model of efficiency, they assumed that only docile workers—those who submitted entirely to the dictates of the machine—could operate them effectively. From this principle, logically, it followed that workers should also blindly obey the dictates of their managers, the industrial "experts" who knew how to organize the workplace along rational lines, thus converting it into an extended model of machine efficiency. In all of this, according to the historian of Taylorism Hugh Aitken, the worker's only role "was to be passive—that of an efficient but self-effacing servant of the real producer, the machine" (46).[1]

Yet what is an absolutely obedient, docile, silent and passive worker if not a mere appendage of the machine that he or she operates? Such a dim, utilitarian view of the matter, though rarely stated outright, was occasionally expressed by the more frankly instrumental-minded representatives of the works management movement. Horace Arnold, who occasionally used the phrase "living tool" to refer to mass workers, is most explicit on this point: "Shall the machinist be regarded solely in this commercial aspect, as a part of the machine-shop equipment, having certain earning potentialities, giving the reasonable expectation of profits to his employer, a means to an end, in a word simply a tool, to be hired at the lowest possible rate, and discarded promptly upon evidence of reduced efficiency? Probably the truest kindness and charity and philanthropy will answer this question in the affirmative, with only circumstantial qualifications, which do not in the slightest degree modify the policy" ("Modern Machine-Shop" 1090). Eighteen years later, in 1914, Arnold and Faurote would find just such an ideal worker ("simply a tool") in Henry Ford's Highland Park automobile factory, which had recently converted all of its labor processes into continuous-flow assembly lines. In their detailed report on the plant, it is clear that Ford's mass production workers should in no way be seen as exercising any sort of authority, or possessing any sort of knowledge, in relation to the machinery they operate. The authors observe: "The Ford Company has no use for experience, in the working ranks, anyway. It desires and prefers machine-tool operators who have nothing to unlearn, who have no theories of correct [methods of work] . . . and will simply do what they are told to do, over and over again, from bell-time to bell-time" (41–42). As Arnold and Taylor would have it, the knowledge and authority embodied in the machines are simply the reflections of the knowledge and authority of the industrial engineers who designed this ultrarational system of production. Ford's workers should therefore be permitted to do, or think, only what the machines—the materialized will of the managers—command.

If it seemed to be asking too much of workers to expect them to think and behave like machines, Arnold and Taylor (and later, Ford) were convinced that paying workers relatively higher wages would solve this problem. High wages were thus used as a disciplinary device to enforce the will of the management. Even with the wage incentive, however, workers were not always willing, in Arnold's words, to "make horses of themselves" ("Production" 922). In tacit recognition of this fact, it would appear, Taylor repeatedly had to remind business managers that "it is only through *enforced* standardization of methods, *enforced* adoption of the best implements and working conditions, and *enforced* cooperation that this faster work can be assured" (83). On the whole, therefore, the techniques of labor efficiency advocated by Taylor and his associates were nothing more than a "desperate attempt to find some way of reconciling the working class to the agonies of mechanized production and transferring its implacable resistance into creative co-operation" (James 51).

Typecast Workers

To rationalize production in any given company, Taylor insisted upon a strict division of labor between workers and managers, which presupposed an absolute separation between the "conception" and the "execution" of the labor process (Edwards 104). Such a division of labor was essential because, as Taylor saw it, "Even if the workman was well suited to the development and use of scientific data, it would be physically impossible for him to work at his machine and at a desk at the same time. It is also clear that in most cases one type of man is needed to plan ahead and an entirely different type to execute the work" (38). Taylor is here concerned with a logistical problem of engineering—the physical impossibility of one worker being in two places at the same time—which he solves by means of a categorical distinction between "types" of men.

For Taylor, though, it is a question not simply of local differences between individual, discrete workers but of differences between entirely distinct classes of human labor power. That is, whenever he speaks of different "types" of men, he is at the same time defining an elite class of "brain workers" in contradistinction to the lower classes of labor, the class of "muscle workers." Such a division of labor in the workplace (between planners and executors) could then be further justified by invoking a conventional discourse of "natural" aptitudes: while some workers are naturally fit to be laborers, so Taylor might reason, others are naturally fit to be managers.

In general, engineers like Taylor and Arnold considered low-wage unskilled laborers—those who occupied the bulk of the mass industrial workforce—to be inherently unsuited to advance to higher-paying skilled jobs. "The typical wage-earner," as Arnold put it, "is, first of all, incapable of managing any business, even his own—much more that of an assemblage of his fellows. . . . If a man is capable of managing, servitude is revolting to him, and he will not continue a day-wage earner" ("Modern Machine-Shop" 1091). Taylor was even more candid when expressing his conviction that the mass worker possessed only a negligible degree of intellectual capacity. In his view, scientific management "is directly antagonistic to the old idea that each workman can best regulate his own way of doing the work. And besides this, the [unskilled] man suited to handling pig iron is too stupid properly to train himself" (63). Taylor elaborates this point in two of his more notorious comments:

> This work is so crude and elementary in its nature that the writer firmly believes that it would be possible to train an intelligent gorilla so as to become a more efficient pig-iron handler than any man can be.... In almost all of the mechanic arts the science which underlies each workman's act is so great and amounts to so much that the workman who is best suited actually to do the work is incapable (either through lack of education or through insufficient mental capacity) of understanding this science. (40–41)

> Now one of the very first requirements for a man who is fit to handle pig iron as a regular occupation is that he shall be so stupid and so phlegmatic that he more nearly resembles in his mental make-up the ox than any other type. The man who is mentally alert and intelligent is for this very reason entirely unsuited to what would, for him, be the grinding monotony of work of this character. Therefore the workman who is best suited to handling pig iron is unable to understand the real science of doing this class of work. He is so stupid that the word "percentage" has no meaning to him, and he must consequently be trained by a man more intelligent than himself into the habit of working in accordance with the laws of this science before he can be successful. (59)

Those who are suited to *handling* pig iron, then, are manifestly unsuited to *manage the process* of handling pig iron, including their own individual process. To be exact, as Taylor sees it, pig-iron handlers' "own" labor process is no process at all, because by definition it is not (and could never be) scientific. Their capacity to perform this kind of work is instead taken by Taylor to be a sufficient proof of their "insufficient mental capacity." Moreover, although stupid workers—like gorillas and oxen—need intelligent experts to train them, for Taylor, the fact that they do not always do what they are told (and are thus less efficient than they could be) only stands as further proof of their stupidity. As a manager himself, Taylor explains that whenever he had to train "a man of the type of the ox" he had to command absolute and unquestioning obedience, for this type of man was "so stupid that he was unfitted to do most kinds of laboring work, even" (61–62).

It is important to note that Taylor here is associating the physical nature of a particular job with the physical qualities of the worker who is engaged in it and then inferring the worker's relative lack of intellectual capacity on the basis of this association. The physicality of the effort required to perform a job is thus retroactively made to serve as confirming the truth of Taylor's initial assumption that, in every conceivable instance, a specific "type" of worker is inherently suited, both physically and mentally, for a particular kind of job.[2] According to this scheme, then, managers should be able to determine a worker's intellectual capacity with accuracy and efficiency, since it is inversely proportionate to his or her bodily capacity. The more physically demanding the job, the stupider, consequently, the worker who is able to perform it reveals himself to be.

Efficient methods of production therefore boil down to a question of the right types of bodies working together, machinelike, to maintain a certain predetermined level of output. Corresponding to this method of production, a system of management that "deals with the worker as a simple tool, a mere commercial commodity," is essential because this kind of system alone is founded "on a correct basis of money values by which the capital of the master joins with the capital of the workmen in the form of their own bodies" (Arnold, "Modern Machine-Shop" 1091). In this scenario, the "living tools," the workers, constitute a material element of the plant machinery because, from the managers' point of view, they are nothing more than the productive capacity of their bodies. Indeed, since Arnold and Taylor believed that capital was most tangibly present in the physical bodies of workers and machinery alike, they were especially impressed by labor processes in which "purely hand operations involving the use of purely muscular power are urged and driven and rushed to the limit of the workmen's strength, precisely as the tools are driven to the limit of their powers" (Arnold, "Production" 922).

Mass-Produced Difference

Although the principles of scientific management may not appear to have any especially racialized, gendered, or ethnic implications, when one reads Taylor's accounts of precisely how they are applied in the workplace, it is clear that he conceived of the engineer's "monopoly of knowledge" as a matter of identifying and manipulating certain physiological qualities supposedly inherent to individual types of workers. If, therefore, these various types of workers can be distinguished on the basis of their particular ethnic, racialized, or gendered characteristics—presumably natural marks of difference—then an expert knowledge of such characteristic types will play a key role in the scientific management of any given industrial firm. Conversely, the degree of rationalization attained by the management can easily be made to appear as, at bottom, a matter of the ethnic, racial, or gendered division of labor in the firm. By simply altering or reshuffling the division of labor along these lines, industrial mass production can resort to (what it takes to be) perfectly "scientific" solutions for its problems.[3]

To illustrate how the distinction between two basic types of workers—intellectual versus physical—could be translated into racial, ethnic, or gendered terms, it is useful to recall one of Taylor's most famous anecdotes, which begins: "The task before us, then, narrowed itself down to getting Schmidt to handle 47 tons of pig iron per day and making him glad to do it" (44). After verbally chastising and then eventually persuading Schmidt—"a little Pennsylvania Dutchman" who doubts his ability to perform such a task—Taylor reflects on the whole process: "This seems to be rather rough talk. And indeed it would be if applied to an educated mechanic, or even an intelligent laborer. With a man of the mentally sluggish type of Schmidt it is appropriate and not unkind, since it is effective in fixing his attention on the high wages which he wants and away from what, if it were called to his attention, he probably would consider impossibly hard work" (46). The fact that Taylor conceives of Schmidt—a hard-working immigrant who speaks broken English—as a "man of the mentally sluggish *type*" suggests that, from Taylor's perspective, certain kinds of workers are naturally predisposed to brute, physical labor. And conversely, their predisposition to this kind of labor is justified by Taylor on the grounds of brute, physical evidence: Schmidt's muscular ability to lift heavy loads of pig iron, combined with his lack of a mastery of English and his outsider status as ethnically marked. His extraordinary physical capacity is here associated with his "foreign" status, and both are taken as proof that he is stupid and thus aptly suited to perform this kind of labor.

The tendency to identify foreign immigrant workers, who were ethnically or racially marked, with various kinds of degraded and unskilled labor was shared by virtually every representative of the works management movement. This tendency continued to exert a powerful influence on managerial thinking within mass production industries well into the twentieth century. In 1915, for example, between 50 and 60 percent of the workforce at Ford's Highland Park plant was made up of "non-English-speaking foreigners" (Lee 193). The Ford Motor Company's use of such workers was distinguished by the fact that, through its Sociological Department, it sought to remake them into "decent" Americans, or rather, as Ford's official historians put it, "to convince irascible Slavs, Italians, or Greeks that the company standards would be pleasanter and healthier than those they had brought from their native lands" (Nevins and Hill, *Ford: Expansion* 335). So, whereas Horace Arnold in the 1890s routinely expressed disdain for such workers as "the low type of the Jewish tailors inhabiting the east side of New York," who were nevertheless essential elements of mass production, twenty-five years later Henry Ford could proudly claim that the majority of his rank-and-file employees were unskilled foreigners who spoke little English (Arnold, "Modern Machine-Shop" 1089; Ford, *My Life* 79; see also Meyer 67–94).[4]

Depending on the type of worker concerned, then, the American Dream of financial success as Taylor imagines it is achievable, but only in the degree to which one can demonstrate one's nonethnic (fully "American") status, one's nonracialization (being racially white), and one's nongendering (being gendered as male).[5] Furthermore, if one happens to be ethnically, sexually, racially or otherwise associated with the "lower" classes, Taylor's scheme celebrates how one's humanity can still be fully recognized as such through the sheer immutability and naturalness of this fact. His utopian vision of a society of brain workers can therefore be read as an attempt to justify scientifically a technocratic ruling elite consisting solely of well-educated white males. In Taylor's words: "The demand for men of originality and brains was never so great as it is now, and the modern subdivision of labor, instead of dwarfing men, enables them all along the line to rise to a higher plane of efficiency, involving at the same time more brain work and less monotony. The type of man who was formerly a day laborer and digging dirt is now for instance making shoes in a shoe factory. The dirt handling is done by Italians or Hungarians" (qtd. in Braverman 129; cf. Ehrenreich and Fuentes 47; Kraut 77–78).

The dramatic growth of vertically integrated mass industrial enterprises between 1900 and 1920 would not have been possible without just such an institutionalized system for coordinating and controlling labor productivity. This system had its theoretical origins in the logistical programs developed by the works management movement, as illustrated by Taylor's "principles of scientific management"; but the program of scientific management itself presupposed, and was in turn enabled by, an implicit theory of the proper (most efficient) types of workers for every level of the industrial firm's operations. In short, then, the emergence of industrial mass production in the United States needs to be understood as vitally linked to—indeed, as not possible without—certain notions of race, gender, and ethnicity that were presumed to be self-evident to Americans during the first half of the twentieth century. It was the relatively independent material science underlying mass industrial methods of production that lent a quasi-natural, self-evident character to the racial, ethnic, and gendered representational categories upon which managers' full control over the workforce relied. In turn, these variously articulated representations of embodied labor power were intricately tied to the organizational structure of the mass industrial firm, providing the material substrate, as it were, for a corporate edifice that appeared to be solely the brainchild of technicians and logistical engineers.

In other words, the organization of highly complex, systematic methods of production in U.S. mass industrial firms—which economists and historians often take to be a purely logistical or managerial phenomenon—in fact required a material base of actual human bodies, the materiality of which, however, it made every effort to disavow in the interests of its properly scientific management. Nevertheless, taken together, the ensemble of material effects that the various forms of scientific management had on the mass industrial workforce was such that the meaning, as well as the lived experience, of work in the twentieth century underwent a sea change. The mass industrial worker had become not only degraded, to use Braverman's expression, but fundamentally racialized, ethnicized, and gendered to a degree that no worker's body was left unaccounted for in the hierarchy of a modern firm's network of operations.

The Deskilling of the Industrial Worker

For a particularly clear illustration of the racializing effects of the Taylor system, one need only examine Thomas Bell's 1941 novel about three generations of western Pennsylvania steelworkers, *Out of This Furnace* (subtitled "A Novel of Immigrant Labor in America"). The entire narrative of Bell's novel is organized around this racial-ethnic stratification of the modern industrial workforce, shifting over time with the changes in the technology of steel production. Bell's omniscient narrator notes that the steelworkers in the Pittsburgh region

> were in the beginning mostly American and English. When the Irish came the Americans and English, to whom sheer precedence as much as anything else now gave a near monopoly of the skilled jobs and best wages, moved to the streets above Main and into North Braddock. The First Ward [directly adjacent to the mill] was taken over by the Irish. But the forces that had brought the Irish to Braddock were still at work. New mills and furnaces were built, new supplies of labor found. The Slovaks came; and once more there was a general displacement.... That the company openly preferred foreigners as laborers, that immigration from western Europe had fallen off, that the hours were long, the work hard and the opportunities for advancement rare, helped explain why the unskilled labor force was predominantly foreign by the beginning of the new century. (Bell 122–124)

This description reveals how the expansion of the steel industry depended upon a steady influx of newly arrived immigrants who would be willing to work in the most menial and low-paying jobs. In addition, by closely tying job-skill classifications to categories of racially and ethnically embodied labor, the managerial middle class came to view the lowest rungs of the mills' workforce in animalistic, subhuman terms. "This strike [of unskilled steelworkers] is not being brought about by intelligent, English-speaking workmen," proclaims a pastor to his congregation "in the 'good' part of town." He continues: "You can't reason with these people. Don't reason with them. You can't, any more than you can with a cow or a horse" (Bell 241–242; cf. Foner, *Industrial Workers* 282, 294).

The experience of one of the central characters of *Out of This Furnace*, Mike Dobrejcak, provides an especially clear picture of the hierarchical relations of steel production, where a separation between the planning and execution of work is strictly enforced. The novel thereby details how a "monopoly over knowledge" accompanies and facilitates the translation of unskilled, degraded labor into (degrading) racial-ethnic types. For example, whenever the General Superintendent of the mill comes to observe Mike and his coworkers in the blast furnace,

> [his] presence disturbed the rhythm, the relationship, between worker and job.... With his appearance the furnace and the men

became separate. It was now his furnace and they its servants, and
his; for its well-being they were responsible now not to the furnace
and to themselves, their pride in knowing how to handle her, but to
him. He took it away from them. They ceased to be men of skill and
knowledge, ironmakers, and were degraded to the status of employees who did what they were told for a wage, whose feelings didn't
matter, not even their feelings for the tools, the machines, they
worked with, or for the work they did. (Bell 166)

Given such a workplace environment where he feels continually robbed of his skills and intelligence by the authority of the General Superintendent, Mike eventually loses his faith in political forms of superintendence as well. After defying company policy by voting for the socialist candidate Eugene V. Debs in the presidential election of 1912, with the hope that this will improve the condition of the working class, he briefly fears the loss of his job if his vote were to be revealed. Yet when nothing happens, instead of feeling relieved that his job is secure, he suspects that, by voting for Debs, he is nothing more than a "flinger of pebbles against a fortress, his impunity was the measure of his impotence" (Bell 190). As his faith in the power of political representation is further shaken, he remarks: "Nobody can help us but ourselves, and if anything is to be done we will have to do it ourselves" (194). Thus, once an ardent believer in the power of elected representatives to improve the lives of their constituents, Mike finally comes to the conclusion that "the mass of men were . . . striving for all their blunders toward worthy goals and failing most often when they put their trust in leaders rather than in themselves" (199).

Over the course of *Out of This Furnace*, Bell establishes a close correlation between these two apparently separate themes: the degradation of unskilled labor and the loss of faith in elected representatives. Whenever his characters sense that their skills and intellects are being ignored in the context of the workplace, they respond by withdrawing their active support from those who claim the authority to represent their interests outside the workplace. Just as "the furnace and the men became separate," where the relationship between job and worker is severed through the power of the General Superintendent, these characters feel separated from their own interests and voices whenever they must depend on representatives to speak "for" them and in place of them.

Their simultaneous efforts to repair these two sets of broken relationships would seem, therefore, to indicate a continuity between forms of managerial control in the workplace and the apparatuses of ideological and political representation in the broader society. To guarantee the smooth operation of a steel mill, its leaders/managers must be able to count on a "controlled" workforce. This is secured through a process of deskilling, which in turn enables a representation of workers as so many racial-ethnic types of embodied labor power. While this process is occurring inside the mill, outside the mill these same workers now suspect that they are being controlled insofar as they naively allow themselves to be "represented," and potentially misled, by their chosen leaders. In each context, control—of one's labor and of one's interests—can be restored only by being dislodged from its identification with a given representational power.

"The Lowest and Most Degraded of Human Beasts"

In contrast to Bell's account of the steelworkers, Upton Sinclair's 1906 novel about Chicago meatpackers, *The Jungle*, supposes that the deskilling of workers will automatically lead them to acquire a faith in the Socialist Party and its representatives. Why exactly this should be the case, however, the novel does not make clear. The fact that it was published thirty-five years before Bell's novel suggests two possible explanations for this discrepancy. On the one hand, the optimistic outlook of socialists in 1906 could have been so profound that socialist writers at the time, such as Sinclair, simply assumed that it would cure every imaginable social ill. On the other hand, in 1906, the full effects of the deskilling of the industrial workforce had not yet become fully known to the general population. Indeed, at that time, techniques of scientific management were only just starting to affect a broad number of workers in different branches of U.S. mass industrial enterprise.

Sinclair's description of the division of labor in the packinghouse stresses that the class hierarchy here is determined in relation to the filthiness of the work performed: "The managers and superintendents and clerks of Packingtown were all recruited from another class, and never from the workers.... Perhaps this state of affairs was due to the repulsiveness of the work; at any rate, the people who worked with their hands were a class apart, and were made to feel it" (*Jungle* 94). To work with the hands likewise means that a worker's intellect must be totally subordinated to the series of bodily operations required for the job. Thus for the packinghouse workers "every faculty that was not needed for the machine was doomed to be crushed out of existence" (127). Whereas the work itself may be dirty and mind-numbing, Sinclair takes this fact one step further, adopting and making more explicit Taylor's racial-ethnic stereotyping of the "Italians and Hungarians" who are suited only for "dirt handling." During a strike, for example, we are told that the packinghouse recruited "negroes and the lowest types of foreigners—Greeks, Roumanians, Sicilians and Slovaks" as scabs to do the dirtiest jobs (247). Again, echoing the remarks of the pastor in *Out of This Furnace*, Sinclair refers to these same workers as "a throng of stupid black negroes, and foreigners who could not understand a word that was said to them" (248) and as "the lowest and most degraded of human beasts" (255).[6]

But it is not enough that Sinclair's workers, to be reckoned as "human beasts," are racially and ethnically marked, perform grueling tasks, and do not understand English. The degradation of the packinghouse workers in *The Jungle* depends equally upon the purely corporeal nature of the work they perform. Sinclair calls attention to this by highlighting the devastating effects of this work on the actual bodies of the meatpackers. The numerous injuries and diseases he cites all share the fact that "the worker bore the evidence of them about on his own person—generally he had only to hold out his hand" (90). Workers' bodies figure significantly in this novel as pieces of evidence of the destructive effects of capitalism. To be a meatpacker, as Sinclair sees it, is to be nothing more than a body that will be entirely consumed by the capitalist machine. Such a body is "unregenerate" in the most literal sense: it generates nothing of itself beyond the profits that result from its total consumption within the packinghouse. Of the novel's protagonist, Jurgis Rudkos, Sinclair tells us that "in the beginning he had been fresh and strong, and he had gotten a job the first day; but now he was second-hand, so to speak, and they did not want him. He was a damaged article, to put it exactly" (114); indeed, "They were simply not counting him at all. He was of no consequence—he was flung aside, like a bit of trash, the carcass of some dead animal" (147).

Sinclair's meatpackers therefore function collectively to display a wholly abject working class that has lost its voice and agency, along with the skills and intelligence that previous generations of workers possessed. Further, Sinclair's notion of degradation differs from that of Bell insofar as it recognizes no possibility of autonomous thought or action on the part of his characters. Where Mike Dobrejcak at least knows that he possesses skills and intellect, and that these are being undervalued both inside and outside the steel mill, Jurgis and the rest of the meatpackers are made to appear completely helpless and ignorant of their condition through the very terms of their representation in the novel.

One way to explain this discrepancy in the way that Bell and Sinclair depict workers' degradation is to note the pivotal role played by Sinclair's zealous, evangelical form of socialism within the overall representational strategy of *The Jungle*. Jurgis first hears the socialist gospel and undergoes his conversion while he is listening to an orator proclaim, "I speak with the voice of the millions who are voiceless" (282). Later, while Eugene V. Debs is speaking at a rally for his 1904 presidential campaign, the narrator reminds us that "the tears of suffering little children pleaded in his voice" (325). Socialists are portrayed here not simply as eminent and gifted public speakers but as those who speak of, for, and in place of an utterly voiceless working class (Rideout 35–36). Since for Sinclair workers and suffering children alike have no voice to speak of, they must (and can only) be spoken for by representatives of the Socialist Party. When the lost voices of abject and helpless workers are finally represented—which is to say, discovered and united—in the voice of the socialist, they become transfigured into what Sinclair calls "the voice of Labor, despised and outraged! A mighty giant, lying prostrate—mountainous, colossal, but blinded, ignorant of his strength" (*Jungle* 286). Sinclair's working class, then, although a mighty giant, is an essentially passive and mindless mass of "unregenerate" mute bodies, "wandering in darkness, and waiting to be delivered" by the truth of socialism (304).

Sinclair's brand of socialism exchanges a faith in Christ and divine revelation for a faith in socialist representation and the electoral process. The bottom-line priority for this version of socialism is not organizing workers into militant unions or waging successful mass strikes but voting the socialist ticket and spreading the good news of the coming of a socialist government. Furthermore, this task cannot rely on the initiative of the workers; for, at least in *The Jungle*, the workers, Sinclair tells us,

> were ignorant and helpless, and they would remain at the mercy of their exploiters until they were organized—until they had become "class-conscious." That was a Socialist phrase; it meant that a workingman had come to perceive once and for all that the interests of his employer and his own were opposite; and then he would join the Socialist movement, and devote all his efforts to opening the eyes of others. It was a slow and weary work, but it would be done—it was like the movement of a glacier, once it was started it could never be stopped. Every Socialist did his share, and lived upon the vision of the "good time" coming—when the working-class should go to the polls and seize the powers of government, and put an end to private property in the means of production. . . . Nowhere else

[than in Chicago] were the unions so strong; but their organizations did the workers little good, for the employers were organized, also; and so the strikes generally failed, and as fast as the unions were broken up the men came over to the Socialists. It was a fine thing to see—one could feel the excitement in the very air, and even the "old party" [Democratic and Republican] papers were forced to admit that the Socialists were holding the most successful political meetings of the present campaign.... The vote was going to be a record-breaker. It would set a mark, and break the conspiracy of silence of the capitalist press—they would have to discuss Socialism, and, even though they told lies about it, more people would begin to ask questions. So it was that the party made its progress, carrying the ground inch by inch, in the face of every obstacle. (*Jungle* 292–293)

Note how Sinclair implicitly rejects as impotent every working-class organization that has not fully accepted the socialist message and submitted to the leadership of the party and its representatives. In addition, although he seems to recognize the legitimacy of only a single form of working-class representation (socialism), the methods he cites for how it will be achieved are identical to those of the "old party" political campaigns that are vulnerable to graft and fraud. Sinclair's faith in the power of the ballot—and in the integrity of the ballot box—is even more surprising given his repeated claim in *The Jungle* that electoral politics is an inherently corrupt institution. Finally, perhaps the most peculiar feature of this passage is that socialism, for Sinclair, appears to signify a struggle directed not primarily against capitalism but against censorship, "the conspiracy of the capitalist press."

Yet if socialists generally have a hard time making their voices heard, the voiceless workers of *The Jungle* have it even harder, for their collective experience amounts to what Sinclair labels "a burden of things unutterable, not to be compassed by words" (281)—hence, their need to be represented and spoken for. Sinclair designed the main character of Jurgis to provide a composite glimpse of the lives of many different meatpackers, compressing as much as possible of the workers' lives into the individual story of Jurgis's life. However, Jurgis's experience turns out to be just as unutterable as that of all the workers he stands for: "That he should have suffered such oppressions and such horrors was bad enough; but that he should have been crushed and beaten by them, that he should have submitted, and forgotten, and lived in peace—ah, truly that was a thing not to be put into words, a thing not to be borne by a human creature, a thing of terror and madness!" (287).

How are such workers to be represented by anyone, including Socialist Party candidates, socialist novelists, or even themselves? Indeed, how could their experience be rendered legible in a novel that insists that this is "a thing not to be put into words"? Instead of suggesting answers to these questions, *The Jungle* only demands of its readers that they recognize and accept two basic principles: first, that the industrial working class is degraded (blind, mute, helpless), and second, that this class needs to be represented somehow, preferably by socialists. In the words of Billy Hinds, one of Jurgis's mentors, all that socialists can do toward realizing this goal is "to agitate and preach . . . to get the people together and organize them . . . to teach them, to make them read and study and think for themselves. We have to train men to write and edit, to speak and debate, to organize and to administer affairs" (308).

By committing the socialists to the task of representing mass industrial workers, *The Jungle* appears to be advocating nothing short of a vast cultural-administrative program of ideological uplift. While this program is directed toward the working masses who are "wandering in darkness, and waiting to be delivered," it is designed ultimately for the benefit of socialists who are campaigning for political office. The point is not to give workers a voice of their own but to elect socialist candidates to be "the voice of the voiceless." In this respect, Sinclair's novel follows one of several popular (conservative) lines of Socialist Party doctrine at the turn of the century.

The People of the Abyss

At this point, one should recall that the socialist program proposed by Sinclair's novel was not the only vision of socialism circulating in 1906. One year after *The Jungle* appeared, his friend and fellow socialist Jack London published *The Iron Heel*, a futuristic novel of the coming socialist revolution and its defeat, in 1932, by a protofascist alliance of monopoly capitalists (the "Oligarchy"). Though one might expect London's treatment of industrial workers to agree with Sinclair's on certain points, *The Iron Heel* seems intended precisely to refute Sinclair's pious neglect of workers' potential and faith in the electoral process.

In London's novel, representation by socialist politicians is doomed from the start. From the enlightened perspective of the twenty-seventh century, the novel's fictitious editor supplements the text of the narrative with a footnote that reads: "Even as late as A.D. 1912, the great mass of the people still persisted in the belief that they ruled the country by virtue of their ballots. In reality the country was ruled by what were called *political machines*" (54). London might well have had in mind Sinclair's joyous outlook—"the vote was going to be a record-breaker"—as well as the latter's description of those optimistic socialists who "lived upon the vision of the 'good time' coming," when he tells us: "Thus it was that in the fall of 1912 the socialist leaders . . . decided that the end of capitalism had come. . . . Everywhere the socialists proclaimed their coming victory at the ballot-box" (131). Such optimism is short-lived, however, for the novel's protagonist, Ernest Everhard, discovers that the Oligarchy does not recognize the legitimacy of any electoral victories that could put a check to their power. Although Ernest is eventually elected to Congress, he soon finds the notion of parliamentary representation to be nothing but a "legislative farce," lacking all integrity, and carried out solely in the interests of the Oligarchy: "'It's no use,' he said. 'We are beaten. The Iron Heel is here. I had hoped for a peaceable victory at the ballot-box. I was wrong. . . . We shall be robbed of our few remaining liberties; the Iron Heel will walk upon our faces; nothing remains but a bloody revolution of the working class. . . .' And from then on Ernest pinned his faith on revolution. In this he was in advance of his party. His fellow-socialists could not agree with him. They still insisted that victory could be gained through the elections. . . . There was no room in their theoretical social evolution for an oligarchy, therefore the Oligarchy could not be" (112). *The Iron Heel* thus does away with the cornerstone of Sinclair's ideological program—the representation of degraded industrial workers by socialist political leaders—and replaces it with a vision of bloody revolution. From this point forward, the notion of "leadership" disappears almost entirely from the narrative, while militant workers and various underground revolutionary groups organize themselves in preparation for a series of armed revolts.

As far as the mass of industrial workers is concerned, London's depiction of them might also be expected to echo Sinclair's. In particular, when this class makes its dramatic appearance in the novel under the heading "The People of the Abyss," it could easily be viewed as simply another version of that category of subhumans Sinclair calls "the lowest and most degraded of human beasts." The bottom ranks of the working class in 1912, Ernest observes, will be an "abyss, wherein will fester and starve and rot, and ever renew itself, the common people, the great bulk of the population. And in the end, who knows in what day, the common people will rise up out of the abyss" (143). Ernest's view of degraded labor here differs from that of Sinclair in a few important respects. The mass of "common people" in this passage is not "unregenerate" in Sinclair's sense, for, as Ernest notes, it will "ever renew itself" (whereas Sinclair's workers are used up and discarded once and for all), and it will "rise up out of the abyss" without necessarily having to rely on the benevolent intercession of socialist political leadership. Also, the date of this uprising ("who knows in what day") evidently cannot be calculated with the help of electoral statistics. Nonetheless, in spite of these differences certain images of the workers in *The Iron Heel* appear to be closely aligned with Sinclair's portrait of the abject wage slave. London notes, for example, that the people of the abyss "lived like beasts in the great squalid labour-ghettos, festering in misery and degradation" (143) and that "they were labour-slaves . . . machine-serfs and labour-serfs" (192).

What is possibly the most famous passage of the novel depicts the first actual appearance of the people of the abyss during a workers' revolt in Chicago in 1913. When they emerge onto a scene of rioting and slaughter in the streets of Chicago, this mass gathering of "the refuse and the scum of life" is characterized by the novel's first-person narrator (Ernest's wife, Avis) in terms that rival Sinclair's repulsive image of the meatpackers:

> It was not a column, but a mob, an awful river that filled the street, the people of the abyss mad with drink and wrong, up at last and roaring for the blood of their masters. I had seen the people of the abyss before, gone through its ghettos, and thought I knew it; but I found that I was now looking on it for the first time. Dumb apathy had vanished. It was now dynamic—a fascinating spectacle of dread. It surged past my vision in concrete waves of wrath, snarling and growing carnivorous, drunk with whiskey from pillaged warehouses, drunk with hatred, drunk with lust for blood—men, women, and children, in rags and tatters, dim ferocious intelligences with all the godlike blotted from their features and all the fiendlike stamped in, apes, and tigers, anæmic consumptives and great hairy beasts of burden, wan faces from which vampire society had sucked the juice of life, bloated forms swollen with physical grossness and corruption, withered hags and death's heads bearded like patriarchs, festering youth and festering age, faces of fiends, crooked, twisted, misshapen monsters blasted with the ravages of disease and all the horrors of chronic innutrition—the refuse and the scum

of life, a raging, screaming, screeching, demoniacal horde.... The people of the abyss had nothing to lose but the misery and pain of living. (London 207)

Again, in spite of the similarities between London's language and Sinclair's, the people of the abyss are not shown here to be passive and helpless victims of their situation. They may be just as degraded as the meatpackers, just as beastly in the impression they make upon the narrator, but apparently they are not "waiting to be delivered" by any representatives of political parties. Instead, these labor slaves are "raging, screaming, screeching" for revenge against their capitalist masters. By pointing out that "dumb apathy had vanished" and that the mass of workers "was now dynamic," London signals a potential for action and initiative that is missing from Sinclair's account of the meatpackers. These workers may be insane and diseased, but because they are shown to possess a certain "dim ferocious intelligence," they are not entirely without thought.[7]

Above all, London's characterization of the people of the abyss is significant because it suggests—in contrast to the image of meatpackers presented in *The Jungle*—that the degraded condition of the unskilled working class does not automatically reduce it to being a passive beneficiary of political and economic struggles waged by others on its behalf. London's narrator goes even further to state that the industrial working class is a positive production of modern capitalism, a class endowed with the power actually to threaten the ensemble of forces that produced it: "In all truth, there in the labour-ghettos is the roaring abysmal beast the oligarchs fear so dreadfully—but it is the beast of their own making" (192). Such a perspective clearly differs from Sinclair's, which can view the working class only as the negative (thus harmless) waste produced by the capitalist profit machine; Jurgis, recall, was simply "flung aside, like a bit of trash, the carcass of some dead animal" (*Jungle* 147).

Representing Things That Think

The representation of the people of the abyss might be understood as an attempt to imagine a condition of abject degradation that nevertheless retains potential for some forms of thought and action. At times, therefore, the picture of oppressed industrial workers London presents in *The Iron Heel* verges on the surreal. For instance, when the narrator, Avis, sees a worker who was injured during the Chicago uprising, their encounter has an uncanny quality: "How distinctly do I remember his poor, pitiful, gnarled hands as he lay there on the pavement—hands that were more hoof and claw than hands, all twisted and distorted by the toil of all his days, with on the palms a horny growth of callous half an inch thick. And as I picked myself up and started on, I looked into the face of the thing and saw that it lived; for the eyes, dimly intelligent, were looking at me and seeing me" (219). Because London's writing here seems forced to pressure the limits of narrative representation, Avis's encounter (if it makes sense to call it one) with the "thing" that is actually a suffering man takes on an uncanny quality. Apparently the defeated and dying worker, who is at least two degrees removed from the humanity assumed by the other characters in the novel, can be represented only as a thing—but notably, as a thing that lives, thinks, looks, and sees.

This passage calls to mind a famous antiwar novel published over thirty years after London's: Dalton Trumbo's *Johnny Got His Gun*, which appeared in 1939. Trumbo's novel portrays the postwar life of Joe Bonham, a working-class World War I veteran who comes back to the United States after being blown apart by a cannon shell. Although the two novels are temporally separated by over three decades, they share an apocalyptic vision of the not-so-distant future, determined in large part by the effects of mass industrial capitalism. In bed at the Veterans Hospital, Joe soon discovers that "he had no legs and no arms and no eyes and no ears and no nose and no mouth and no tongue. . . . He was nothing but a piece of meat like the chunks of cartilage old Prof Vogel used to have in biology. Chunks of cartilage that didn't have anything except life so they grew on chemicals. But he was one up on the cartilage. He had a mind and it was thinking. That's more than Prof Vogel could ever say of his cartilages. He was thinking and he was just a thing" (Trumbo 62–63). The novel recounts Joe's experience of being "just a thing," but a thing that lives and thinks. In this respect, *Johnny Got His Gun*, for all its thematic and stylistic differences, picks up where London's ambivalent fascination with the people of the abyss left off.

So, what if Joe Bonham or the people of the abyss could speak? In what terms could their speech be represented? More to the point, how could they be represented as speakers in the context of narratives that explicitly position them outside the sphere of representational possibilities? The pertinent question here is not "What would they say?" but rather "How could they be represented as saying—anything?"

In a sense, we hear Joe Bonham speak throughout the whole of *Johnny Got His Gun*, since the novel is made up entirely of a single interior monologue. We learn, however, that what Joe desires most is the ability to communicate with others and thereby recover an "environment" and a basic relationship with those around him. When he conceives a way to nod his head in Morse code, his joy gives some measure of his isolation: "All he had to do in order to break through to people in the outside world was to lie in bed and dot dash to the nurse. Then he could talk. Then he would have smashed through his silence and blackness and helplessness. Then the stump of a man without lips would talk" (Trumbo 162). When the doctors realize that Joe is trying to speak to them, the first thing they ask him is "What do you want?" Having returned to language—and thus faced with the task of accounting for his desires—Joe tells the doctors that he wants to teach others through the power of his example or, more exactly, through the example of his present abject state. By nodding his head in Morse code, he tells the doctors that he would like to be "an educational exhibit":

> People wouldn't learn much about anatomy from him but they would learn all there was to know about war. That would be a great thing to concentrate war in one stump of a body and to show it to people so they could see the difference between a war that's in newspaper headlines and liberty loan drives and a war that is fought out lonesomely in the mud somewhere a war between a man and a high explosive shell. . . . He would make an exhibit of himself to show all the little guys what would happen to them . . . and he would have a sign over himself and the sign would say here is war and he would concentrate the whole into such a small piece of meat and bone and hair that they would never forget it as long as they lived. . . . Say to the farmers here is something I'll bet you haven't seen before. Here is something you can't plow under. Here is something that will never grow and flower. The manure you plow into your fields is filthy enough but here is something less than manure because it won't die and decay and nourish even a weed. . . . It has a brain. It is thinking all the time. Believe it or not this thing thinks and it is alive and it goes against every rule of nature although nature doesn't make it so. You know what made it so. (224–227)

Without being able here fully to do justice to this extraordinary passage, consider a single strand of its discourse. Joe is requesting the freedom to exhibit himself (or what remains of his body) to the public, but this request is couched in terms of the work of disguise, burial, repression, and forgetting. In what appears to be a reversal of the process of working-through in mourning, Joe is asking to communicate the loss of his "self" in relation to others without actually speaking about it. Specifically, he wants, not to communicate "about" the loss in the intransitive sense, but in the transitive sense, to communicate the very fact of the loss itself, the loss of his ability to communicate. To communicate the loss in this manner is essentially to re-create it, and to do so interminably in such a way that those who saw him "would never forget it as long as they lived."

Joe's desire to exhibit himself, then, instead of a working-through of grief, should be understood rather as a working-*back* toward its cause and toward his present war-torn state, "one stump of a body," which he sees as constituting a truthful and expressive "work" in its own right. Even if this stump is seen by spectators only as an index of the past—namely, the unrecuperable loss of what "used to be" Joe—for Joe himself it is both this and a typical product of the present-day work of modern warfare. Having apparently forgotten his enthusiasm over the use of Morse code, in this more basic act of revelation Joe imagines a form of expression that would communicate simply through the singularity of what it displays: an exhibition for the public, but one that ultimately produces a certain public (educated about the reality of war) in and through the mere staging of the exhibit. In Joe's notion of expression, "communication" is thus broken down into its more demonstrative etymological cousins: a communal gathering, communing with others, the convening of a community, people in communion with one another.

At this point, the representational strategies of *Johnny Got His Gun* and *The Iron Heel* converge. For both London and Trumbo the degraded and abject state of modern industrial workers/soldiers serves as a prophetic, voiceless symbol of a destructive world to come, and precisely not, as it does for Sinclair, as proof of the workers' need for representation by socialist politicians. Neither London's nor Trumbo's narrative conveys undue anxiety over the potential unrepresentability of working-class suffering. On the contrary, the symbolic force of Joe Bonham and the people of the abyss is strengthened as a result of the uncanny silence imposed upon them in their formal and narrative roles. For example, when Joe's request to exhibit himself to the general public is denied by the doctors with the response "What you ask is against regulations[.] Who are you[?]" he learns what has driven the doctors to their decision (Trumbo 234–235). As a stump of war-torn flesh, a mere "thing" that nevertheless thinks, Joe realizes that his unspeakable condition embodies—exactly as *The Iron Heel* prophesied in its apocalyptic vision of mechanized warfare and mass slaughter—"a perfect picture of the future":

And then suddenly he saw. He had a vision of himself as a new kind of Christ as a man who carries within himself all the seeds of a new order of things. He was the new messiah of the battlefields saying to people as I am so shall you be. For he had seen the future he had tasted it and now he was living it. . . . He saw starved cities black and cold and motionless and the only things in this whole dead terrible world that made a move or a sound were the airplanes that blackened the sky and far off against the horizon the thunder of the big guns and the puffs that rose from barren tortured earth when their shells exploded.

That was it he had it he understood it now he had told them his secret and in denying him they had told him theirs.

He was the future he was a perfect picture of the future and they were afraid to let anyone see what the future was like. (240–241)

The Matter of the Masses

In the novels of Trumbo, London, and Sinclair, the mass worker's experience of degradation is at the core of a broader problematic concerning the viable forms of workers' representation in literary and political contexts. As workers' degradation increases through the means used to increase the speed and efficiency of industrial production, the availability of forms to represent them adequately in a novel or a political party appears to diminish. Sinclair's novel deals with this problem by converting a traditional but inadequate form of political representation (electoral) into a religious faith, while London and Trumbo deal with it by first openly criticizing, then finally abandoning, conventional political and artistic means to represent the working class. Yet all of these writers use what they consider the unspeakableness of this class's degraded state as an occasion to illustrate the destructive effects of modern capitalism. In each of these novels, though in different ways, industrial workers ultimately come to figure as educational exhibits, much like Joe Bonham.

From this standpoint, Clara Weatherwax's 1935 novel about Aberdeen, Washington, lumber mill workers, *Marching! Marching!*, takes the representation of the mass worker in a surprising new direction. In Weatherwax's novel workers are shown to be similarly degraded and not amenable to conventional forms of literary and political representation. However, through its formal and stylistic innovations, the novel illustrates one way in which the degradation of the mass worker could be represented successfully in the thoughts and actions of the leading characters of a fictional narrative. Beyond this, however, it also seeks to show how the degraded mass worker may indeed be representable for political purposes, in the form of a political movement that is intimately associated with the rank and file it claims to represent. Although it won the *New Masses* award for the best "novel on an American proletarian theme" in 1935—which led it to be viewed, by some critics, as nothing more than "a pastiche of 'proletarian' clichés" (Aaron 300)—the Communist Party itself does not figure prominently here. As several of the novel's characters are former Wobblies (members of the IWW), Wobbly and communist ideologies receive equal recognition over the course of the narrative, though official representatives from these organizations do not appear.

Mass industry, we now know, could not be considered sufficiently "modern" without the contributions of Frederick Taylor. Thus, for the lumber mill workers of *Marching! Marching!* "there were always efficiency experts all over the place pulling the stopwatch on them . . . speeding them up, dangling the bonus system before them" (Weatherwax 97–98). With "efficiency" comes increased mechanization, together with the increased importance of workers' bodies in the production process. If Taylor could judge Schmidt a "man of the mentally sluggish type" because of his muscular build and broken English, the foreman in a whaling station, we learn, follows the same principle when hiring his workers: "The boss had felt him all over like a horse: chest, back, arms, thumping him on the muscle. 'You betcha!' the boss had said . . . 'Heap plenty work here for good boys like you. Sabe? For *good* boys!' Shouting loud as if a man were deaf when he didnt understand English quickly" (104). While one might expect such a bestialized image of the worker ("like a horse") to lead to more pathetic depictions of working-class misery à la Sinclair or London, Weatherwax shows that these workers—including those who are subjected to the discipline of efficiency experts—can resort to unconventional tactics to establish a slight measure of control on the shop floor: "the way we can talk low to each other with our eyes and shoulders even when they're sticking the stopwatch on our necks, right while we're busting the small of our backs bending over the machines" (92–93).

Whereas other novels simply identify degradation with embodied labor power, *Marching! Marching!* implies that the worker's physical and racial-ethnic exploitation on the job manifests a collective experience of the entire industrial working class and, as such, one that can be viewed as a potential resource for the organization of this class. This is because the shared experience of embodied labor materially connects the individual worker to other similarly exploited workers.[8] The narrator remarks that such experience "stayed in the worker-mind like carvings in stone" (63). "All were simply present in him. Japanese, Filipinos, whites, Negroes, Mexicans ... experience hammered into them by clubs and toil" (113–114). Together, then, the workers in *Marching! Marching!* constitute and inhabit a thoroughly industrialized environment insofar as their corporeal experience of the workplace determines the primary quality of their experience in general. Every aspect of their lives is portrayed, in one form or another, as a reflection of their bodies' experience. The material solidity of the solidarity of workers, the novel hints, would thus be a necessary consequence of their collective experience of the workplace. In addition, their experience as a class is echoed by the apparently collective form of the narrative itself, which lacks clearly identifiable protagonists. Even the language of Weatherwax's account seeks to blur the distinction between the materiality of the workers' individual bodies and that of their shared environment. With the butchers in a whaling station, for instance, "slime blood grease slop ... stiffened their socks and crawled into their skin, under their black, broken, stinking toenails" (104), while the trees around lumberjacks are habitually "scratching bruising flesh without the nerves' knowledge" (14).[9]

Following this particular idea of collective working-class experience, Weatherwax represents exploitation most often in the form of threats to the safety and integrity of the worker's body. Paula Rabinowitz rightly notes how "the excessive violence of the workplace" depicted in the novel "dismembers and disfigures the workers, whose labor inscribes their bodies with deformities" (105). Weatherwax's narrator repeatedly reminds us how in a lumber mill "the day's run of risks included smashed feet, cuts, falls, sawed fingers, drowning, ruptures, 'accidental death'" (187). In this regard, her portrayal of the "scientifically managed" workplace harks back to Sinclair's description of the meatpackers whose damaged bodies were held up as evidence of the horrors of industrial capitalism: "Each man was stamped with the signs of his labor. Sawyers with gone fingers and hands, not like crabs, never grow new members.... Peaveys and timber hooks gouge channels in a man's body like drainage ditches: feet get crushed where the timbers fall" (24–25).

One of the most remarkable stylistic features of *Marching! Marching!* is that it does not merely describe such injuries when they occur to workers but strives to reproduce their dismembering effects in the text of the narrative itself. It does this by breaking apart the syntax of its speakers' voices when characters are either injured or threatened with injury. For example, when a lumberjack named Tim is decapitated by a free-flying wire saw, the narrator reports, "At the place where his face and head at the place where it—the top was sliced neatly off" (Weatherwax 15). The narrator's voice and thought here are cut short, cut into (or in two) and textually dismembered, as it were. Shortly after this incident Tim's co-workers are trying to make sense of the accident they witnessed, but the coherence of their thoughts, like the image of Tim's head, are syntactically split apart within themselves: "Tim God Jesus Tim's dead what was it we dead we were going he's dead" (22). This is the last line of the novel's first chapter, a fragment without a period suggesting that the speaker is separated indefinitely from his own, unfinished thought. Even clearer illustrations of Weatherwax's use of such a technique appear when exploited workers first begin openly to confront their bosses: "Then when you. . . . You fixed it so she—. . . . She said she thought maybe after I came she'd drop in the river and you'd probably see that I. But I guess you. I guess she got so she didnt care. I didnt know all this until. Wait a minute. I got to say it so it makes sense" (31).

Through these various stylistic devices, Weatherwax aims to produce a form of narrative that would be capable of representing the experience of the mass worker's degradation—an experience that, appearing to other writers to be politically unrepresentable, was by implication artistically unrepresentable as well. By providing her fictional workers with significant narrative voices—albeit unconscious, disjointed, muted, or incoherent voices—that they have lacked in other novels, Weatherwax draws on hitherto unacknowledged possibilities for the literary representation of the mass worker. Indeed, while the opening lines of *Marching! Marching!* seem to return us to the familiar realm of mute and unspeakable working-class misery—"the [tree] stumps standing up bare and black, forests made voiceless, without leaves or life" (Weatherwax 9)—the narrative equally stresses that this voiceless environment includes elemental forces that somehow find ways to contest their abject condition, such as the sounds made by a wooden rocking chair "squeaking shrill and sharp, as if a voice in the wood were protesting [a] body's weight" (41).

The question remains, of course, whether the novel succeeds in its apparent aims. These are, first, to represent through a literary narrative a working class whose experience of mass industrial degradation seems to place it beyond the reach of conventional novelistic and political forms of representation, and second, to represent this class as being "self-representable," which is to say, as a class that generates within itself the means and the occasions to speak for, or on behalf of, its own members and interests. The first of these involves testing the limits and possibilities of artistic and political forms of representation, while the second more narrowly involves rethinking the concept of "voice" and the role it plays—or might be imagined to play—in both of these forms of representation.

To arrive at a satisfying judgment of *Marching! Marching!*'s success with regard to either one of these aims would obviously be an immense undertaking. Nevertheless, a few provisional conclusions on the status of voice in the novel may suffice for the moment. The workers here are frequently portrayed as speaking without realizing that they are doing so, or as thinking that they are speaking when in fact they are not. This is largely because their bodies interfere with—by shaping and ultimately controlling—what they say and how they say it. When one of the main characters, Pete, gets injured in a fight with his coworkers at the lumber mill who mistake him for a company stool pigeon, his effort to speak for himself in defense illustrates an experience typical of all the workers in the novel: "'Go on,' Pete said in the roaring inside his skull without being aware it was blood, not words, coming out of his mouth" (Weatherwax 17); "'Wait!' he said shouting after them. 'I got to tell' and stopped. Without a doubt it was himself making that thick groggy noise. Nobody looked back. He licked his lips slowly. He must have got the taste of blood and dirt in his mouth, the taste bringing awareness of cuts and swellings, because he grimaced and spat" (19). While there is nothing unusual about the experience of choking on one's own blood, the style of Weatherwax's description here extends to her representation of speaking characters throughout the rest of the novel, even those who are not injured. At one point or another, all her characters struggle to find their words, suggesting that, in order to speak, they must first overcome the various impulses of the body to express its needs. Because the narrative recounts many similar instances of choked-up speech, for Weatherwax it seems that the body and blood of workers are potentially always competing with their words and thoughts. When the body asserts its superiority, as it does here, even Pete's sense of self is temporarily shaken, suggested by the phrase "without a doubt it was himself making that thick groggy noise."

In the end, then, silence and disorientation appear unavoidably, if not ideally, to characterize the embodied condition of Weatherwax's fictional lumber workers (Rabinowitz 107, 111). In the case of Mario, a key figure of the novel and a militant union organizer, the last we hear of him he is lying in bed after having been assaulted by company thugs, where "he lay beyond speech in a void of silence" (Weatherwax 192). However, just when it seems that *Marching! Marching!* confines its imaginative range to yet another version of the helpless, abject mass worker, we learn that even lumber workers who must struggle to "find" their words manage to find other resources—such as simply looking at one another—to communicate among themselves: "Anybody that opened his mouth to spit or say something... got an ant flying in.... the air was choked, reddish with wood dust and flying ants and their busted-off wings. So talking went slow, but when a guy looked at anybody he could see they were all thinking around pretty much the same things" (20).

Capital Incarnate

One peculiar feature of all these novels is that their authors seem artistically inspired by the complex and apparently inhuman character of mass production itself, even in the case of those processes of industrial production that are clearly responsible for the degradation of the mass worker. In this respect, their writing resembles that of professional industrial journalists of the same period who wrote quasi-romantic accounts of mass production, enthusiastically detailing and advocating the advancement of its techniques. For example, when describing the complex operations of an auto-chassis assembly line at Ford's Highland Park factory, the engineering journalists Horace Arnold and Fay Faurote, apparently at a loss for words, resorted to metaphors of divine creation that ascribed a virtual life to both the mechanized process and the objects it produced: "These excite the liveliest interest and admiration in all who witness for the first time this operation of bringing together the varied elements of the new and seemingly vivified creation" (135). The novelists discussed in this chapter—on the whole, no doubt, a less sympathetic group of observers—likewise conveyed a sense of almost dumbstruck awe in their representations of the machinery of large-scale capitalist industry.

Similar instances of Arnold and Faurote's romantic, mystical view of the power of industrial machine technology appear frequently in Sinclair's *The Jungle* and Weatherwax's *Marching! Marching!* They are especially prevalent in novels about steelworkers in western Pennsylvania, such as Bell's *Out of This Furnace*, William Attaway's *Blood on the Forge* (1941), and Phillip Bonosky's *Burning Valley* (1953). Perhaps this is because, from the point of view of its imaginative observers, the most horrifying aspects of industrial mass production were the result of the seemingly superhuman scale of its operations. Writers like Attaway, Bell, Bonosky, and Sinclair, then, could condemn the former only by paying a kind of indirect tribute to the latter. Much like narrative films that aimed to criticize the inhumanity of mass production—such as Fritz Lang's

Metropolis (1926) or Charlie Chaplin's *Modern Times* (1936)—these novels could do so only by representing the modern factory as a grandiose, sublime spectacle (Giedion 126).

The expansion of U.S. industrial enterprises that had been spurred by two major technological innovations during the period from 1900 to 1920—Frederick Taylor's "scientific management" and Henry Ford's continuous-flow method of production with assembly lines—deepened the division of the industrial labor force into two, mutually exclusive categories: "brain workers" and "muscle workers." In response to these developments, novelists began increasingly to depict the industrial workplace as an abstract technological structure, essentially consisting not of human beings but of materialized (and mechanized) networks of power. Those writers who specifically portrayed "muscle" workers in mass production industries tended to celebrate their absorption in the process of production itself, as if such workers had now become a part of the material environment of the workplace (like buildings or machines). In their view, a new, triumphant figure of the mechanized mass worker seemed to have finally replaced the abject, powerless, and helpless worker of the recent past. Rather than simply bemoan the dehumanizing conditions of mass production, these portrayals instead hailed the worker's identification with the new technologies that were to be found in the modern factory.

From one angle, it was obvious why certain novelists, journalists, and sociologists would see in this new type of worker a positive sign of progress. In 1924, Charles Reitell, writing for the *Annals of the American Academy of Political and Social Sciences*, described the new mass worker that he found in the automobile industry: "Quickly—over night as it were—the machine, gigantic, complex and intricate, has removed the need of muscle and brawn. As Frederick W. Taylor puts it, 'The Gorilla types are no more needed.' Instead we have a greater demand for nervous and mental activities such as watchfulness, quick judgments, dexterity, guidance, ability and lastly a nervous endurance to carry through dull, monotonous, fatiguing, rhythmic operations" (188). Instead of exploiting the brute physical force of workers' bodies, modern mass production seemed only to exercise and cultivate those positive mental qualities of its workers—attention, dexterity, and alertness—that were considered generally useful personal skills. This could easily be taken, then, as proof of the fact that the processes of mass production, through technological advancements, tended to develop in a manner that was not only less degrading but positively beneficial to workers. In other words, it was precisely because modern machinery appeared to be so "gigantic, complex and intricate" that the degraded and dehumanized mass worker (Taylor's "Gorilla types") seemed, in Reitell's eyes, to be a thing of the past.

Yet from another, less sanguine perspective the figure of the mechanized mass worker appeared to be losing its recognizably human qualities. To observers such as Thorstein Veblen, if one could not exactly claim that this new worker was degraded, it was equally no longer possible to claim that machine technology enhanced the worker's intellectual skills: "The machine throws out anthropomorphic habits of thought. It compels the adaptation of the workman to his work, rather than the adaptation of the work to the workman. The machine technology rests on a knowledge of impersonal, material cause and effect, not on the dexterity, diligence, or personal force of the workman, still less on the habits and propensities of the workman's superiors" (Veblen 148). In clear contrast to Reitell's view, Veblen here asserts that the "impersonal, material" knowledge demanded of the mass worker has nothing at all to do with his "dexterity, diligence, or personal force." Rather, for Veblen, because of the increased use of machine technology in the industrial workplace, the only new characteristic of this "new" worker is that he can now be considered "a factor involved in a mechanical process whose movement controls his motions" (146). That is, instead of the worker being able to demonstrate the independent and superior force of his intellect through the control he exercises over a complex process of production, this very "process comprises him and his intelligent motions" (146). Thus, if any intelligence is demanded of the new mass worker, it is only ever one of "a peculiar character": an extremely attenuated form of intelligence that "requires close and unremitting thought, but it is thought which runs in standard terms of quantitative precision" (147).

The novels examined in the next chapter represent the specifically technological degradation of mass workers as though it were a natural (and therefore acceptable) product of modern industrial capitalism. The figure of the mechanized mass worker one encounters in this group of novels reflects what Antonio Gramsci called "a new type of man suited to the new type of work and productive process" (286). Such a worker, in Veblen's even more prescient analysis, had learned "to think in the terms in which the machine processes work" (149). In these novels, if the figure of the mass worker is shown to be *empowered*, this is because it is taken to be a materialized expression of the power of modern industrial capitalism—which is to say: capital incarnate.

2 / The Empowered Worker and the Technological Representation of Capital: "Out of this furnace, this metal"

The writers examined in the previous chapter were faced with the dilemma of having to represent an industrial workforce that was otherwise unrepresentable by unions and political parties. This problem seemed to be resolved by a second group of writers, who were convinced that mass workers actually could be represented, only this time not in symbolic but in iconic terms: namely, as representations of capital itself. In the view of this second group of novelists, the mass worker was primarily a technological phenomenon, produced as the quasi-natural offspring of modern industrial capitalism. If they tended to imagine the mass worker as an empowered figure—a heroic testament to the power of modern industry—this is because they assumed that mass workers embodied and displayed the triumphant forces of capital in general. Thus their novels represent the mass worker as being essentially akin to the material environment of the industrial workplace: the tangible realization of a fantasy of purely technological power. As one machine among others, this figure of the worker seems designed to articulate nothing more than the technological and logistical conditions of mass production.

Like the group of novels considered in the previous chapter, each of the novels explored in the present chapter describes the calculating and inhuman quality of the techniques adopted by modern industry to exploit its workers. However, the present group of novels adds one important twist to this message: the figure of the mass worker that appears in them is oddly strengthened, rather than destroyed, by the experience of industrial exploitation. In Thomas Bell's 1941 novel, *Out of This Furnace*, for instance, the mass worker is closely identified with the machinery of the modern steel mill: "*Out of this furnace, this metal*" (412), his heroic narrator proclaims of himself. Likewise, the heroic protagonists of Robert Cruden's *Conveyor* (1935) and Lawrence H. Conrad's *Temper* (1924) emerge from the factory experience similarly hardened (or "tempered") by the monotonous work they perform with heavy machinery. As a group, these novelists glorified the supposedly virile and superhuman aspects of the factory environment. Against such a backdrop, their fictional depictions of the degraded mass worker came gradually to assume the outlines of its heroic other, as if such workers had become fully functional parts of the machines they operated. This chapter explains how, and to what degree, the technological changes that were occurring in the mass industrial workplace played a role in shaping this new, positively valorized image of the mass worker in fiction.

During the thirty-year period that separated the publication of Upton Sinclair's *The Jungle* from the novels of Bell and Cruden, a fundamental change in the techniques available for representing the mass worker in narrative fiction had occurred. Remarkably, a wholesale reversal was taking place in the representation of the mass worker in narrative fiction. The very same negative aspects of mechanized production that had signified the worker's degradation were now coming to be understood as positive signs of the worker's productivity. And, strange as it may seem, this reversal was occurring at exactly the same time (1905–1940) that the mass worker was also being represented as a helpless and abject victim of the forces of industrial production. Over the course of this period, novelists who wrote about mass workers developed strategies for positively reinvesting several of the motifs associated with the growth of industrial capitalism in the United States—motifs of mechanization, efficiency, and continuous-flow production. Reflecting these writers' ambivalent response to the technological changes that were reshaping the modern workplace, the machinery that had previously been associated with the figure of the degraded mass worker somehow became an essential part of its heroic portrait.

The aim of this chapter is to chart and make sense of the process whereby novelists who wrote about mass workers made a series of subtle shifts in their approach to representing modern, mechanized labor practices. By charting precisely where and how they redistributed the figurative and ideological points of emphasis in their novels, the chapter seeks to account for how the "powerless" worker was transformed, as if by magic, into the figure of the "empowered" worker.

Because of the Ford Motor Company's exemplary status as setting a standard for mass production industries, the chapter begins by surveying the changes in working conditions that were occurring there during the 1920s and 1930s. This is followed by an analysis of *Conveyor*, Robert Cruden's 1935 novel about assembly-line work at a fictionalized version of Ford's River Rouge plant. Cruden's revalorization and glorification of the speedup is of particular interest here. The chapter then briefly juxtaposes and contrasts representations of the speedup in Cruden's novel with those found in Upton Sinclair's *The Jungle* (1906) and Thomas Bell's *Out of This Furnace* (1941). The bulk of the chapter, however, is devoted to a close analysis of Lawrence H. Conrad's 1924 novel *Temper*, about a degraded worker in an automotive metal shop who is miraculously transformed into a champion of modern industry. In conclusion, the chapter considers the ways in which William Rollins, Jr.'s, 1934 novel about a textile workers' strike, *The Shadow Before*, was able to appropriate and mobilize this figure of a heroically mechanized mass worker for progressive ends. In doing so, Rollins's representation of the mass worker reflected a stylistic tendency that was common to many Depression-era radical novels. In this regard, it can also be read fruitfully in conjunction with several of the novels we will be considering in chapter 4.

In all of these novels, mechanization and continuous-flow production—forces clearly greater than those of the individual worker who is subjected to their discipline—are held ultimately accountable for producing a new, distinctly modern variety of mass worker. In each case, the narratives differ from one another only over the question of the nature of this "mass." For Sinclair it is degraded and helpless, while for Conrad it is malleable and acquiescent; for Cruden and Bell, it is productive and bold, while for Rollins it is organized and militant. Yet as a group these writers all take the mechanized environment of the industrial workplace as the key to explain the origins of a unique and hitherto unknown type of mass worker. The "empowered" worker seems, in their eyes, to be produced through methods of mass production as surely as any Ford automobile.

An especially clear illustration of the empowered figure of the mass worker can be seen in the character of Yank, the tragic protagonist of Eugene O'Neill's 1921 play *The Hairy Ape*. O'Neill introduces Yank by showing him reveling over his literal identification with the machinery of the industrial workplace. "Sure I'm part of de engines!" Yank exclaims to his fellow stokers in the boiler room of an ocean liner (116). Yank not only identifies with his harsh workplace but genuinely thrives while performing backbreaking work among the machines in the lowest decks of the ship. Embodying the hypervirile aura associated with the force of modern technological power, Yank also ridicules those of his coworkers who complain about their grueling conditions:

> Why de hell not! Dey move, don't dey? Dey're speed, ain't dey? Dey smash trou, don't dey? Twenty-five knots a hour! Dat's goin' some! . . . I move wit it! It, get me! . . . De engines and de coal and de smoke and all de rest of it! He can't breath and swallow coal dust, but I kin, see? Dat's fresh air for me! Dat's food for me! I'm new, get me? Hell in de stokehole? Sure! It takes a man to work in hell. Hell, sure, dat's my fav'rite climate. I eat it up! I git fat on it! It's me makes it hot! It's me makes it roar! It's me makes it move! . . . It—dat's me!—de new dat's moiderin' de old! I'm de ting in coal dat makes it boin; I'm steam and oil for de engines; I'm de ting in noise dat makes yuh hear it; I'm smoke and express trains and steamers and factory whistles; I'm de ting in gold dat makes it money! And I'm what makes iron into steel! Steel, dat stands for de whole ting! And I'm steel—steel—steel! I'm de muscles in steel, de punch behind it! (116)

Between the time O'Neill's play was premiered and the outbreak of World War II, the mass worker began to appear in novels more and more often as an icon embodying the wonders of modern U.S. industry. The notion, however, that workers may also exercise power as independent human agents, pitted against the blind machinery of mass production, seldom surfaces in these texts. On the contrary, as a commodity like any other, the image of the worker one encounters here is no longer easily recognizable as "human." For these writers, rather, it would seem that the humanity of the mass worker ought to be entirely (and heroically) subsumed by the technological character of modern capitalism.

Mass workers could be defined, exploited, and fictionally represented as material instruments of production only in the wake of a revolution that took place at the start of the twentieth century in the field of labor-management relations. With the rise in popularity of the principles of Frederick Taylor's scientific management, a more pronounced division of labor on the shop floor pitted managers against workers to a degree that had not been seen, or even conceivable, prior to the creation of large-scale, vertically integrated, monopoly capitalist firms.

After 1913, when Ford introduced continuous-flow methods of production with assembly lines, this same division of labor became more deeply embedded in the physical and technological structures of the modern plant itself. The power dynamic between workers and managers was now materialized, and technologically articulated, in the form of moving conveyor belts. "After World War I," C.L.R. James reminds us, "the Taylor system, experimental before the war, becomes a social system, the factory laid out for continuous flow of production, and advanced planning for production, operating and control" (39). The control that managers sought to maintain over workers' rate of production could henceforth be exercised through the speed of the production line, rather than through more traditional forms of verbal incitement. "Never had there been such a device for speeding up labor," exclaims the narrator of Upton Sinclair's 1937 novel about Ford autoworkers, *The Flivver King: A Story of Ford-America*. "You simply moved a switch, and a thousand men jumped more quickly. It was an invisible tax, like the tariff, which the consumer pays without being aware of it" (27).

The Ford Motor Company's giant River Rouge plant, which became fully operational in the early 1920s, marked the pinnacle of these developments, inspiring a diverse range of novelists, journalists, and industrial sociologists to account for the peculiar new type of mass production worker they found there. In the minds of such writers, as well for other observers, the tremendous physical scale and commercial impact of the River Rouge plant represented the most advanced stage not only of Fordist production methods but of the automobile industry as a whole. Hence, a single, unique site of automobile manufacturing, the River Rouge, soon became identified with the phenomenon of mass industrial production itself—an image it would retain throughout the period from 1920 to 1940. The novelists we will examine in this chapter chose to represent these new, behemoth-like plants, both literally and metaphorically, as abstract technological structures. In their fictional portraits of these factories, the relationship between workers and managers consists not of human beings, exactly, but of networks of mechanized power.

The New Worker

In his 1924 report entitled "Machinery and Its Effect upon the Workers in the Automobile Industry," Charles Reitell explains how workers in modern mass production industries are in the process of becoming adapted to the peculiar form of labor required to operate heavy machinery: "The workers by the millions in mills and factories are being shaped to meet the demands of these rigid machines." The specific demands these machines make upon the worker include "dexterity, alertness, watchfulness, rhythmic and monotonous activities, coupled with a lessening of much of the older physical requirements." In recent years, Reitell asserts, these new requirements have been "registering results that portray a new type of worker in industry. Mankind has built this steel giant—the machine. He is finding the giant more powerful than its maker" (181).

In what sense is this "giant"—the machine—more powerful than those who create and operate it, in Reitell's view? And to what particular kind of machine can Reitell ascribe such extraordinary power? Reitell has in mind large, automated forms of machinery that require nothing but simple standardized operations on the part of workers to function. These are not only the machines that fill the floor space of modern industrial factories but, more importantly, the machines without which industrial production on a mass scale would never have been possible in the first place. By reducing workers' tasks to a narrow set of standard operations involving monotonous repetition of the same basic movements, automated machinery, Reitell argues, denies mass industrial workers the sense of personal accomplishment associated with more traditional (craft) occupations: "The regular, rhythmic stride of the machine absolutely precludes the worker from showing off his individual ability in any definite field of activity. Automatic machines put padlocks on self-expression" (185). As a result, he infers, the increased use of such machines in mass production industries has led to an overall lessening of the need for either traditional skills or brute physical strength among the workforce in these industries (184). These machines are more powerful than their makers, then, because they have effectively absorbed both the "brains" and the "brawn" that used to belong exclusively to workers (cf. A. Williams).

The automobile industry of the 1920s, as Reitell saw it, exemplified the most advanced stage of this technological development. "Here is an absolutely new industry, free from all traditional methods," he claims. Because this particular industry more than others depends on the use of automated machines, it has created a new system of production that "lends itself nicely to almost complete standardization. The outcome could be little else than a far reaching change upon those who do the work in this gigantic industry" (182). Although Reitell cannot yet predict what this change will amount to exactly, he provides a list of what he takes to be its symptomatic features: "The ability to meet ('to hit') and maintain a constant machine pace; to be able to eliminate all waste and false motions; to follow without wavering printed instructions emanating from an unseen source lodged in some far off planning department—these constitute the requirements of a successful machine tender. The percentage that his actual production is below the standard production set for him is the measurement of the specific tender's inefficiency" (183). Reitell's definition of the new worker reads like those descriptions of the ideal mass production worker one could have encountered twenty years earlier in various statements of the works management movement. Contrary, then, to Reitell's claim that the contemporary autoworker signals a radical break from industrial workers of the recent past, the basic similarity between his account of the autoworker and Taylor's ideal of a "trained gorilla" suggests that the principles of the works management movement had finally been brought to fruition, and thus had been embodied, by the fully mechanized process of production in the automobile industry.

The River Rouge Plant

The uniquely modern mass worker of large industrial enterprises is perhaps best illustrated by the figure of the Ford autoworker, beginning around 1920, when the Ford Motor Company opened its immense River Rouge plant. Both admirers and critics of Ford were unanimous in their belief that this huge plant "symbolized a new industrial era" (Nevins and Hill, *Ford: Expansion* 279). Indeed, because the Rouge was "one of the largest industrial establishments in the world . . . [it] became a superb example of modern integrated production" (Chandler, "General Introduction" 14), which is to say, "the magnificent manifestation of Ford's fundamental policies of mass production and vertical integration" (Chandler, "Ford Sticks" 97). The River Rouge plant outstripped all of Ford's rivals through its high level of vertical integration (control over the basic elements of production and distribution), its high degree of mechanization, and the sophistication of its machinery. Just as Ford's moving assembly lines had influenced the preceding generation of automakers, the Rouge not only influenced the design of other auto manufacturing plants but set new standards for industrial mass production as a whole. The Rouge thus consolidated and exemplified an entire system of production—best known simply as "Fordism"—that would have an impact on the organization of large industrial firms throughout the remainder of the twentieth century (Nevins and Hill, *Ford: Expansion* 297).

The Rouge plant also inspired the imaginations of those who visited and wrote about it, producing a sublime effect through the sheer size and complexity of its design.[1] For example, after visiting the plant, the

English writer J. A. Spender remarked that its various structures "are in their own way works of art.... They have the artistic quality of stirring the imagination till it falls back exhausted" (Nevins and Hill, *Ford: Expansion* 282). To cite another typical account, the description offered by John H. Deventer, awestruck by the vast scope of the manifold operations of the Rouge, claimed that, even to trained engineers, the first impression of the plant was "one of vastness and complexity" (Nevins and Hill, *Ford: Expansion* 282). After this initial impression, then, the educated visitor "sees these units not only in their impressive individual and astounding collective magnitude, *but he also sees each unit as the part of a huge machine*—he sees each unit as a carefully designed gear which meshes with other gears and operates in synchronism with them, the whole forming one huge, perfectly-timed, smoothly operating industrial machine of almost unbelievable efficiency" (288). These descriptions of the Rouge plant—evidently straining the writers' imaginative resources—illustrate at the local level what Reitell asserted about the modern automobile industry as a whole: that "man no more marvels at the nature of the labor effort expended in the automotive industry. He stands dumbfounded, however, before the complexity and intricacy of the machines" (185). Such a dumbfounded gaze could easily be translated into an even more romantic glorification of the apparently inhuman character of mass production itself. Edwin P. Norwood, whose accounts of the Rouge were prone to moments of intoxicated enthusiasm, identified Ford's plant with a sublime state of "progression—never ending. Of many journeys made in this amazing place not one has ever reached complete conclusion. Always there has been more to be seen, more to know about, somewhere beyond.... That ever-changing romance which has its setting on the River Rouge" (xi–xii).

Making Bigness Creative

After several years of expansion, including periodic technical overhauls, the River Rouge plant reached its maximum size in the years 1929 to 1936. More than just a large automobile plant, the Rouge was an "industrial city" spread out over 1,115 acres. Its ninety-three separate structures, which included 160 acres of floor space, were linked together by ninety-three miles of railroad tracks and twenty-seven miles of conveyors. During its peak periods of production, the plant employed 120,000 workers, whose hours had to be scheduled in complex staggered patterns to avoid congestion at the plant gates during shift changes.[2]

Ford's plan to integrate production by gaining control over his sources of supply and means of distribution was part of a carefully calculated strategy to ensure his dominance in the automobile industry. According to Ford, because all the elements of production—raw materials, machinery, means of transportation, and workers—"were in a large sense one," he was convinced that the company could "relate and control them, forging a new and superior type of industry." As he himself put it, vertical integration was therefore a means of "buying insurance against non-supply," which allowed the company to sustain maximum levels of production in the face of unexpected shortages in supply, high prices, or strikes. The fully integrated Rouge, "symbolizing self-sufficiency," thus became Ford's "prime objective" in the years of its initial planning and construction during World War I (Nevins and Hill, *Ford: Expansion* 201).

The basic purpose of vertically integrated production was to allow an enterprise to regulate and adjust the "flow" of its output—a term that originally referred to processes within the factory alone but was soon expanded to encompass every aspect of the firm's operations (Nevins and Hill, *Ford: Expansion* 202–203). The ideal of continuous flow that Ford realized on a small scale through the use of assembly lines at his Highland Park plant led him to want to "command flow throughout the entire manufacturing cycle, and make bigness creative not only in its separate parts, but as a whole" (204). In a 1924 publicity brochure, the Ford Motor Company boasted of its newly integrated system of production at the River Rouge plant: "Here is conversion of raw material to cash in approximately 33 hours" (qtd. in Nevins and Hill, *Ford: Expansion* 288). By 1929, this total time would be reduced to just five hours (288). The Rouge, then, was designed and operated strictly with a view to realizing "that ever-sought-for ideal—steady flowage at a dependable pace" (Norwood 16).

This kind of flow, of course, does not simply occur on its own. At the Rouge, Ford used a combination of technological, managerial, and covert methods to achieve and sustain it. All of these methods, however, were ultimately focused upon a single, critical factor: the worker, whose labor needed to flow in accordance with the precise rhythms of the entire factory. Since Ford's workers—being humans and not machines—could potentially disrupt this flow at any time, the tasks they performed and the rate at which they performed them needed to be regulated and controlled from one instant to the next, down to the most minute movements. A logical result of the strict and exacting measures that were taken to ensure such total control, then, was that the ideal River Rouge worker, in the eyes of Ford's managers and outside observers alike, came increasingly to resemble the machinery of the plant itself.

Technologically, the flow of production within the plant required a large variety of conveyor mechanisms. The plant's conveyor policy was guided by "a constant reaching out after new ways of making endless-chain deliveries; of putting power and yet more power-driven machinery behind, beneath, or above all loads" (Norwood 18). Hence, "in conveyors alone," write Ford's historians, the Rouge became "a wonderland of devices," consisting of "gravity, belt, bucket, spiral, pendulum, gravity roller, overhead monorail, 'scenic railway' and 'merry-go-round,' elevating flight—the list was long both in range and adaptation to special purposes" (Nevins and Hill, *Ford: Expansion* 287). All of these conveyors together created the impression of an "ever-increasing maze," a "never-failing flow of parts from machine to machine and from department to department" (Norwood 2, 2–3). "As the arterial system of the human body carries blood, so does this convolution of machinery penetrate to almost all departments" (7).

At the managerial level, the company's harsh methods of supervising its workforce, involving cruel and arbitrary disciplinary measures, harked back to an earlier era of factory rule through brute tyranny. The head of the Rouge plant, Charles E. Sorensen, was the most notorious of these tyrants, and he encouraged (or often forced) his foremen to follow his example. According to the company's historians, "As Ford reduced prices on cars, there was inevitable pressure from Sorensen down to weed out men, to keep the vast plant moving at its maximum pace. The entire [plant] felt the strain." Such dictatorial methods of control at every level of the plant's operations made the day-to-day experience of working there "relentless, harassing, and to many hateful" (Nevins and Hill, *Ford: Expansion* 296). The rules enforced inside the plant "were the rules of an army"; one of Sorensen's regulations even "required complete silence" of workers throughout the course of their shift (514). In addition, under orders from Sorensen, the supervisors from various departments would regularly compete with one another to surpass the output of the other shifts, driving their workers to the limit of their capacity (519). As W. Allen Nelson, a worker at the Rouge plant, recalls: "Men actually worked until they dropped in front of their machines trying to contribute to [the production goals of their foremen]. They just went to it until they were exhausted" (296).

Finally, the River Rouge plant employed a small army of time spotters, "service men," and all-purpose labor spies. The service men patrolled the plant, enforcing its many rules, rooting out labor "agitators," and generally treating the men "like dogs," according to one Ford worker (Nevins and Hill, *Ford: Expansion* 592). Time spotters zealously reported those workers who appeared to be "stealing time," creating in workers' minds "the haunting fear that their every movement was being watched" (515). Harry Bennett, the infamous head of Ford's Service Department, supplemented his staff by hiring thugs from Detroit's underworld to spy on workers. William C. Klann, a floor boss at the Rouge, openly admitted to these conditions in the plant, stating, "We always had spies or agents to get information—on Communism, union activities, and general employee attitudes toward the management" (538).[3]

The Speedup

Because of the size and complexity of the Rouge, those who worked in it typically felt "a sense of being lost in inexorable immensity and power" (Nevins and Hill, *Ford: Expansion* 295). Indeed, this sense of being lost in a giant, inhuman structure corresponds exactly to what Henry Ford considered to be the nature of any large mass industrial enterprise: "A great business is really too big to be human. It grows so large as to supplant the personality of the man. In a big business the employer, like the employee, is lost in the mass. Together they have created a great productive organization which sends out articles that the world buys.... The business itself becomes the big thing" (Ford, *My Life* 263–264). Ford realized his vision of "the big thing" in the form of the River Rouge plant. Workers who were sent there from the older Highland Park plant had to be "made over" while adapting to the intensified nature of production in the new environment. One plant supervisor bluntly characterized the Rouge as "a place of fear," and another former Ford manager explained: "It was a hard-boiled policy at Highland Park but it didn't compare with the intensity that was at the Rouge. Everybody was on edge. They ran around in circles and didn't know what they were doing. Physically everybody was going like a steam engine but not so much mentally" (Nevins and Hill, *Ford: Expansion* 296).

During the brief postwar recession, which lasted from the summer of 1920 to the late spring of 1921, the pace of work in the Rouge plant increased considerably, beginning what would amount to the most intense long-term speedup in the company's history (Nevins and Hill, *Ford: Expansion* 518–519). At this same time, the rules of the plant also started to be enforced by more severe and arbitrary methods (589). As a result of these changes at the plant, Alfred Chandler notes, "by the mid-1920's Ford's name was already becoming synonymous with many of the most notorious of labor malpractices, such as the speedup of work, the dropping of the older, higher-paid men, arbitrary discharges, and so on" ("Unionizing" 194). Workers in the plant "were subject to discharge at any time and for any reason. They had no tenure and no appeal" (Nevins and Hill, *Ford: Expansion* 534). Because the pace of work increased to ever greater speeds, it became more common for workers on automated assembly lines to fall behind the required levels of output, which foremen and floor bosses could easily notice from the accumulation of stock at a worker's station (296). To keep up with the swift pace of production, then, the worker's movements had to become "purely mechanical" (Adamic, *Dynamite* 394). This characterization of the worker's mechanized experience is no doubt familiar to us today, since it is associated with any type of labor process involving automated machinery. Nevertheless, in the 1920s and 1930s, it was most often—and most negatively—identified with working conditions at the Ford Motor Company specifically (Chandler, "Unionizing" 194).

Robert W. Dunn's 1929 report on working conditions in the automotive industry, *Labor and Automobiles*, singles out Ford's River Rouge plant to illustrate the glaring fact of the speedup: "In 1919 in the motor assembly plant, on certain conveyor-lines the unfinished motors moved by a given point at the rate of 40 an hour; by 1925 they were moving at the rate of 60 an hour. On other lines in 1919 the rate of speed was 120 an hour; in 1925 . . . it had been increased to 180 an hour. *And this with the same machinery.* The difference was made up in human energy, for which the workers received no substantial increase in wages" (qtd. in Adamic, *Dynamite* 401). In the 1920s, it was common for observers of the auto industry to describe its workers as being generally "bound to the conveyor the way the galley-slaves were bound to the vessel" (Arthur Feiler, qtd. in Adamic, *Dynamite* 402). Yet early in the decade, and throughout the next twenty years, the Ford Motor Company acquired a unique reputation among autoworkers as the most vicious employer in the industry (Cruden, *End* 3).

Even after the recession of 1920–1921 had passed and consumer demand had returned to the auto industry, Ford maintained its policy of continually speeding up production at the River Rouge plant. During the brief crisis, therefore, Ford had discovered a method guaranteed to produce automobiles at an ever-lower cost, which would serve as the

FIGURE 1. Jacob Burck, "New Model—1932." Cartoon illustrating workers' negative perception of the Ford Motor Company. *Daily Worker* 1932. Rpt. in *The End of the Ford Myth*, International Pamphlet 24 (New York: International Publishers, 1932).

company's routine mode of operation, in good times and bad, for the next twenty years. In turn, by setting a standard for the rest of the industry, Ford's brand of speedup became the model followed by the other large auto manufacturers in the late 1920s and throughout the Great Depression of the 1930s (Cruden, *End* 4).

Heroic Machines

Robert Cruden's 1935 novel about Detroit autoworkers, *Conveyor*, is perhaps the best illustration of what could be called a Fordist fictional narrative. In it, Cruden details the experience of Detroit autoworkers who were subjected to the speedup. His fictional portrait of Ford autoworkers underscores how they felt materially chained to their assembly lines as just so many cogs in the industrial machine. In Walter B. Rideout's assessment, the novel, though only "a crudely fictionalized report on working conditions" in Ford's River Rouge plant, "gives the fullest picture of the nerve-racking task of keeping up with an assembly line"

(181, 210). By the time the novel was published in 1935, Cruden (a.k.a. James Steele), who actually worked on the assembly line at River Rouge, had already given up writing fiction to pursue a career as a labor activist and journalist. He went on to work as a publicity writer and editor for the union of rubber workers in Akron, Ohio, during the period of their mass sitdown strikes in 1936 (Wixson 157, 304, 541n69).

Although Cruden's novel is well known to historians of Depression-era leftist literature, it has never received thorough analysis as the quintessentially Fordist novel that Cruden intended it to be. Instead of understanding it in relation to the material environment of the River Rouge plant, in which many of Ford's technological and managerial innovations were first introduced, from the time of its appearance up to the present cultural historians and literary critics with strong political investments in 1930s "proletarian" fiction have seemed interested only in the degree to which the novel articulates the ideals of the U.S. Communist Party. This oversight or neglect on the part of scholars is somewhat surprising, given that the novel explores several aspects of the automobile industry as a whole in Detroit, Cleveland, and Flint. In addition, it was published just one year before the CIO began its organizing campaign in this industry. These qualifications alone make the novel significant as one of the few attempts to express, in the deliberately reflexive form of a literary narrative, those things that actual workers of the period were struggling to organize themselves against, particularly the speedup on production lines. While a few fictitious unions do appear in the novel, they prove to be more or less crippled in their attempts to organize workers (reflecting what was then the actual state of the United Auto Workers Union [UAW] as a member of the conservative American Federation of Labor [AFL]). As a result of the methods Ford used to increase labor productivity, the workers in the River Rouge plant—and those in Cruden's fictional equivalent, the "River Rohte" plant—sensed, correctly, that the auto company was attempting to turn them into machines, to integrate them into the ideal of "continuous flow" production as merely the fixed elements of a complex network of conveyors. The following analysis of the novel therefore pays close attention to its depiction of the speedup, the principal form of control used by Ford to ensure labor productivity.

The protagonist of *Conveyor*, Jim Brogan, works in a variety of auto assembly-line jobs in the Detroit area before finally getting a job as a "trimmer" at the Rivers Motor Company, the fictional equivalent of the Ford Motor Company. The hub of the Rivers corporation is its sprawling "River Rohte" plant ("Rohte" is a Germanified version of "Rouge"), a vertically integrated, all-inclusive complex of factories linked and combined into one mammoth operation, where the many different stages of automobile production are coordinated through an elaborate system of technological and managerial control mechanisms.

On Jim's first day on the job, when he enters the grounds of the plant and the building in which he will work, an omniscient narrative voice details the scale and character of the enterprise:

> Across the yard was the powerhouse, a gigantic structure whose silver stacks shone in the sun. Inside, its huge dynamos purred while the wide stretch of plant pulsed with the generated energy. Then there were the steel mills, the glass plant, the cement plant, the blast furnaces poking up above the others. To the north of them were the assembly building, the rolling mills, the machine shop, and the motor building, to which he was assigned. ... He stepped inside ... [and] found himself on a broad road, extending as far as he could see towards the other end of the building. Flanking it was a mass of machinery which, in the distance, became a forest of moving steel. Beside him men were working swiftly lifting crankshafts from an overhead conveyor, clamping them quickly into a gauge, which they read in a flash of a second, and then quickly reaching up and placing the crankshafts on to the hooks on the conveyor. The conveyor was moving rapidly, as Jim could see, and the men had all they could do to keep their arms and bodies in constant motion keeping up with it. None of them even gave him a glance—they were all reaching up, clamping, peering at the indicators, slinging the heavy piece up again. Behind every few men a boss paced back and forth. (*Conveyor* 118)

This "mass of machinery," a "forest of moving steel" that typifies large-scale Fordist production, makes up only one part of the plant's network of facilities. Jim's first impression of the interior of the factory is marked by images of men and machines speeding to keep pace with the conveyor, men who do not even notice him, so focused are they on keeping "their arms and bodies in constant motion." The bosses pacing behind the men—an apparently minor detail here—will turn out to be key players in this narrative, which emphasizes how autoworkers perform their tasks under rigorous personal scrutiny, achieved through an extensive hierarchy of supervisors: "The day boss, the department boss, the job foreman, the straw-boss, the job-setter—they were in and around all the time" (177; cf. 154–155, 201–202).

In addition, if the whole scene resembles a Tayloristic fantasy where the principles of scientific management have been fully implemented, it is not surprising to find Jim's body, carefully estimated for its physical qualities, at the core of such a fantasy. Upon being hired, Jim's scientifically managed physical examination by an army of doctors gives some measure of the degree to which Rivers's workers will be subjected to supervisory control as they execute their assigned tasks. Much like the separate pieces of a machine, each part of his body is worked on by a specialized doctor who is skilled in the examination of that part alone, all while "Jim stood naked and chilled, growling to himself, 'What do they think I am, a horse or somethin'?'" (*Conveyor* 116).

Indeed, to keep up with the pace of production, Jim must become something of a horse. Just as an autoworker gauges a crankshaft, the bosses on the shop floor constantly observe, test, and calibrate the worker's performance to match the speed of production. *Conveyor* thereby illustrates how the rationalized assembly line produces ideal autoworkers just as efficiently as it produces automobiles. An intended effect of this speedup method of control is that those who prove to be inefficient (not fast or accurate enough) can be easily identified and separated from the efficient, thus providing a conveniently "objective" rationale for layoffs and other cost-cutting measures. Competing with its rival, Universal Motors, the Rivers Motor Company issues a national speedup policy in the form of "orders from headquarters," to be passed down the chain of command of bosses till it reaches the "human dynamos" at work on the production line (*Conveyor* 164). When Jim is forced to adjust the speed of his work, he is immediately "dizzy from the pace—fifteen pans of stock a day, 850 push rods an hour, 15 a minute, one every four seconds!" (165). Only later does he understand the true motive behind the company's use of the speedup, which, as he puts it, has "got ev'rybody doin' almost two men's work now. Quite a savin,' ain't it?" (210).

The speedup in Jim's case is achieved not by an accelerated conveyor belt but through a "pace-setter," a worker whom the company employs with the explicit aim of increasing the output of the other workers in a department through the example he sets. When Jim and his coworkers have so far managed with great effort to produce fifteen pans of stock per day, by the midday lunch break the pace-setter is up to twelve and a half pans. "Never a stop. Never a moment's hesitation—in with the rod, pull, release, in, pull, release, minute after minute, hour after hour, his muscles working with the machine as though a part of it" (*Conveyor* 208). With the pace-setter eventually producing nineteen pans in this efficient, machinelike manner, Jim's supervisor announces at the end of the day that from now on the remaining workers will be expected to produce a minimum of eighteen pans per day.

In its depiction of the speedup, it is worth noting that *Conveyor* does not attribute the phenomenon to the company's use of purely technological means. That is to say, Jim's bosses do not simply increase the speed of the machines or the conveyor belts; instead they employ a man who works *like* a machine to demonstrate to Jim and his coworkers that it is humanly possible for them also to work like machines. This variety of speedup still relies on broader technological factors, but in this case the primary technological function is represented specifically by the bodies of the workers themselves. The company invests value into the physical efforts of their bodies just as it would invest in the electrical and gas-driven motors that drive the machines. Over the course of the narrative the autoworkers thus sense that they are expected to become more and more machinelike in the execution of their tasks, knowing that if they fail to keep up with the pace-setters they can easily be replaced by others who will. In light of the company's increasingly unrealizable demands, Jim's coworkers wryly note that "they'll even get machines for repairin' machines" (180) and that "the next thing we know they'll be pushin' brooms up our behinds so's we can sweep the floors when we go an' get stock" (189).

The experience of the autoworkers represented in *Conveyor* reveals how the smooth running of a highly mechanized, continuous-flow production plant ultimately depends upon the degree to which human labor power itself can be mechanized to guarantee its reliable and predictable effects. The ideal autoworker—one whose regular performance most closely approximates that of a machine—will henceforth be integrated as a controlled factor among the plant's various technological inputs. While the total output of the combined workers becomes ever more strictly a matter of their bodies' capacities and limits, the individual worker's performance is tested, calculated, and evaluated not according to supposed human standards but according to those of the machines he or she operates.

In Cruden's narrative, then, instead of primarily displaying "human" qualities, the mass worker represents a new type of humanity that has been saturated with the technology of the industrial workplace. Even the main character of the novel, Jim Brogan—whom Cruden no doubt intended to exemplify workers' inherent human dignity in the face of their exploitation by mass industry—is presented as one who thrives in the mechanized environment of a Fordist factory. His first impression of the River Rohte plant is notable in this regard: "On each side of Jim men were working quickly, silently, glued to the square foot of their machines, their bodies flexing in the rhythm of production. Jim smiled at them all, wanted to tell them that he was going to be one of them before the day was out. The hum of machines and the sharp crash of the presses were a triumphal march to his ears, it was so good to be at work again!" (*Conveyor* 119). While this passage expresses Jim's obvious pleasure to be working after a long layoff, a similarly "triumphal" and joyous image of the stationary bodies of workers "flexing in the rhythm of production" recurs throughout the novel, serving as a leitmotif to suggest their habituation to this form of labor. The narrator, for example, repeatedly observes that the autoworkers' muscles are "flexing in rhythm with their machines" (191), that "the men, rooted in a square foot of ground, flexed their muscles in furious rhythm, faster, faster" (201), and that Jim frequently considers how "it was good to feel his muscles flexing with the steel" (152). Furthermore, outside the factory Jim and his wife Marie typically experience their bodies through analogies to the machines in the plant. We are told that Jim's "brain throbbed like a punch press" (40) and that his "heart beat like an outworn punch press" (114), while Marie's body is "running on her nerves, like an automobile on its battery" (171).

Though one might expect such a descriptive trend to culminate in a humanist critique of the degradation of workers (along the lines of the classic theories of fetishism and reification put forth by Marx, Lukács, and Braverman), *Conveyor* instead glorifies the mechanized worker while castigating the tyrannical bosses who drive their men like so many galley slaves. That is to say, in Cruden's narrative, machine technology and the Fordist assembly line function not as the stock villains they are usually taken to be—the inhuman symbols of workers' alienation and oppression, the instruments of their total subjugation under the forces of capitalism—but as the real heroes of the novel, particularly in those moments when workers and machines are shown working together in productive harmony. The bosses, on the other hand, emerge as the true villains of the story—not because they are bosses but because, insofar as they perform their duties as bosses (yelling at the men), they interfere with and unsettle the harmonious understanding that joins the workers to their machines.

For instance, when Jim eventually manages to adjust his pace to the speedup, the narrator deems his workstation "a perfect unit in the machine-filled building as it throbbed through the morning, throbbing with the feverish heat of production" (*Conveyor* 155). From Cruden's perspective, the only thing that threatens the productivity of this "perfect unit" is the bosses who constantly berate the men, shouting commands at them to go faster. Although the workers must obey these commands, those like Jim who are able to increase and maintain their pace soon reestablish a more "rational" unity with the machines—and they do so, moreover, in spite of the presence of the bosses, who now appear to be a superfluous and unproductive element hampering the smooth operation of the factory.

In fact, just before the end of the novel, when Jim finally realizes that the autoworkers need a union to represent their interests, it is still not clear whether *Conveyor* is concerned in any way with the specifically technological exploitation of the mass worker in highly mechanized industries. For at the height of the speedup, when the bosses are at their most ferocious, Jim is shown to be happily productive, making machines with machines, working as if he were himself a part of the machine he operates: "The work went with a will—the building shook with the throbbing machinery. Jim felt gayer at work than he had for many months—his hand flashed on the handle, was off again in a moment, while his other hand whisked in and out of the groove like a part of the machine itself—rrr-sst-ping, rrr-sst-ping, pull, release, pull, release, again and again, fifteen times a minute, once every four seconds—rrr-sst-ping" (*Conveyor* 200). In Cruden's novel, finally, the mass worker is represented as belonging essentially to the machine technology of the industrial workplace. Far from being alienated by the tedium of highly mechanized labor, the autoworkers in *Conveyor* find their true reflections in the machines they operate (Foley 350).

Sublime Cannibalism

From the standpoint of an earlier novel such as Upton Sinclair's *The Jungle* (1906), the technology of the highly mechanized meatpacking factory does not only alienate the workers depicted in the narrative; it literally destroys them. Published thirty years before Cruden's novel but anticipating many of its representational strategies, *The Jungle* offers the earliest—and most gruesome—fictional account of assembly-line mass production. The continuous-flow production famously associated with Ford's assembly lines was in fact modeled on the disassembly lines of the Chicago packinghouses (Edwards 116–118). When Ford visited these meatpacking plants early in the century, he was inspired by their speed and efficiency, achieved through an innovative coupling of human labor power with machinery. In addition, the packinghouses were some of the earliest vertically integrated firms, setting a trend that their younger cousins in the auto industry would soon follow. Sinclair, for example, tells us of the "Beef Trust" that "it was reaching out for the control of other interests, railroads and trolley lines, gas and electric-light franchises, the leather and the grain business of the whole country" (*Jungle* 297).

When Jurgis Rudkos, the novel's protagonist, first visits the packinghouse in which he will work, the narrator's account of the continuous-flow operation could be mistaken for the picture of the River Rohte auto plant published thirty years later in *Conveyor* (substituting crankshafts for pigs):

> It was all so very business-like that one watched it fascinated. It was pork-making by machinery, pork-making reduced to mathematics.... [The pig] was then again strung up by machinery, and sent upon another trolley ride; this time passing between two lines of men, who sat upon a raised platform, each doing a certain single thing to the carcass as it came to him.... Looking down this room one saw, creeping slowly, a line of dangling pigs a hundred yards in length; and for every yard there was a man, working as if a demon were after him. At the end of this pig's progress every inch of the carcass had been gone over several times, and the pig was a work of art. (Sinclair, *Jungle* 31)

Jurgis is struck by the sheer scale of the enterprise as well as by its evidently scientific organization. The reduction to "mathematics" of a task that Jurgis had performed in rural Lithuania is what particularly impresses him in this scene. Because the labor of the meatpackers is subjected to the same mathematics, they are forced by the speed of the machinery to keep pace with the production line. "They worked with furious intensity, literally upon the run—at a pace with which there is nothing to be compared except a football game. It was all highly specialized labor, each man having his task to do [which] would consist of only two or three specific cuts" (33). The overall scene thus leaves Jurgis with a feeling of sublime awe very similar to that which Jim Brogan felt when he first saw the interior of the motor building at the River Rohte plant: "It was a thing as tremendous as the universe—the laws and ways of its working no more than the universe to be questioned or understood. All that a mere man could do, it seemed to Jurgis, was to take a thing like this as he found it, and do as he was told; to be given a place in it, and a share in its wonderful activities, was a blessing to be grateful for" (*Jungle* 35; cf. Norwood 3).

In stark contrast to Jim Brogan's story, however, this awe-inspired view of the packinghouse is merely a setup for the narrative of Jurgis's destruction. While both characters are grateful to be given a place among the machines of these vast enterprises, and both are figuratively identified with—and personally identify themselves with—the technology of their respective workplaces, for Jurgis the fate of the meatpacker is ultimately reflected by that of the livestock that are herded into the packinghouse to be killed and dismembered. In other words, where Jim is shown to be nurtured by the machinery he operates, growing faster and more efficient until his labor transforms him into an extension of the machines he works on, Jurgis is portrayed as a type of animal, an unwitting victim of the packinghouse who is gradually being slaughtered by the very work he performs there. This is because the packinghouse workers, as Sinclair depicts them, "are not human beings at all, but simply parts of a machine for producing wealth" (*Jungle* 118). Although this same statement could be revalorized and applied to the autoworkers of *Conveyor*, when it appears in *The Jungle* it is meant not to celebrate the achievements of modern industry but to suggest the brutality of the process through which human labor power becomes mechanized and embedded within the material structures of the workplace. Indeed, *The Jungle* repeatedly condemns this process for destroying precisely what Cruden praises it for producing: the figure of the mass worker. In contrast to Cruden's triumphant portrait of mechanized autoworkers, Sinclair's depiction of the meatpackers makes them pathetic victims of mechanization, "simply the worn-out parts of the great merciless packing machine" (*Jungle* 115)—an image that is literally the same as, but figuratively opposed to, Cruden's "perfect units" of productivity that are "like a part of the machine itself" (*Conveyor* 155, 200).

Likewise, while both authors take the speedup to be one of the quintessential features of mechanized mass production, for Sinclair the effect it has in a modern packinghouse is not invigorating but as deadly to the meatpackers as the work they perform on animals:

> For murder it was that went on there upon the killing-floor, systematic, deliberate and hideous murder—and there was no other word for it, and nothing else to be said about it. They were slaughtering men there, just as certainly as they were slaughtering cattle; they were grinding the bodies and souls of them, and turning

them into dollars and cents.... [In the sausage-rooms] now and then some one would lose a finger in the dangerous cutting-machines;... when that happened they would stop the machine, but only for a minute or so; if they could not find the finger they would let it go and call it sausage. And that was grinding up men, as anyone will admit; yet it was not one bit more actually grinding them than the system of "speeding-up." (*Jungle* 82)

Sinclair here wants to obliterate the distinction between the literal and figurative senses of the term *grinding*. Or rather, where it is a question of understanding the actual effect of the speedup, he claims an exclusive authority for the literal over the figurative sense of *grind*. In doing so, Sinclair defines the speedup as a form of mechanized human slaughter, thus foreclosing the possibility that it might connote an ideal of fast and efficient work, as it does for Cruden.

Figurative language, however, plays a pivotal role in *The Jungle*'s representation of the meatpackers.[4] When workers in the sausage rooms are literally ground up by the cutting machines and the speedup, their severed limbs are renamed "sausage," a term that for Sinclair illustrates a deceitful but apt use of figurative language. The fact that the company must *call* the final product sausage already proves that its real ingredients do not correspond entirely with those implied by its market name. That is, the sausage represented in *The Jungle* is shown to be actually (literally) made up of rotting animals, the poisonous flesh of diseased pigs, and dismembered human body parts. Yet the meatpacking industry relies on a host of such metaphors to turn a profit. "Mushroom catsup," "potted chicken," "potted ham," and "devilled ham" are a few of the packinghouse products whose actual contents Sinclair makes a point of revealing. Consistent with this trend of his narrative, Sinclair represents the workers as so many "processed" products of the industry, merely raw materials to be worked on by the company and consumed in the form of profits. For example, sausage makers are described as being "precisely the color of the 'fresh country sausage' they made" (*Jungle* 124), and in the case of workers who fall into open vats, we are told that "sometimes they would be overlooked for days, till all but the bones of them had gone out to the world as Anderson's Pure Leaf Lard!" (91).[5]

"Out of this furnace, this metal"

Strangely enough, thirty-five years later, what Sinclair considered to be a worker's worst nightmare appeared in the celebrated form of the American Dream in *Out of This Furnace* (1941), Thomas Bell's novel about steelworkers in western Pennsylvania. Initially, Bell's narrative seems to be headed toward *The Jungle*'s familiar thesis on the destruction and dehumanization of the mass industrial worker. For instance, of Mike Dobrejcak, one of the novel's main characters, the narrator observes that "exhaustion slowly numbed his body, mercifully fogged his mind; he ceased to be a human being, became a mere appendage to the furnace, a lost, damned creature" (Bell 167). A generation later, however, Mike's son Dobie is working in the same mill when the CIO completes its victorious drive to organize steelworkers. To Dobie, "the C.I.O. men were thinking and talking like Americans . . . the kind that's got *Made in the U.S.A.* stamped all over them" (410). For the steelworkers of Dobie's generation, American Industry has evidently become a kind of brand name in itself, connoting honesty and rugged authenticity. Proud to have fought for the recognition of the union in his mill, and to be finally represented as a union worker himself, Dobie reflects: "I'm almost as much a product of that mill down there as any rail or ingot they ever turned out. . . . I want certain things bad enough to fight for them, bad enough to die for them. Patrick Henry, Junior—that's me. Give me liberty or give me death. But he meant every word of it and by God I think I do too. *Out of this furnace, this metal*" (412). Here again is an affirmative statement of the sort one would expect to find in Robert Cruden's *Conveyor*. Yet if it were to appear verbatim in the context of Sinclair's novel it would unquestionably signify the horrific lot of the mass industrial worker who is "a mere appendage to the furnace." To be a product of the mill like "any rail or ingot they ever turned out"—even to consider oneself metallic in a figurative sense—would prove for Sinclair that the mill had succeeded in "processing" its human workers. What Bell regards as an expression of the workers' courage, toughness, and resolve, Sinclair would interpret as signaling the loss of their humanity, their reduction to a basic element of raw material to be degraded and consumed in the production of steel.

How, then, is one to account for such a discrepancy? In part, the narrative of *Out of This Furnace* is designed to show the gradual improvement of conditions that workers were able to force upon the steel industry between 1885 and 1937. This alone might explain why Mike Dobrejcak's experience of degradation is transformed, 250 pages later, into Dobie

Dobrejcak's CIO-inspired statement of self-affirmation (Foley 381, 388, 393). However, when *Out of This Furnace* is placed alongside a novel such as Cruden's *Conveyor* that directly links mechanized labor to a positive image of the mass worker, a different alignment of representational strategies emerges. From this standpoint, both Cruden's and Bell's narratives appear to endorse the very same features of the industrial workplace that Sinclair singled out for being especially worthy of criticism: the speedup and the transformation of the worker into a productive machine. In the context of these two narrative perspectives—Sinclair's on the one hand, Bell's and Cruden's on the other—almost identical representations of workers are invested with diametrically opposed meanings.

Rising Up from the Mass

So how exactly did novelists refine, refit, and retool the figure of the degraded mass worker to transform it into the glorified figure of the productive, highly mechanized mass worker? The best way to answer this question is to examine in detail a novel that openly dramatizes this very change at the level of its narrative structure, Lawrence H. Conrad's *Temper*. Published in 1924, *Temper*—an "assembly line-ennui novel," in Laura Hapke's view (175)—tells the story of Paul Rinelli, an Italian immigrant recently arrived in Detroit who works in the foundry of an auto assembly plant. In spite of his managerial aspirations, Rinelli is finally pressured into accepting his degraded condition, realizing that his life is worth less than the steel auto parts he makes.

Conrad's often overlooked novel is of particular interest because, like *An American Tragedy* (1925), Theodore Dreiser's novel about corporate, bureaucratic control and its peculiar meat grinder–like effects on workers, its narrative centers on a working-class protagonist who strives to move up the ladder at his factory job. By 1924, many large U.S. industrial firms had reorganized their production methods by applying some version of Frederick Taylor's managerial principles. Even though Conrad's apparent intention is to suggest that Taylorism generally affirms, by technologically redefining, the "humanity" of industrial workers, his narrative instead illustrates that just the opposite is the case: that Taylorism, once it is fully implemented (particularly in a Ford-style factory environment), produces only degrading and dehumanizing effects upon the industrial workforce, reducing managers and laborers alike to fixed pieces of the plant's machinery. However, apart from its elaborate depiction of shop-floor brutality between supervisors and workers, one of the most remarkable features of this novel is that Conrad's protagonist, by the end of the story, learns fully to accept the degrading and menial character of the work he performs as his only option in life. Moreover, significantly, he learns this lesson not in spite of but as a direct result of his constant battles with managerial authority.

Paul Rinelli is trying to get ahead in the United States. He is told by one of his mentors that to get all the way "to the top of the ladder," as he puts it, he must first be "burning up with the desire to become the organizer and director of human machinery in the mass" (Conrad 71). Of course, to do this Paul must find a way out of his current job at the auto plant, where, as he knows, he is himself only a part of the mass of human machinery. Thus, from the start, Conrad's narrative depicts Paul as a mass worker who is struggling to leave the mass behind him, to demassify himself by rising above it and becoming its "organizer and director."

Yet Paul's ambition to rise out of the mass is itself conceived in mass industrial terms. According to Paul's mentor, a pharmacist named Smith, being an organizer and director of human machinery requires "years of study and fighting and advertising if you are going to sell yourself to the world at a premium.... That is what you want to do. Make a big sale! Clip coupons off from your personality" (Conrad 72–73). Smith is telling Paul not just to view himself as a high-priced commodity but to make his personality the focus of his commodification. As Smith knows, Paul has no marketable skills and no education and has not yet become a U.S. citizen (a situation that remains unchanged throughout the novel). The only thing of his own that Paul has to sell is this obscure phenomenon called "personality," his supposedly unique disposition and idiosyncrasies. Till the end of the narrative, he imagines his self quite literally as a product for sale on the open market. "What he had needed," Paul later reflects, "was some way to express himself, some kind of work into which he could put himself and through which he could give himself—sell himself—to the world" (171).

In the foundry of the auto plant, Paul finds few opportunities for the kind of self-expression he has in mind. At first, he tries to resign himself to the job with the comforting thought that his work requires no thought at all. Early in the novel, the omniscient narrative voice—which often doubles as Paul's interior voice—tells us (as Paul tells himself): "You should be glad you don't have to think at your work; he had learned that much. You should be glad to let your hands go ahead and do the work; that's what they were for. They even called all the men *machine-hands*. That was easy enough to understand" (Conrad 10). Yet whatever consolation Paul derives from knowing that he is merely a "machine-hand" is short-lived, for he discovers that his ability to think is strangely affected by the work he performs with his hands. After a few months on the job, he notices "a cloudiness in his head that had never been there before. He couldn't use his mind in the ways that he used to" (57).

Even more frightening than this, Paul senses that the highly mechanized environment of the factory is beginning to invade and take control of his whole being:

> There was another thing that he could feel: that beating that always comes inside of you when you are in the factory. It made your heart-beat change, and your breathing change until you got into step with it. Every man's body on every machine swung backward and forward with it—not with each other; with *it*, the beating. It was the thing that the bosses had to change when they wanted to get more production, and they found it a very hard thing to do. It came into you through the floor upon which you stood, through every lever that you put your hand upon, through every breath that you breathed, and even through all of the clamor that kept your ears filled with the good sound of men at work. It came into you through your eyes every minute of the day as you watched every other thing beating in time with it. Some of it came from the touch of the hard, rough foundry-steel that brought it in from another shop, from a mill, from a mine. Perhaps it even lodged there in the machines, which were themselves made somewhere in time to its beat.
>
> When Paul felt it coming over him again, he could tell what it was doing to him. It was slowing him down; all of his movements, even the movement of his mind. His fine imaginings could not endure it; they had to move as swiftly as a flashlight. Already as he sat there upon the garbage-can, he could feel the muscles of his legs trembling in response to the vibration that was all about him. He gave his attention to his breathing to see if it was still normal. The feeling of the shop was creeping over him like a great dread. He looked down at his hands and found them half closed, curled around one another, and a feeling in the palms as of levers soon to be grasped. (Conrad 82–83)

In spite of his efforts to be his own person, and thus to "own" his personality, Paul's mind and body get the better of him when he is in the foundry, where he feels literally possessed by his job. His breath, pulse, muscles, hands, perceptions, and thoughts are here shown to be involuntarily realigning themselves to synch up with the operations of the machines around him.

This extraordinary passage is just one of several in the novel that depict the process through which Paul's entire existence becomes ever more solely a function of the factory's machinery. It is also worth noting that this picture of the factory does not include the figure of a pace-setter (an efficient, machinelike worker) but instead represents the speedup as being directly tied to the "beating" of the machines, "the thing that the bosses had to change when they wanted to get more production." In the industrial workplace of *Temper*, evidently, machine technology alone sets the standard for "human machinery in the mass," without considering the labor of actual human beings.

Paul Rinelli is horrified by the idea that he could spend his life working in such an environment. He therefore keeps reminding himself that he and his fellow workers "weren't machine-hands and sweepers and furnace-tenders because they wanted to be. No, indeed. They were just doing that kind of work temporarily, while they waited for something better to open up. They all said so" (Conrad 18). Determined not to get trapped in his job at the foundry, Paul fosters his initial and stubborn ambition to rise out of the mass—the naïveté of which, however, resounds unmistakably in his frequent lectures to his wife: "We are going to be something in this big country. We are going to be something up near the top somewhere. There are just millions of places on the way up, and we are going to take them steadily, we are going to keep going upward as long as we live" (182), and again, "You see, it is all like a big ladder. You start in and climb up, and when you get to the top, you are happy. Down here there is only misery. But up at the top there is joy all day long. We have got to climb up" (260).

While such speeches may seem intended to provoke ridicule, Conrad's decision to portray Paul's hopes and dreams in this fairy-tale manner works to establish the basic conflict at the heart of the narrative. Simply put, the question is: How can Paul continue to work in the foundry at the auto plant (where "there is only misery") and at the same time affirm his conviction that he is climbing to the top of U.S. society (where "there is joy all day long")?

The Making of "Human Machinery"

The solution proposed by *Temper* is that, since Paul obviously cannot work in one place while climbing toward another, he must find a way to recast his misery into joy and thereby renounce—or rather temper—his aspirations. Underlying the story of Paul's shifting outlook toward his job, then, are signs of a broader shift in the fictional characterization of the industrial mass worker: namely, a shift away from *The Jungle*'s focus on workers' misery toward the joyous experience of productivity represented by the workers in *Conveyor* and *Out of This Furnace*.

Thus Paul, like the steel he works on, must first be "tempered." This process initially occurs through the effects of his workplace environment. We are told, for instance, that "the shop was stamping him, getting a grip on him, that he would never be able to resist" (Conrad 202). Paul's sense that he is being "stamped" is further illustrated through a series of industrial fantasies that increasingly occupy his thoughts while he is at work. Watching the men around him in the foundry, it eventually dawns on him that "the men were like the fires they tended. There was a roar and a blast to each of them. They were alive and seething inside. They handled one little rod of steel with the same great blast of energy that the furnaces used to heat it. What a wonder to hold your own with men like that!" (192). Later, we are told that "he thought that there was a relation, a kinship, between the men and the fires, that proceeded out of their contact with each other. When a man took hold of one end of a bar, the other end of which was in the fire, he thought he could see a complete connection, that made the man and the fire one" (195). It is one thing for Paul to want to hold his own with these men but quite another for him to posit a mystical identity between the workers, their materials, and the furnaces. In Paul's awestruck imagination, what begins as a figurative resemblance between these (men being "like" the fires) evolves into "a relation, a kinship," until finally, through some cryptic power of osmosis, it acquires the status of a "complete connection." This series of inferences does not merely reveal the deepening of Paul's supposed insight; it also sheds light on the preliminary stages of what one might call a "phenomenology" of the mass worker's reification.

At this point, though, Paul still seems very much the dreamer the novel has portrayed him to be. His fantasy life continues to thrive, particularly when he is at his job, where he finds increasing evidence to support his idealizations of the industrial workplace. The more sure of these he becomes, the more they begin to shape his everyday experience of working with steel. For example, when Paul is transferred to a job in the blacksmith department, he begins to identify himself concretely with the steel he works on: "He saw that the steel was a wonderful substance, and that each white-hot ingot that they put before him had some strange power in its heart that made it valuable. That was its temper. It was the treatment you gave it that increased its temper and made it more valuable. Paul thought that there was something of the muscle of the blacksmith that traveled down the handle of the sledge and added strength to the great blocks of metal" (Conrad 222). Here at last the "temper" of the novel's title materializes to signify the inherent value of steel, its "strange power," which must be augmented through the "added strength" the blacksmith pounds into it.

If in part this type of power is still an abstraction rooted in Paul's imagination, he is soon to learn its more literal truth (cf. Veblen 217n4). His new boss, the head blacksmith Cameron, informs him, "We handle the men just like the ingots, in here. Now you've got good stuff in you, but there's a run of slag somewhere down through the center that will have to be worked out gradually" (Conrad 225). The slag Cameron detects in Paul is precisely his habit of daydreaming on the job, which is both unproductive and potentially dangerous for a blacksmith working with hot ingots. So when Cameron announces to Paul, "You are going to get tempered just as surely as my name is Cameron," the head blacksmith is not speaking metaphorically (230). His words are a warning to Paul to stifle his imagination while he is at work in the foundry.

Cameron's warning only echoes what the narrator's (or Paul's interior) voice has been saying all along. From the very start of the novel, the ideal of a "tempered" worker had subtly taken shape and begun to exert its force, opposing Paul's tendency to fantasize about his work. Early on, for instance, Paul is working at an upright lathe that shaves steel pistons. The job excites him to such a degree that a bosslike narratorial voice suddenly interrupts and takes charge of the scene: "This is a factory; men work here. You've got to be a man. Look at them. What are they like? Hard, hard, very hard. You've got to cut out that silly stuff. You can't go dreaming around here like a kid in school. There's only one kind of man that we need here. We need them all alike. That makes it easier. We can handle them like little pencils of iron. We can handle them like pistons, and shave them all down to the same size. Any man is a fool who tries to be different. Any man is happy in the head who goes dreaming around. Cut it all out. Be like men are. Be hard!" (Conrad 39). A "hard" worker, the speaker insists, is one who does not dream on the job. He should be happy in the body, not in the head. Moreover, he blends in with all the other workers in the factory who, in their hardness, resemble standardized steel pistons that have been shaved "down to the same size."

Since Paul has not yet become hard in this sense, Cameron treats him as he said he would—like a hot steel ingot. He "tempers" him by literally beating him up. Using his fists, he pounds Paul into submission with the aim of increasing the value of Paul's labor in the work of the blacksmith shop. At the end of this humiliating experience, Paul's dreaming is effectively stopped, thereby releasing that "strange power" within him to generate value from his labor. Beginning at this point in the narrative, we are told that he "found himself being a different kind of a person, and it seemed to him that his whole body had been so violated by Cameron's beating that, when it healed, it became a new thing.... He no longer roared inside, and his life did not burn with a blast.... He threw himself back upon the general movement of things, and let it carry him" (Conrad 232).

Paul's secular epiphany marks the beginning of a new narrative focus: the story of the "new" Paul, or better, the story of a mass worker who has learned the value of submission to the "general movement" of the industrial workplace. Like any epiphany or quasi-religious awakening, this one is accompanied by Paul's testimony explaining that he is a changed man. He recognizes, for instance, the rebellious quality of his now dormant fantasy life, as he tells his wife, "My nature is finer than the kind of work they make you do in the shop. I think that most of our trouble was brought on by the fact that my nature was in rebellion against my surroundings" (Conrad 261). The narrator further describes Paul's new way of viewing the class stratification of U.S. society. Having discarded the image of the ladder along with his dreams, Paul now "could see no up and down about it." The different classes in his view were "merely different. Each class had to live in its own way. And probably the most interesting thing that each man had to do in life would be to find out what that way was" (283).

From this point forward, the remainder of the novel is devoted to tracking Paul's effort to discover how those of his class "had to live." Since he no longer feels the need to rise out of the mass of human machinery, his lectures to his wife are now meant to justify his tenure at such a dangerous and low-paying job, with Paul asserting that "a man in the shop is not any worse off than a man outside" (Conrad 287). Likewise, the concluding pages of the novel reinforce the notion that Paul has consciously decided to accept and even enjoy his fate as a mass worker: "I am going to be happy ... just as the old negro in the shop is happy, because I know what my lot is, and I am not afraid to live in it.... I have found a way of living that is the best for me, and I am not afraid to live in it" (304).

The "Life-Blood" of Industry

If this development of Paul's character sounds somewhat forced or peculiar—given the fact that the bulk of the narrative focused on his socioeconomic aspirations—it is important to recall the impact of Paul's first impressions of the factory: the beating of machines that permeated and took control of his mind and body. When these early impressions are brought into relation with his apparently defeatist remarks at the end of the novel, it seems fair to conclude that, throughout *Temper*, Conrad's concern has been to show how an otherwise resistant worker can be turned into a fixed piece of "human machinery in the mass" and then learn to like it. In the end, Paul not only appears sufficiently tempered to be a good, tractable worker but feels a nostalgic longing for the mechanized world of the factory, a place that he once felt was "creeping over him like a great dread." As he tells his wife, "If I stay with the company, they will always treat me decently. And besides, I like it. I have been lonesome for the blacksmith shop all the while I have been at home. It is not only that man Cameron that makes it a wonderful place; it is the big machinery and all of the men I know there. . . . And the men move around the machines like pygmies, and some of them are wrapped around with clouds of smoke, and others look like wonderful things made out of metal as they stand in front of the fires, with the fierce, bright light on their faces" (289–290). Apart from the question of how Cameron makes the foundry "a wonderful place" (in fact, by beating his workers), it seems that Paul's imagination is not entirely suppressed even in this later stage of his story. For when he pictures his fellow workers as "wonderful things made out of metal," this is a style of representation that stems directly from the mystical identity that he used to posit between the workers and their machines. The apparent liberation of Paul's fantasy life at this point in the novel would thus seem to support Antonio Gramsci's (strained) assertion that the mass industrial worker, after being fully adapted to the methods of mechanized production, is free to think. Gramsci writes, "Once the process of adaptation has been completed, what really happens is that the brain of the worker, far from being mummified, reaches a state of complete freedom. The only thing that is completely mechanicised is the physical gesture; the memory of the trade, reduced to simple gestures repeated at an intense rhythm, 'nestles' in the muscular and nervous centres and leaves the brain free and unencumbered for other occupations" (309).

In his new and improved role as the contented mass worker, Paul is free to recall his earlier fantasy of an identity between workers and machines and to reinvest it with a purely positive significance:

> The eternal grinding and pounding of the great machines brought him back to a sense of the old life. He could feel his pulses leaping again to get themselves into tune with the throb of the mighty hammers, with the roar of the furnaces, with the vibrations of the very concrete floor itself. He drew in a great lungful of the stinging smoke, and felt his spirit revive and roar within him like a forge when the bellows begins to pump. . . .
>
> The waves of heat lapped over him, penetrating all of his clothing in an instant, and bringing out the tingle of sweat upon his legs. He felt that he was being baptized again in the life-blood of industry. . . . He stretched out his chest, drinking the spirit of the place down into his lungs. . . . Through his hand, still gripped tightly upon the steel banister of the stairs, the spirit of this wonderful metal was creeping up his arm, up into his shoulder, along his body. He was beginning to feel once more, the "iron in his blood." (Conrad 299–300)

Where previously the identity of worker and machine posed an ambiguous threat to Paul (since it included a mixture of dangerous and destructive elements), it is now recast and represented in this passage as a life-giving, mystical fusion. Paul is here portrayed as if he were fully integrated with the machinery of the factory. "Being baptized again in the life-blood of industry," this "Paul" has been transfigured and has become a part of the factory itself, for he now heeds the call of the "iron in his blood." He belongs to the factory not primarily because he misses the camaraderie of his fellow workers but because, as a mass worker, he believes he has been transubstantiated into the materials of the very machinery with which he works.

Temper thus brings the fictional representation of the mass worker closer to the heroic portraits one encounters in the later novels of Cruden and Bell. Through the successive phases of Paul Rinelli's individual development as a character, the narrative rehearses a struggle between two opposing literary images of the modern mass worker: that of Sinclair, for whom mechanized labor is always associated with the worker's degradation, versus that of Cruden and Bell, for whom mechanized labor both produces and reflects the worker's strength, courage, and resolve. Insofar as Paul learns unconditionally to accept his role in the mechanized workplace of the auto plant, to "let it carry him" by suppressing his conflicting desires, he loses the ability he once possessed to recognize the technological (nonhuman) sources of his exploitation. As these become less noticeable to him, they acquire an ambiguous, apparently neutral status, which in turn makes them available for reinscription and redeployment in the novel, only this time charged with a different (positive) range of ideological and narrative values. The stage is thus set for Paul to feel his spirit "revived" by the factory, to get in touch with the now life-affirming "iron in his blood," and, finally, to be heroically displayed as a joyous, productive machine among machines.

A comparison of the representations of the speedup in Conrad and Cruden is instructive in this regard. In *Temper*, at a time when Paul is still resisting the dehumanizing environment of the auto plant, the speedup is described (though not explicitly named) much as Sinclair would have described it: as being purely a function of the integrated network of machinery, which sets the pace of the factory's production independently of human controls. Yet later in the narrative, as Paul comes to feel at home among the machines, nothing appears to suggest that the speed of his work has a negative effect upon the quality of his life. That is, he no longer even acknowledges the existence of the technological speedup. In contrast to this, the speedup is represented in *Conveyor* as being solely the result of human controls. Cruden's narrative perspective, much like that of Paul Rinelli after his submission to the harsh conditions of the workplace, does not recognize a possible source of harm to the workers in the machines and conveyors themselves. The specific form of exploitation achieved through the technological speedup simply disappears from Cruden's novel, although it is amply replaced by the dictatorial authority of an army of bosses and supervisors.

It would seem, then, that the narrative erasure of one type of speedup (through machinery) has prepared the way for its replacement by another (through humans) in fictional representations of the industrial workplace. The narrative of *Temper* illustrates one of the possible ways through which the realities of technological exploitation could be made to appear benign, insignificant, or nonexistent in novels about industrial workers. By fusing his protagonist with the technological materials of the workplace, Conrad may have imagined that he was simply representing Paul Rinelli's "joy"—the joy of an essentially human worker to whom machinery is no longer a threat. On the other hand, since whatever remains of Paul's supposed humanity has been absorbed into, and in turn saturated by, the materials and machines of his job, the novel also (perhaps unintentionally) suggests that the "humanity" of the mass industrial worker is in the process of being revolutionized by the power of mass industrial technology.

In any case, if it makes sense to speak of such a thing as "mass industrial" humanity, the three protagonists of the novels of Cruden, Bell, and Conrad—Jim Brogan, Dobie Dobrejcak, and Paul Rinelli—could be viewed as its literary prototypes, each one of them highlighting a different aspect of the figure of the mass worker who has become fully habituated to the experience of mechanized labor.

Mechanized Masses

Between the extremes of degradation and revitalization, novelists of this period found many other ways to represent the effects of machinery upon industrial workers. William Rollins Jr.'s 1934 novel about New Bedford, Massachusetts, textile workers who organize a strike, *The Shadow Before*, similarly depicts both the factory's workers and its managers as though they are strangely akin to the machinery that surrounds them. However, instead of using this device as a form of evidence to prove either the existence of working-class misery or the achievements of modern industry, Rollins's novel posits a necessary causal relation between mechanized labor and militant workers' movements. That is, *The Shadow Before* is of particular interest here because it illustrates how the discipline imposed on workers by these new technological and managerial requirements would inevitably lead to spontaneous forms of factory strikes.

One of the most notable stylistic features of the novel is its use of familiar modernist techniques to represent narrative actions and events. Rollins frequently alters the typography of his text to evoke the effects of movement and noise. A typical example is his description of a fire engine passing through a street at night: "Far away, coming nearer, sounded a fireengine, hooting down the Drive; rushing, *shooting,* HOOTING DOWN THE DRIVE; (Harry jumped up, his heart pounding) UNDER THE WINDOW, SHRIEKING TO THE NIGHT. ON AND ON, *into the City;* on ... and on" (271).

While there is nothing unique about this kind of typographic mimesis—which by 1934 had become a standard trait of more daring fictional narratives—Rollins significantly extends its use to portray the thoughts and speech of workers amid the suffocating commotion of machinery in the textile mill. The following passage depicts the character of Micky, a textile worker and future strike leader, trying to talk to her coworker, Doucet, while she is working in the mill:

> The sound of [Micky's] voice, penetrating sound, rasping through the roar, roar, roar, clamp them on; clamping, roaring; snapping, roaring—. [Ramon] Viera came walking through it, moving up the aisle toward them.
> "What do you think of your new boss?" Doucet shouted.
> Micky glanced over her shoulder. Her smile faded and she turned to her machines. Her lips moved in reply as her fingers played up and down the spindles; but the tiny sound was swept away in the sea of sound. Her eyes faded in the eyes, machines, figures of girls, UP and down; clamp them on; snap them off; UP; down. UP; down. Doucet moved on down the line.... UP; down. UP and down; to the ends of the room, reaching to Ramon's shoulder, the obedient host of machines roared, roared, jerked UP and down, his eightyfive girls clamped the bobbins on, twisted the thread, snapped them off; heads moving, fingers moving, shouts and throbbing, human arms, machine arms. (94)

In this passage, the girls at work are clearly meant to be seen as belonging to the "obedient host of machines" of the mill, their arms being figured as "machine arms." Furthermore Micky, the individual, is absorbed into the collective mass of textile workers and machinery, as we are told that her "eyes faded in the eyes, machines, figures of girls" around her in the mill.

This image of the workplace not only suggests that Micky's visual perspective is saturated by the commotion of the mill. In conjunction with similar passages, it also indicates that her figurative "vision"—her thoughts and memories—are interwoven and structured by the noise of her workplace: "In the blur of her moving hands, in the jerking bobbins, was the memory of his slim figure, sharpcut ... overseeing the girls, girls, clamping them on; snap one off—; *God, I hate you,* she breathed, moving her fingers up and down, I hate you, I ... Her head sank back; she bit her lip (snapping a bobbin off)" (Rollins 105). As Micky's conscious thoughts and memories are constantly interrupted by the machine she works on, the motions and sounds of the machinery are joined to the expression of her thoughts, apparently to punctuate the textual form of the narrative itself. Thus by deliberately industrializing not just the thematic representation of his characters' experience but the actual form of his narrative as well, Rollins seeks to conjure on the formal level of his text the same effects that the fictional mill has upon the workers who inhabit it.⁶

The mill's manager, Thayer, is also subjected to the effects of the machinery, to such a degree that at times he resembles the portrait of Paul Rinelli that emerges at the end of *Temper*, a mass worker "baptized in the life-blood of industry." Rollins describes Thayer against the backdrop of the mill's machines: "Clamp them on; snap them off.... The sound, muffled by the closed doors of the mill rooms and his office, seeped into Thayer, an overtone to his conversations, his work, his thoughts. Like the rhythm of his pumping blood, the rhythm of his respiration, came this dull sullen rhythm, unnoticed, but lifesustaining; and when it stopped, as when his breathing and his heart stopped, that would be the end. But there would be no end. Clamp them on; snap them off" (Rollins 141–142). By representing Thayer as one literally driven by the force of the machines he oversees (of which "there would be no end"), Rollins connects the plant's management to its workers on the basis of their shared habituation to the mechanized workplace they both occupy. Yet over the course of the novel this common experience serves ultimately to distinguish the workers from their managers. That is, where the speed and efficiency of the factory have the effect of turning the workers into militant strikers, the cacophony and tension of its administration turn the managers (including the company's owners, officials, and stockholders, as well as the town's judges and police officers, along with the rest of the capitalist class) into sadistic perverts.⁷

Such stylistic devices—used to evoke a scene of class conflict within a more general and shared industrial environment, where both parties to the conflict appear equally mechanized—also contribute to the image of the "mass" of workers that figures so prominently in *The Shadow Before*. The novel in fact provides two different (ideologically familiar) versions of this mass. The first of these characterizes the textile workers before they are organized for their strike. At the end of a normal workday, when they are leaving the mill, the workers assume a form that seems threatening on account of its apparent formlessness: "In the doorways that faced three sides of the huge pebbled court, dark figures, jammed into formless bodies, swayed, bobbed, grunted in talk; in every dark doorway a mass of pale jerking faces.... Six doorways vomited men, women, children, wave after wave, separating, running, running.... They jammed together again at the gate, damming it with an everwidening torrent" (Rollins 112). This menacing and unruly mass, however, is viewed by the union organizers in the novel as a potentially revolutionary force, representing the struggles of the whole of "mankind." In the eyes of Marvin, a textile worker and one of the lead organizers, "The workers... were a mass: even though he personally knew and liked Fred and Slim and Mary and Albertine: they were a sweeping mass that was mankind:... He saw the incongruity of his [biblical] heaven, lifeless finite goal, against the living fluidity of mankind. What had a dead tale of the desert... to do with the living struggling mass?" (174–175). The narrative transformation here of the workers into the "living struggling mass" of mankind, when earlier they appeared as mere "formless bodies" and "a mass of pale jerking faces," depends on the submersion, absorption, and cohesion of its individual members—Fred, Slim, Mary, Albertine—into a force greater than themselves.

In other words, for Rollins the creation of a revolutionary mass of workers is based on a process that is virtually identical in its essential characteristics to what occurs in the modern industrial workplace. When individual workers are forced to adapt to the rigors of mechanization and continuous-flow production, they seem to become transformed into a single, collective force of labor power. The moment the textile workers of *The Shadow Before* come together to form a mass on strike, therefore, their narrative depiction starts to resemble that of the factory—a sea of impersonal machines that are technologically coordinated and running in synch: "They closed in a tight mass in the center that widened, widened, as more and more poured out; until at last they filled the court, a dark, agitated, compact mass.... Their voices, sharp, deep, or shrill, fused in a mighty rumble" (151). The tightness of this mass reflects the image of the uniform "hardness" of the steelworkers in *Temper*, just as the fusion of their "sharp" voices suggests Paul Rinelli's ultimate fusion with his factory's machinery. Again, though one might expect such an image to convey, however slightly, the dehumanizing effect of mechanization on workers, Rollins instead uses it to strengthen the bond of affiliation that links his militant workers to their machines. For instance, during the strike, "At committee meetings [Micky] listened carefully to discussions, aware of the formation of a portentous pattern. And when rarely she spoke herself, she felt her words enter the weave.... [The strike] engulfed her as the mill had engulfed her, the irregular stampede of picketers in and out her office had replaced naturally the continuous even throb of the machines back in the high dark room" (247). Rollins's language here suggests that the "portentous pattern" Micky senses is in fact the mapping of a terrain that both the strikers and their opponents share—namely, the mill. If her speech in this setting can still "enter the weave" like the bobbins she recently handled, it stands to reason that, from her perspective, the stream of picketers can "naturally" replace the throbbing machinery of the mill.

Although Rollins's narrative at times gestures toward a more critical view of the relation between workers and machinery, the momentum already established in the opposing direction—identifying workers with machinery—finally dominates its representation of the textile mill. In one of the few exceptions to this trend, the strike leader Marvin, while observing millworkers, ponders how they must go "to 'their' machines, the machines they belonged to according to the bosses" (110). Marvin here questions the relation workers have to "their" machines, contrasting this to the relation imposed upon them by the mill's bosses, for whom the machines possess "their" workers. In each instance, it is a matter of determining a certain proprietary relation. Marvin's thought suggests that this relation in its present state should be inverted: instead of the machines owning the workers, the workers should own the machines.

Yet by the end of the novel—the company having broken the strike, while the union continues its apparently futile efforts—such a vision seems even more unlikely than it did at the start. The narrative concludes with Micky imagining the fate of the workers who are still at "their" machines in the mill. The bold image she conjures, however, is designed to be read as a prophetic warning of the coming revolt of textile workers. This is suggested not only through a text made up entirely of capitalized letters, but especially through Rollins's choice to leave the end of his narrative suspended in the form of a fragment: "THE GIRL WITH AUBURN HAIR MOVES FINGERS, SNAPPING ONE OFF AND BRUSHING IT BACK AND CLAMP ONE ON 'YOU DON'T GET TIME TO BREATHE!' SHE SHOUTS AND CLAMPS ONE ON.... THE GIRLS BESIDE HER GIGGLE CLAMP THEM THEN THEY SOBER ON AND MOVE THEIR FINGERS SNAP THEM UP AND DOWN THE SPINDLES OFF AND UP AND DOWN THE CLAMP THEM HIGH DARK ROOM THEY MOVE THEIR FINGERS ON AND SNAP THEM OFF AND CLAMP THEM ON AND" (389). These last words of the novel, "CLAMP THEM ON AND," without a mark of punctuation, imply a future action that would "snap them off," as well as the potential for more revolutionary deeds on the part of the workers.

This fragmentary image at the end of the novel implies an ambiguous range of possibilities. It could be taken to mean that the machines will continue to run indefinitely, but it may also mean that some unspeakable force has already interrupted their steady flow. The open form of the fragment, then, signifies both a kind of caesura and a continuation. In a 1935 *Partisan Review* symposium on the subject of "proletarian literature," the critic Edwin Berry Burgum, discussing the political significance of the proletarian novel, cited the recent trend of formal experimentation in novels such as *The Shadow Before*, arguing that "this 'open' form ... is not 'open' in the romantic sense since the direction is established. ... Therefore, every proletarian novel craves its sequel" (11). If Rollins's choice to supply a fragmentary ending for *The Shadow Before* means that his novel should similarly be read as craving its sequel, in Burgum's twofold sense—namely, a sequel in the form of a conclusive revolutionary action, which in turn would require the production of more proletarian fiction—it is still unclear what will become of Rollins's fictional textile workers. Although they may be destined one day to own the machines of the mill, the general representational strategy of his narrative suggests that they will do so only insofar as they adopt the characteristics of the very machines they seek to control.

Getting to the Point of Production

The notion that mass workers could adapt to highly mechanized forms of labor and ultimately become heroic machines in their own right is a common theme of all the novels examined in this chapter. However, the ambivalence of Rollins's narrative on this point suggests that the process of the worker's mechanical "retooling" is not so straightforward as it may have seemed to Cruden, Bell, and Conrad. "The adaptation of habits of life and of ideals and aspirations to the exigencies of the machine process is not nearly complete," observed Thorstein Veblen in 1904, "nor does the untrained man instinctively fall into line with it. Even the best-trained, severely disciplined man of the industrial towns has his seasons of recalcitrancy" (191n9). Although Veblen's observation reflects a relatively early stage of mass industrial development—thus we might assume that, thirty years later, workers would have become more adapted to what Veblen terms "the machine process"—the characterization of the mass worker in *The Shadow Before* (as well as in Weatherwax's *Marching! Marching!*, discussed in the previous chapter) reveals that this adaptation is still marked by the worker's peculiar "recalcitrancy."

On the whole, the novels examined in the first part of this study, "The Making of the Mass Worker," have underscored the degrading and dehumanizing effects that the managerial and technological conditions of mass production had upon U.S. industrial workers in the first decades of the twentieth century. Their representations of the figure of the mass worker—though different from one novel to the next—share a central point of reference, in relation to which the other elements of their narratives are more or less subordinated. Namely, they all agree that the making of the mass worker occurred at the actual point of production in the factory and that it consisted of three interrelated forces that operated on and through the body of the worker, in various degrees and combinations. These involved, first, the general intensification of the labor process that resulted from the reorganization of production by Taylorist and Fordist methods; second, the dominant role played by automated forms of machinery in the determination of specific labor processes; and third, the deskilling of traditionally skilled industrial occupations, which led to the blurring, homogenization, or disappearance of older craft distinctions.

In addition to sharing this theme—which could be termed "degradation through commodification"—the novels we have so far examined also provide various indications (more or less explicit, depending on the novel) that the mass worker was never simply "made" by these forces of U.S. industrial capitalism. That is, at no point do the workers represented in these novels ever fully submit to and absorb the effects of such degrading forces. This in turn may reflect the broader historical fact that, at each stage of their development in the crucible of the modern industrial workplace, actual (nonfictitious) mass workers never entirely lost the means or the inclination to resist being treated simply as machines. In response to being "made over" to suit the technical requirements of mass production, industrial workers, pushed to a certain limit, inevitably refused to allow their laboring bodies to be bought, sold, and used as mere commodities. Rather, from one factory shop to the next, they proved over and over again that they were not the "living tools" Horace Arnold imagined them to be ("Modern Machine-Shop" 1090).

The novels discussed in the second part of this study—"Strategy and Structure at the Point of Production"—are therefore narratives of troublemakers in a much more explicit and literal sense. In short, they are novels about workers who found or invented effective ways to resist being treated as commodities at the point of production. Compelled by the demands of mass production to become passively "made over," the workers represented in these novels deliberately choose to make trouble. They do this through a variety of large-scale and small-scale acts of resistance, with methods that are both overt and covert. In our study of these novels in the following two chapters, we will consider all such acts under the general heading of "sabotage," while the methods informing these acts will be considered under the general heading of "direct action."

The basic motives underlying industrial workers' use of sabotage and their faith in the principles of direct action are perhaps nowhere better illustrated than in a speech that the IWW organizer and poet Arturo Giovannitti made to a group of striking textile workers in Lawrence, Massachusetts, on January 20, 1912. Giovannitti informed the strikers: "Nobody cares for you. You are considered mere machines—less than machines. If any effort is made to improve your lot and to raise you to the dignity of manhood and womanhood, that effort must come from yourselves alone" (qtd. in Adamic, *Dynamite* 168).

Instead of resigning themselves to, accepting, or positively valorizing the physical and mental discipline imposed upon them by the machinery with which they work—as do most of the workers in the novels we have discussed in this chapter—the mass workers whose representations we will study in the next two chapters will be both *disempowering* and *powerful*. Such workers conceive of the modern industrial workplace as a vast material structure, composed of impersonal economic and political powers that are embodied in the concrete form of machinery. They know that this structure, and the machines that both reflect and enable it, need to be shut down or disabled (disempowered) at the actual point of production inside the factory if they are to acquire any power of their own. Neither labor leaders, unions, politicians, or political parties will be of any use to workers in this respect, since none of these has direct access to the machinery inside the factory (hence, direct access to machinery is the necessary precondition for direct action). Yet they also recognize that once they have succeeded in crippling the material structures of the industrial workplace, they will have acquired a position of economic and political strength that will be at least equal, if not superior, to that of their employers. The economic and political power that was materially embodied in the means of production—which they have effectively paralyzed—will now be transferred to them. They will become *powerful* workers in the precise degree to which their actions succeed in disempowering the basic mechanism of mass industrial production.

PART TWO

Strategy and Structure at the Point of Production

Up until now, we have examined only the ways in which U.S. industrial workers in the period from 1900 to 1940 came to be viewed as a homogeneous mass of human labor power. Industrial engineers, politicians, labor leaders, and novelists throughout this period imagined that workers in mass production factories, who were forced to adapt themselves to the exigencies of the machine process, had become more or less indistinguishable from the machinery which they operated.

This process of massification, however, is only one half of the story of the mass worker. In spite of the ongoing efforts of scientific managers and business entrepreneurs to protect large industrial concerns against the threat of labor unrest, the vulnerability of these giant enterprises to workers' acts of resistance at the point of production steadily increased as a result of the vertically integrated nature of their operations. The very systematicity by which the various forms and stages of their production processes were coordinated with one another made them highly sensitive to any sort of interference (Arrighi, "Marxist Century" 47–48; Veblen 14–15).

A perfect illustration of this phenomenon may be seen in the following description of Ford's Highland Park plant in 1914, when the bulk of the plant's production departments were converted to continuous-flow processes:

> Intricately adjusted lines of motion, indeed, reached far outside the factory walls. Precisely the right amounts of coal, iron, nickel, brass, leather, rubber, lubricants, gasoline, and other commodities had to be delivered to Highland Park in a hundred ever-flowing rivulets, delivered at just the right time. In the coal fields of West Virginia, the ore bed of the Mesabi, the nickel mines of Canada, men toiled to the end that none of the streams that fed the Ford assembly line, and the imitative lines of other great factories, should slacken. If one tributary ran dry, the whole complex was paralyzed. As long as all the streams ran to the specifications of the engineers, a car came off the assembly line every ten minutes—every five minutes—every two minutes. (Nevins and Hill, *Ford: The Times* 475 [cf. 369n, 472])

As Ford's historians observe, if any branch of this integrated network of operations functioned improperly, it could alter the balance of elements throughout the entire system, potentially even putting a stop to production. Thus, "if a few key men were late, half the factory was late" (Nevins and Hill, *Ford: Expansion* 514). The workers in these huge plants realized early on that, because Fordist mass production methods "operated as a system of related parts," when the relation between any of the parts changed, everything else was forced to change along with it (Edwards 121).

Seeds of Revolt

A direct by-product of the extreme systematicity that characterized Ford's production cycle, therefore, was that the day-to-day operations in the company's plants required extreme levels of discipline among their assembly-line workers (Ford, *My Life* 111). Nevertheless, the more Ford and other industrialists tried to monitor and control the basic movements of their workers, the more resistance they encountered.

Because labor power is embodied in human beings, any attempts to transform it into a pure mechanism will always be met with some degree of resistance. Yet apart from the many physiological causes one could cite to explain mass workers' acts of resistance, there was also the issue of their psychological dissatisfaction with their jobs, due to the monotonous tasks they performed day in and day out. While skilled workers could at least see how their labor and talents went into the building of a finished product, semiskilled or unskilled workers on assembly lines were deprived of this basic awareness and the feeling of accomplishment that went along with it. As a result, all the wage incentives and time studies imaginable could not arouse mass workers to take a personal interest in the labor they performed. Besides, if assembly-line operatives became too intellectually involved in their work, they were liable to fall behind in the execution of their assigned tasks; and if this happened, they knew they would have to endure various disciplinary actions, reprimands, and punishments at the hands of their supervisors.[1]

The fact that the mass worker felt no satisfaction from his job but instead sensed the desire of his employer "to reduce him to a trained gorilla" could, in Antonio Gramsci's words, "lead him into a train of thought that is far from conformist" (310). And just when mass workers were beginning to think in such ways, they were also realizing how vital each and every one of them was to the process of production in their various factories, for they were reminded of this every minute they spent on the job. Being subjected to constant supervision by foremen, assembly-line workers knew that they would be personally admonished as soon as the pace of their work dragged behind or exceeded that of the rest of the workers in their departments (Arnold and Faurote 247; see also Nevins and Hill, *Ford: Expansion* 296). Because he had to endure such rigors on a daily basis, the mass worker in the Fordist factory "soon realizes that he is not only being measured but that this work is a link in a long chain of operations, which link, if it does not function properly, is quickly noticed by management and by other workers" (Reitell 187).

In short, the more dissatisfied the assembly-line workers in these highly integrated plants became, the more they realized how easy it would be for any one of them to disrupt the flow of production. Ironically, while foremen tried to discipline the workers under their command to keep up with the pace of the conveyor belt, their efforts only led these workers to hate their jobs more and to recognize at the same time that, in fact, there was something they could do to challenge the tyranny of the "line production system" (Federal Trade Commission 29; Gartman 147–178). That is, these workers were learning—because their supervisors were constantly reminding them—that they could destabilize the general system of production just by slowing down or speeding up the pace of their work by even a slight degree. So every time they were admonished by foremen for falling behind the assigned rate of production (which had been unilaterally set by the company), mass workers were also learning that each of the tasks they performed as individuals was essential to the smooth operation of the factory as a whole.

If even a small group of line workers suddenly decided to stop working for any period of time, the linkage of their labor to that of all the other workers through the technology of the conveyor belt meant that every other worker on the line would be affected by their decision. Workers at earlier and later stages of the production process would have to cease work as well, either because those who were working further down the line would run out of jobs to do or because, for those who had completed earlier stages of the work, their finished jobs would quickly pile up, forcing them to stop as well (Edwards 127–128). Hence, the more that large companies expanded through vertical integration—linking their production operations with supply, distribution, and sales networks—the more they exposed themselves to the risks associated with a noncooperative workforce. Conversely, the potential for even minor outbreaks of labor unrest to disrupt production increased dramatically in direct proportion to the size of the vertically integrated firm. This extreme form of leverage that mass workers acquired—and that they knew they could use to resist the prerogatives of management at the point of production in the factory—was simply unheard of before mass industrial firms began to rely on machine technology to synchronize the different branches of their operations.[2]

By the 1930s, mass workers in a variety of industries had learned that they could appropriate the machinery of continuous-flow production to their own advantage. The technology of the conveyor belt, for instance, could be used as a weapon in their ongoing struggles with management over the issues of union recognition, the speedup, seniority rules, and layoffs (Torigian 338). The modern machinery and technology-driven methods of production associated with the system of Fordism in mass production industries were thus a double-edged phenomenon: They provided owners of large enterprises with a hitherto unknown measure of control over the pace of work and overall rates of production, but they also further exposed these same companies to the effects of workers' acts of resistance at the point of production.[3] In David Gartman's words, the very technologies that had been developed to control the mass autoworker "actually exacerbated the contradiction between capital and labor and increased the power of workers to act upon it. By revolutionizing the labor process, auto manufacturers in some ways inadvertently strengthened the hand of their class opponent in the shops" (147).

Workplace Bargaining Power

The unique form of power workers came to acquire in mass industrial factories was therefore the result of structural changes to the production process that had been implemented during the first thirty to forty years of the twentieth century and not the result of an ideological or political mind-set that, presumably, mass workers could have adopted during this same period. The ability they possessed to disrupt the system of mass production did not stem solely from a peculiar or heightened sense of class consciousness on their part; it had just as much to do with the integrated nature of production with assembly lines. Giovanni Arrighi reminds us that the strike wave that swept through U.S. mass production industries between the mid-1930s and the late 1940s "began as a spontaneous response of the rank-and-file of the industrial proletariat to the attempts by capital to shift onto labour the burdens of the Great Slump of the early 1930s. The main and indeed the only pre-existing organization of the industrial proletariat of any significance (the AFL) did nothing to initiate the strike wave. It became active in organizing and leading the movement only when the latter had proved capable of standing on its own and of generating alternative organizational structures, which became the CIO" ("Marxist Century" 47–48). Arrighi's final point here is central to his broader argument, since he refuses to grant any positive influence of labor parties and organizations on rank-and-file movements during the period in question. Indeed, the role of Marxist ideology is shown by Arrighi to have just the opposite (retarding) effect upon twentieth-century U.S. working-class struggles. Thus, instead of attributing industrial labor unrest in this era to any specific upsurge or ideological tendency in Marxist-socialist thought, he contends that "the foundation of the self-mobilization and self-organization of the industrial proletariat was wholly internal to the proletarian condition" (49; see also Torigian 329–330).

In a 1982 study, Arrighi introduced the concept of what he calls "workplace bargaining power" to describe the primary source of workers' power within vertically integrated companies, in contradistinction to their "marketplace bargaining power" ("Crisis" 82–91). Where the latter term refers to labor's ability to control its selling price in the marketplace, the former refers to the power it acquires as an internal feature of the production process (that is, as a part of the organic value composition of the firm). According to Arrighi, as the process of deskilling and mechanization spreads to all sectors of production in industrial capitalist societies, wage labor fights for its declining *marketplace* bargaining power (MBP) economically, through unions, and politically, through labor parties. Yet this is a Sisyphean task, whose problematic character is very seldom posed in discussions of working-class history. What is needed, Arrighi suggests, is an analysis of the same process from the point of view of labor's *workplace* bargaining power (WBP), since the very factors that steadily undermine its MBP can be seen to strengthen its WBP. That is, the larger the production unit, the more difficult it is for unions to organize the firm's workforce (lower MBP); but by using their strategic position at key junctures to disrupt the flow of production in the plant, the workers themselves can inflict a greater amount of damage to the capital of the firm (higher WBP). Therefore, as the organic value composition of the firm rises, its rising dependency on fixed-capital forms—such as machinery and plant structures—has the effect of raising its workers' WBP (Arrighi and Silver 191–207).

Arrighi and Beverly Silver's analyses convincingly show how the decline of labor's MBP has been historically accompanied by a dramatic rise in its WBP in a variety of different industries and periods throughout the twentieth century. The conclusions to be drawn from the work of Arrighi and Silver have several important implications for twentieth-century labor movements.

First of all, the growth of labor's WBP in the United States between 1900 and 1940 was due first and foremost to structural changes in production processes, and only secondarily (if at all) to the popular acceptance of Marxist ideology or the increased size of working-class organizations and political parties during this period. That is, U.S. labor's increased bargaining power throughout these years was primarily a result of its increased embodiment within—in order to fulfill the needs of—capitalist production, rather than a direct outgrowth of its class consciousness in the intellectual sense.

Second, as the strength of their MBP began to decline around the turn of the century, unions and progressive political parties became less reliable as means for U.S. mass workers to acquire bargaining power in relation to their employers. Moreover, the goals of each of these became increasingly differentiated from one another. In the immediate aftermath of their major organizing victories in the late 1930s, the industrial unions affiliated with the CIO began to adopt exclusively mediational roles between the conflicting interests of labor and capital, thus acting to restrain labor's WBP at the point of production. By contrast, socialist political parties in this same forty-year period became more and more convinced that the best way to achieve their goals was by means of coercion and authoritarian bureaucracies, whose organization mimicked the very capitalist power structures they professed to challenge.

Third, and finally, as labor's WBP rose throughout the first half of the century, U.S. corporations' reliance on a workforce made up predominantly of first-generation immigrants was either partly or wholly superseded by the emigration of capital. Spurred by financial speculation and labor unrest at home, in the late 1940s large U.S. corporations began focusing a greater share of their attention on strategies for expanding production on an international scale. Transnational capitalist development and financial speculation in this period should therefore be understood as attempts to restore corporate profitability, which was threatened by the WBP that mass industrial workers had recently acquired at the point of production.

Industrial Unionism and the Critique of Representation in the Progressive Era

In the face of the broad, coordinated, and well-publicized offensive that the works management movement had been waging against the very idea of skilled labor in the early years of the twentieth century, many AFL leaders at this time still insisted that the federation's tradition of skilled "craft" unionism was perfectly suited to meet the needs of the new throngs of mass industrial workers. Considering the obvious discrepancy between the AFL's approach to organizing workers according to their various skills and the fact that workers in mass production industries were being rapidly and systematically stripped of whatever skills they might have once possessed, progressive unionists at the time responded with calls for a new form of "industrial" unionism. This relatively new approach to organizing labor was based on the idea that mass industrial workers should be represented according to that which the greatest number of them had in common: namely, the industry in which they worked. It thus set out to unite all the workers who were employed in a single industry, regardless of their individual occupation, instead of dividing them into a multitude of separate craft unions according to their different skills. The demand for industrial unions not only expressed the practical need to organize the swelling ranks of the new and generally unskilled workforce in mass production industries; it also signaled a critique of the AFL's long-standing tradition of representing human labor power according to workers' various skill levels and crafts (which were quickly becoming obsolete in any case).

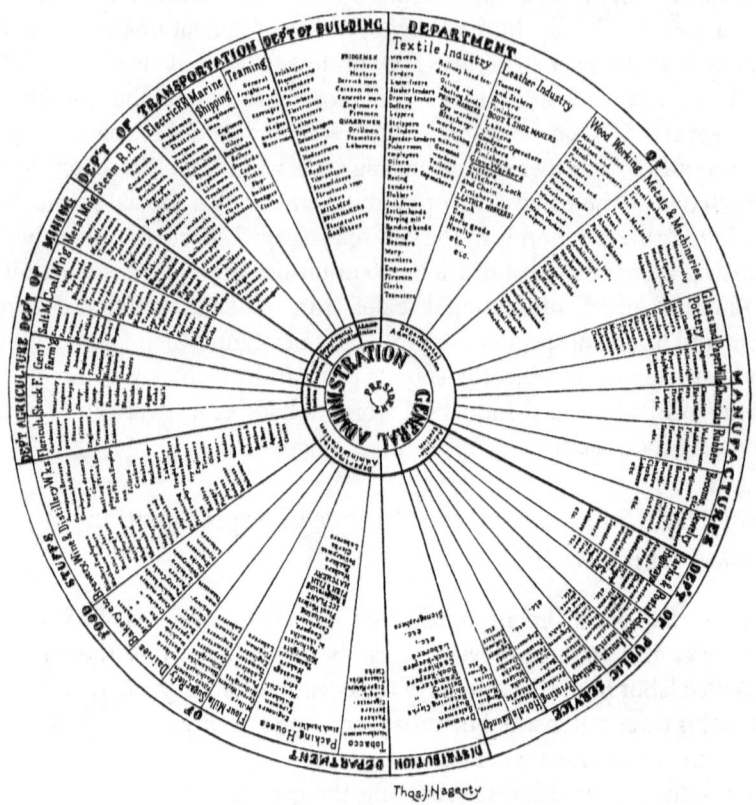

FIGURE 2. Thomas J. Hagerty, "Father Hagerty's 'Wheel of Fortune'." Illustration of the structure of the industrial system. *Voice of Labor* Mar. 1905. Rpt. in Joyce L. Kornbluh, *Rebel Voices: An IWW Anthology*, new and enl. ed. (Chicago: Kerr, 1998).

In the opinion of progressive unionists, those within the leadership of the AFL who resisted the need to change course—as well as, more radically, the need to overhaul the entire structure of the federation to accommodate mass industrial workers—could now justifiably be condemned as labor "misleaders." To oppose the monopoly that the AFL exercised over the organized labor movement, and to push for a genuine form of industrial unionism, a coalition of progressive unionists and socialists meeting in Chicago in January 1905 founded a new alliance of industrial unions, the Industrial Workers of the World (IWW).

At the IWW's first convention in June of 1905, its founders articulated where they stood with respect to the basic problem of the AFL craft unions. In their view, such unions "aid the employing class to mislead the workers into the belief that the working class have interests in common with their employers" (Industrial Workers of the World, "Preamble" 12). Because the more militant advocates of industrial unionism did not entertain any hopes that the AFL would restructure itself to become an industrial organization, they simply dismissed the entire federation out of hand. The "labor misleaders" and "labor lieutenants" who represented the dominant, conservative interests within the AFL thus became the subject of the harshest attacks from the rank and file of the industrial union movement (Brissenden 87–89).

Rejecting the AFL's parliamentary procedures, which they viewed as inherently corrupt, the militant wing of the industrial union movement instead advocated various forms of "direct democracy." In their minds, the practice of direct democracy would eventually come to replace the obsolete institutions of representative democracy that the current generation of unskilled industrial workers had inherited from skilled craft workers in the nineteenth century (Brissenden 158; Foner, *Industrial Workers* 142, 144).

According to the members of the IWW, two basic tools were required to transform the country's existing representative democracy into an industrial (direct) democracy: direct action and sabotage at the point of production in the factory. In his pamphlet *The I.W.W. in Theory and Practice*, Justus Ebert defined *direct action* as "industrial action directly by, for, and of the workers themselves, without the treacherous aid of labor misleaders or scheming politicians. A strike that is initiated, controlled, and settled by the workers directly affected is direct action.... Direct action is combined action, directly on the job to secure better job conditions. Direct action is industrial democracy" (qtd. in Kornbluh, "With Folded Arms" 35). One extremely popular type of direct action among mass industrial workers was acts of sabotage on the job, which could take a number of different forms. The IWW generally adhered to Emile Pouget's definition of this term. Pouget was a spokesperson for the syndicalist movement among industrial workers in France, which paralleled (and slightly predated) the IWW-led industrial union movement in the United States.[4]

Sabotage could be practiced in virtually any workplace environment, though it was most often—and most effectively—carried out by mass industrial workers in the act of performing their jobs, including those

FIGURE 3. Ralph Chaplin, "We Are Coming Home, John Farmer—We Are Coming Back to Stay." Cartoon illustrating the IWW's advocacy of sabotage. *Solidarity* 30 Sept. 1916. Rpt. in Joyce L. Kornbluh, *Rebel Voices: An IWW Anthology*, new and enl. ed. (Chicago: Kerr, 1998).

who were working under the direct scrutiny of supervisors. For example, workers might covertly slow down their pace to put a "crimp" in the system of production wherever they were working. They might also "work to rules"—that is, perform their jobs exactly as they had been instructed, making absolutely no allowance for unforeseen occurrences—in order to clog up the flow of goods or services without having to risk being punished or reprimanded by their supervisors. This type of resistance at the point of production also came to be known by the phrase "striking on the job" (Adamic, *Dynamite* 395).

In sum, then, the members of the IWW, together with other advocates of industrial unionism in the Progressive Era, were fighting to establish a new form of representational practice—a practice that would ensure that mass industrial workers retained the power and authority to represent themselves, their own interests and concerns, at the point of production in the factory. Ideally, as they saw it, mass workers should no longer have to cede control over the mechanism of their representation in the workplace to anyone else, such as labor leaders, politicians, or business managers—each of whom claimed the right and the authority to represent workers, but for their own unique purposes.

The Sitdown Strike and the Mass Worker in the 1930s

The movement for industrial unionism that is often identified with the rise of the IWW reached its peak just as it was being torn apart by a systematic campaign of suppression on the part of the federal government, which lasted from 1917 to 1922, during which time most of the movement's leading figures were either arrested or deported. Fifteen years later, in 1934, the push to establish industrial unions for mass workers was reinvigorated by a debate that broke out at the AFL's annual convention in San Francisco.

In the intervening years, the AFL's tradition of craft unionism had continued to prove itself inadequate as a strategy to organize mass industrial workers. The "pure and simple" or "horizontal" style of craft unionism, which the AFL had been promoting since its inception, linked workers *across* industries according to their various crafts. By contrast, an industrial or "vertical" union would link workers of various crafts and different skill levels *within* a single industry (Adamic, *Dynamite* 446). Though it was practically self-evident that this second, vertical form of union was best suited for organizing mass industrial workers, the proceedings of the AFL's 1935 convention reveal that even this was a contentious issue, dividing the AFL leadership between conservatives and a progressive group of industrial unionists.

In the meantime, mass industrial workers had already started to take matters into their own hands. A new tactic—the sitdown strike—was gaining popularity among workers in industrial plants where production processes had been rationalized along Fordist lines (in the era of the IWW, a similar and related tactic was called a "folded-arm strike"). In 1933, for example, assembly-line workers at the Hormel Packing Corporation in Minnesota carried out a three-day strike during which they stayed inside the plant but refused to work. However, it was the rubber workers in Akron, Ohio, whose use of the sitdown strike brought fame and publicity to this new tactic, which seemed perfectly suited for mass industrial workers (Torigian 331–333).

For a number of reasons the sitdown strike specifically had become, virtually overnight, the preferred tactic for mass workers who were struggling to organize. First of all, because they had few existing sources of associational power (unions) to assist them, mass workers were accountable to no one but themselves (Torigian 334). The sitdown tactic thus allowed them to bypass standard union procedures for calling and voting on strike actions. They could strike whenever and wherever they chose and then worry about building up their union's membership rolls once the strike was already under way. Moreover, before the rise in popularity of the sitdown tactic, efforts to organize these workers were generally limited to "factory-gate speeches" or meetings at workers' homes, both of which were vulnerable to company persecution. It thus seemed nearly impossible to organize mass industrial workers until the sitdown strike tactic proved that these workers could successfully outflank the many union-busting resources that companies had at their disposal (Kraus 92, 158; Torigian 335).

Sitdown strikes were often quick to begin and end. They were generally free of violence (from either side), and workers did not have to resort to picket lines or worry about how to keep scabs from taking their jobs. Furthermore, from their location inside the plant, strikers were able to use their knowledge of the plant's machines and production processes to ensure a victorious outcome. Because they had no union leaders or officials to distrust, they were less likely to be "sold out." Moreover, since, in the case of unorganized workers, the idea of a "strike sanction" from the union's executive council was not a relevant concern, they had the option to strike whenever they pleased. Consequently, the sitdowns gave them a tremendous sense of self-importance, for just one worker's grievance, or that of a small number of workers, could potentially shut down an entire plant. Beyond these advantages, the sitdowns also provided a welcome interruption from the boredom and tedium of work on the assembly lines. They were happy social affairs where workers could get to know one another. In many instances, workers who rarely if ever had the opportunity to speak to each other learned that they held concerns, values, and interests in common. In addition to being dramatic and thrilling events in their own right, the sitdowns fostered a broader sense of solidarity with workers elsewhere, drawing community support from various sectors of the labor movement. In the eyes of mass industrial workers, the sitdown strike thus seemed to embody a purely democratic action. It was a way to apply pressure to giant, impersonal corporations that was anarchic and pragmatic in equal measure.[5]

In addition to exploiting the high degree of workplace bargaining power possessed by workers in mass production industries, the sitdown strike tactic opened a debate within the U.S. labor movement over the extent to which strike actions ought to be planned and carried out by rank-and-file workers themselves (Adamic, *My America* 407). Spontaneous uprisings of striking workers occasioned a fierce debate over the degree to which union leaders ought to encourage or discourage such actions at the point of production. Underlying this debate, however, was an even more complicated set of questions concerning the issue of representation in the industrial workplace. Who has the authority to speak for whom? Who can decide where and when workers should be allowed to talk back to their supervisors? Why do workers need unions to represent them when they have the power to shut down and occupy the factories in which they work and to speak for themselves through such actions? As Adamic clearly recognized:

> The fact that the sitdown gives the worker in mass-production industries a vital sense of importance cannot be overemphasized. Two sitdowns which completely tied up plants employing close to ten thousand men were started by half a dozen men each. Imagine the feeling of power those men experienced! And the thousands of workers who sat down in their support shared that feeling in various degrees, depending on their individual power of imagination.... One man's grievance, if the majority of his fellow-workers in his department agreed that it was a just grievance, could tie up the whole plant. He became a strike leader; the other members of the working force in his department became members of the strike committee. *They* assumed full responsibility in the matter: [they] formed their own patrols, they kept the machines from being pointlessly destroyed, and they met with the management and dictated their terms. *They* turned their individual self-control and restraint into group self-discipline—which probably was the best aspect of the sitdown. *They* settled the dispute, not some outsider. (*My America* 408–409)

Consequently, by the end of the 1930s, even many radicals and left-leaning industrial unionists came to frown upon the indiscriminate use of the sitdown strike (Vorse 10). It was simply too easy for any worker who wanted to sit down on the job to do so; and because the production process was so highly integrated, the effects of even the most minor of these acts of sabotage could be far-reaching. From the perspective of union leaders, these spontaneous actions at the point of production were useful only if they fit within the framework of the union's broader strategic aims. As soon as they "went too far" and exceeded the union's specified aims, organizers were left scrambling to recover control over them. What had once been a radical innovation—one that seemed destined to revolutionize the capital-labor relation in the modern industrial factory—was now seen by both union officials and company managers as merely the sign of an undisciplined workforce.[6]

3 / The Disempowering Worker and the Aesthetic Representation of Industrial Unionism: "I am the book that has no end!"

The statement in the subtitle of this chapter—"I am the book that has no end!"—is made by a fictitious ocean liner filled with mass industrial workers who are on their way to the battlefronts of Europe at the start of World War I. Appearing as the final sentence of Ernest Poole's IWW-inspired novel of 1915, *The Harbor*, the exclamation signals the newfound radicalism of the modern industrial worker, figuratively conveyed in the machinery of a large ship making its way around the world. Why, though, do these workers, whose voices are united in the single call of the ocean liner, insist that they are a *book*, a specific type of aesthetic representation? Moreover, what exactly would a book "that has no end"—either no last page or no definite purpose—reflect about the nature of industrial workers' movements in 1915?

This chapter explores the ways in which a third group of novels about U.S. industrial workers—all published between 1905 and 1915—began to depict acts of workplace resistance. These novels, in other words, sought both to portray and to explain modern workers' efforts to decommodify their labor power. They did this by producing fictional representations of people who were refusing precisely to be represented—by existing trade unions, political parties, and business managers—as nothing more than an inert, powerless, and relatively homogeneous mass of unskilled labor.

The chapter begins by providing a brief overview of the artistic and cultural productions of the IWW, a radical movement of U.S. workers that flourished in the first two decades of the twentieth century. It then looks more closely at a specific example of IWW artwork: the spectacular theatrical production of 1913 entitled *The Pageant of the Paterson Strike*, which was staged and performed by mass industrial workers themselves. Through an analysis of the reception and controversies surrounding the Paterson Pageant, this first part of the chapter establishes a general framework for analyzing the complex status of aesthetic representation in IWW-era novels. The remainder of the chapter is then devoted to close readings of three novels that were affiliated in various degrees with the agenda of the IWW. Proceeding chronologically, it starts by studying Leroy Scott's *The Walking Delegate* (1905), about New York City ironworkers who are on strike. Scott's narrative focuses on the apparent conflict between workers' structural forms of power on the job and theatrical displays of workers' power in the union hall. Through the clear juxtaposition of its characters, Scott's novel lays out the basic points of difference between these two modes of expressing working-class power. Guided by Scott's theoretical concerns, the chapter moves on to explore how Arthur Bullard's novel about Lower East Side garment workers, *Comrade Yetta* (1913), attempted to bridge the perceived gulf between representations of workers and their inclination to direct action. However, as our readings of these two novels will show, both Scott's and Bullard's novels manage to resolve this conflict only through appeals to the sublime nature of working-class solidarity. The chapter concludes, appropriately, with a reading of Ernest Poole's novel about New York City dockworkers, *The Harbor* (1915), whose narrator-protagonist brilliantly illustrates what this chapter has been examining under the heading of "the mass worker sublime."[1]

In contrast to the two groups of novels we examined in Part One of *Troublemakers*, these three IWW-era novels make a point of showing the degraded, mechanized worker engaging in acts of resistance. The mass workers represented in them are still exploited in the same ways that workers in other novels are. However, they differ from these other images of workers in one crucial respect: they are neither defeated nor ennobled by the mechanized labor processes in mass production factories. Instead, their experience of this new environment is marked by their continued acts of resistance. Recall for a moment how the "powerless" and "empowered" workers examined previously were either destroyed or strengthened by their working conditions. In contrast to these, the "disempowering" workers we will consider here are both oppressed and strengthened in the mass industrial workplace. However, what especially sets them apart from other figures of mass workers is that they are also emboldened to take direct action to better their working conditions.

The members of the IWW, or Wobblies, saw themselves as belonging to "One Big Union" made up of all the industrial workers in the United States, in solidarity with industrial workers around the world. The primary aim of the IWW was simply to organize those workers who most desperately needed to be organized. These consisted mainly of low-wage, unskilled (or recently deskilled), and immigrant industrial workers whom the AFL routinely ignored, in the areas of manufacturing, construction, marine transport, lumber, agriculture, and mining.

In novels about Wobblies, modern mass workers were depicted for the first time as subjects of their own labor power rather than as objects of capitalist production. The workers in these fictional narratives struggle to decommodify themselves, for they are portrayed as rejecting both the political (symbolic) and technological (iconic) modes of representation that might otherwise have been used to commodify them. Since established political parties could not symbolically represent them as constituents without first reducing them to mute and helpless wage slaves, and since trade unions could not represent them other than as iconic products, or offshoots, of capital itself, the IWW encouraged industrial workers to resist any attempts by others to represent them in such terms. In turn, the aesthetic representations of industrial workers produced by writers and artists affiliated with (or sympathetic to) the IWW portrayed these workers as actively disempowering anyone—politicians, capitalists, or labor leaders—who sought to gain power over them by representing them for their own purposes.

In addition to shunning political parties, Wobblies rejected the economic and ideological aims of the established trade unions in the United States. Essentially, these consisted of the craft-oriented unions of the AFL, which, like their political counterparts, were all based on the relatively abstract and easily corruptible principles of representative democracy. According to the IWW historian Paul Brissenden, the typical Wobbly "was exceedingly skeptical of the value of undiluted representative democracy for either a labor union or a political state. He suspected that any official might, and probably would, be disloyal. He realized how difficult it is for any organization which depends on representatives to maintain a body of such representatives who really represent" (158). From the IWW's point of view, the established AFL unions only exacerbated the divisions between "labor leaders" and the workers they were supposed to represent, just as existing political parties served to broaden the gap between representatives and their constituents. Thus, while writing off the AFL as the "A.F. of Hell," or the "American Separation of Labor,"

FIGURE 4. Ralph Chaplin, "The Hand That Will Rule the World—One Big Union." Cartoon illustrating the IWW principle of solidarity. *Solidarity* 30 June 1917. Rpt. in Joyce L. Kornbluh, *Rebel Voices: An IWW Anthology*, new and enl. ed. (Chicago: Kerr, 1998).

the Wobblies also frequently refused to ally themselves with the Socialist—or "slowcialist"—Party (De Caux 19, 21; Luhan 193). For the IWW, these unions and political parties, in addition to being filled with parliamentarian reformists, were all equally hampered by corruption, graft, authoritarianism, and bureaucracy. Such organizations, they believed, could only restrict the power the working class already possessed at the point of production in the industrial workplace.

Rejecting the forms of representation offered by these traditional institutions, the IWW instead defined its own concept of representation as one in which, fundamentally, only workers would have the power to represent themselves. This ideal of self-representation was to be realized through workers' solidarity across various crafts and industries and through their "direct action"—strikes and other forms of sabotage—at the point of production in the workplace. "'Strike when you like and wherever you like,' was a key slogan of the IWW," according to the historian Philip S. Foner (*Industrial Workers* 136). Such acts of resistance,

FIGURE 5. Sam, "The General Strike." Photomontage illustrating the IWW principle of solidarity. *One Big Union Monthly* July 1919. Rpt. in Joyce L. Kornbluh, *Rebel Voices: An IWW Anthology,* new and enl. ed. (Chicago: Kerr, 1998).

practiced systematically in every branch of industry, the Wobblies held, would eventually provide the industrial working class with "representatives who really represent" and would thus establish a more genuine form of participatory democracy, by workers and for workers.

Finally, the IWW opposed the signing of time contracts between workers and employers because, in addition to restricting workers' freedom to call sympathetic strikes (which undermined the principle of solidarity), such contracts prevented workers "from striking at any moment that appeared favorable to them and unfavorable to the employers" (which undermined the principle of direct action) (Foner, *Industrial Workers* 37). By insisting that they avoid signing labor contracts, the IWW encouraged mass workers to defy the most basic measures taken by employers to commodify their labor power in the workplace. It was through their direct action, rather than through labor contracts, that mass workers would learn to speak *for themselves*, in order to say that they refused to be treated as representations *of capital*.

FIGURE 6. Ralph Chaplin, "Now He Understands the Game." Cartoon illustrating the IWW's critical view of parliamentarianism. *Solidarity* 11 Nov. 1916. Rpt. in Joyce L. Kornbluh, *Rebel Voices: An IWW Anthology*, new and enl. ed. (Chicago: Kerr, 1998).

In sum, the IWW saw in the modern industrial working class a political power that was free of political representation (by a party), as well as an economic power that was free of economic representation (by a trade union). Far from being an antipolitical movement, then, the strategy of the Wobblies might be better understood as antirepresentational. Their economic and their political principles were equally grounded in a critique of representation—a critique that assumed that any type of economic or political representation of mass workers on the part of others would potentially undermine the power that these workers had acquired in the workplace.

One consequence of this thoroughgoing distrust of representation was that each novelist who wrote about Wobblies had to confront a

FIGURE 7. Machia and Reeder, "Organize on the Job Where You Are Robbed." Cartoon illustrating worker's choice between direct action or parliamentarianism. *Industrial Worker* 23 Mar. 1911. Rpt. in Joyce L. Kornbluh, *Rebel Voices: An IWW Anthology,* new and enl. ed. (Chicago: Kerr, 1998).

complex problem: namely, to sort out and make sense of the relation, and inevitable confusion, between economic, political, and aesthetic forms of representation. How, for example, should they represent a Wobbly as a character in a fictional narrative who goes on strike and refuses to work, and thus one who is refusing to be represented *by others* as a "worker"? Would a fictional representation of a mass work stoppage among Wobblies depict "workers," strictly speaking, or would it instead depict people in the act of refusing to be represented merely as "workers"?

The phenomenon of refusing to work is not one that is easily recognized, or valorized, as a worthwhile subject of study within narratives that are presumed to be about the activity of performing work. (If it were, a text like Herman Melville's 1853 short story "Bartleby, the Scrivener" might occupy a more distinguished place in the canon of working-class fiction.) Furthermore, the figure of the "worker" was the very representational category upon which the basic programs and goals

FIGURE 8. "Direct Action Makes Capitalism See Stars." Cartoon illustrating IWW's advocacy of direct action. *Industrial Worker* 6 Feb. 1913. Rpt. in Salvatore Salerno, *Red November, Black November: Culture and Community in the Industrial Workers of the World* (Albany: State U of New York P, 1989).

of trade unions, progressive political parties, and capitalist managerial bureaucracies all similarly relied. Each of these, though for quite different reasons, claimed the right to speak for and represent "workers." Could novelists therefore represent Wobblies without at some point being forced to invoke—and thereby trap them within—this same category of representation that they themselves had clearly rejected? Could these writers find an adequate way to represent Wobblies in their novels while avoiding what one historian of IWW art, Franklin Rosemont, called "the shameless glorification of workers *as workers*" ("Short Treatise" 437)? In short, how could the demands of Wobblies to represent themselves in *economic* and *political* terms be reconciled with the demands of writers of fiction, who needed to find a way to represent them in *aesthetic* terms?

The Artwork of the Future

Although Wobblies' acts of self-representation may have seemed to protect them against the danger of misrepresentation by others, they could easily amount to (or be mistaken for) a mere lack of representation. Indeed, how could the existence of their socioeconomic power actually be proved if no social institutions or organizations had the authority to speak for them? To solve this problem, the IWW relied on aesthetic forms of representation that they themselves produced and controlled, since these could express the power of industrial workers without hindering the growth of their movement. The proliferation of IWW artwork, songs, and literature would thus partially make up for the lack of acceptable forms of political and economic representation. In addition, these aesthetic forms of representation would themselves be politicized by the Wobblies and used to represent the industrial workforce for both political and economic purposes (Bird, Georgakas, and Shaffer 23).

In the years since its effective demise, the legacy of the IWW has come to be most frequently associated with the "Little Red Songbook," a collection of songs, subtitled "Songs to Fan the Flames of Discontent," that Wobblies originally wrote and sang and that today make up the traditional canon of progressive U.S. folk music.[2] The IWW used these songs not only to maintain morale among striking workers but to instill a feeling of solidarity among their ranks, and in many instances actually to organize them in their workplaces.

In addition to their songs, Wobbly artists produced a great wealth of cartoons, leading Franklin Rosemont to argue that the IWW facilitated "a remarkable art movement—beyond question the greatest and most influential in the history of American labor." For Rosemont, the Wobblies were especially unique among U.S. workers' movements for having created "a vital art of their own, rooted in struggle at the point of production and aimed at hastening the self-emancipation of the working class" ("Short Treatise" 435).

Wobbly songs and cartoons should be seen, not as mere adjuncts to a movement that was primarily focused on achieving its stated economic and political goals, but as an equally important means of self-representation for those workers who were a part of it. Just as the Wobblies' artistic efforts were directly informed by their struggles as industrial workers, these same struggles could be more tangibly communicated to other workers, and the IWW's ultimate goals could be more clearly articulated, in the various artistic efforts of its members. Furthermore, beyond serving a narrowly didactic purpose, their aesthetic productions represented a range of hopes and desires that otherwise might have found no adequate means of expression. Hence, Rosemont adds, Wobbly artists often "transcend[ed] the didactic limits of their work" simply because

FIGURE 9. Various IWW "Silent Agitator" stickers. Rpt. in Joyce L. Kornbluh, *Rebel Voices: An IWW Anthology*, new and enl. ed. (Chicago: Kerr, 1998).

they sought to represent the IWW's "spirit of poetic revolt and utopian revery" ("Short Treatise" 437).

Through the IWW's widespread use of songs, poems, and cartoons, many of its members were convinced that they were participating in something much greater than a traditional union guided by economic interests alone. The labor historian Philip S. Foner has called attention to how the official organs of the IWW at the time exulted in their movement's broad and inspiring cultural character, in large part due to its songs (*Industrial Workers* 156–157). Indeed, the entire aesthetic program of the Wobblies bolstered their sense that they were ushering in a true social transformation of epic proportions. By representing their own real struggles, their aesthetic expressions were also helping to represent, and thus to objectify, the ideal of a workers' society that their movement was dedicated to creating.

In this respect, finally, IWW songs, cartoons, and novels were not just expressions of individual workers' dreams and desires but concrete and practically useful representations of their collectively shared ideals. Their artistic productions, in other words, were used to express a revolutionary ideal that—because of the sublime character it had for many Wobblies—might have otherwise remained inarticulate.[3] As the IWW historian Salvatore Salerno explains: "While the IWW's art forms exposed the limitations of craft unionism, the futility of political reform, and the hypocrisy inherent in the dominant values of civil society, they also actively shaped a conception of a workers' culture that would bring a brighter day in which workers directly administered to the needs of society" (Salerno, *Red November* 140).

The Pageant of the Paterson Strike

If it makes sense to use the phrase "total work of art" to describe any of the IWW's various artistic productions, then the single, sold-out performance of *The Pageant of the Paterson Strike* on June 7, 1913, at New York's Madison Square Garden, would certainly seem to justify it.[4] The brainchild of the radical journalist John Reed, in collaboration with Mabel Dodge, a wealthy New York salon hostess, and William D. "Big Bill" Haywood, the cofounder and leader of the IWW, the pageant, held to raise money and publicity for the Paterson, New Jersey, silk workers' strike, combined Wobbly songs, speeches, elaborate artwork, and theatrical sets and lighting.[5]

FIGURE 10. Program cover artwork for *The Pageant of the Paterson Strike.* Courtesy of the Robert F. Wagner Labor Archives. Rpt. in Joyce L. Kornbluh, *Rebel Voices: An IWW Anthology,* new and enl. ed. (Chicago: Kerr, 1998).

In addition to featuring IWW leaders, the starring role in the pageant was played by 1,029 actual silk workers who traveled from Paterson, New Jersey, to Manhattan to perform a reenactment of the roles they played (and were still playing) in the strike, following a script they wrote for themselves. In effect, then, the pageant literally staged a representation of workers in the act of representing themselves, both aesthetically and economically, at one and the same time. For the workers who performed in the pageant, aesthetic and economic modes of representation had finally seemed to come together (in a tangible, though momentary, fashion) to suggest that the two most significant aspects of the IWW's movement for industrial unionism were, in reality, identical.

While lavishing praise on it, contemporary reviewers described the pageant not only as a faithful representation of the ongoing struggles of Paterson's silk workers but as the invention of an entirely new genre of avant-garde, socially conscious, multimedia art. One typical review, quoted in the magazine *Survey*, characterized it in the following terms: "The pageant, in which a thousand strikers participated, went the 'human document' one better; it gave a real acquaintance with the spirit, point of view and earnestness of those who live what a 'human document' tells; it conveyed what speech and pamphlet, picture and cartoon, fiction and drama fall short of telling. The simple movements of this mass of silk workers were inarticulate eloquence. And the words of [the IWW leaders], in their efforts to give typical strike speeches, added nothing to the effect which the workers themselves spontaneously gave" ("Pageant as a Form" 214). Note how the reviewer contrasts the pageant's flesh-and-blood "showing" to the comparatively lifeless "telling" associated with the text of a so-called "human document." The pageant here (in this respect, much like Wagnerian "music-drama") is accorded a superior ability to tell a story because it does not have to rely exclusively on forms of linguistic enunciation to do so. Its multifaceted, synesthetic medium is taken to overcome the inadequacies inherent to language itself. Moreover, in contrast to the spoken language of their leaders' speeches, the spontaneity of the workers—their direct action on the stage to represent themselves—is identified as the source of the pageant's unique significance, such that the "inarticulate eloquence" of the mass of workers can presumably tell far more than the words of their representatives ever could.

About three months after the start of the Paterson strike, the idea for the pageant was conceived at a small party in Greenwich Village, where Bill Haywood, Mabel Dodge, and John Reed met each other for the first time. Shortly before this party, Haywood had published an article describing how the silk manufacturers, "through their control of outside [New York] newspapers, were able to bring about a general conspiracy of silence" regarding the events in Paterson, thus cutting off the potential financial support for the strikers that could have been earned through publicity ("Rip" 205). According to Mabel Dodge's recollection of the evening, Haywood informed the guests at the party that "the newspapers have determined to keep [news of the strike] from the workers in New York. Very few of them know what we've been through over there—the drama and the tragedy.... God! I wish I could show them a picture" (Luhan 188). Dodge, her imagination sparked, suggested to Haywood, "Why don't you bring the strike to New York and *show* it to the workers?... Why don't you hire a great hall and re-enact the strike over here? Show the whole thing" (188). In response, Reed stood up and shouted, "I'll *do* it!... That's a *great* idea... We'll make a Pageant of the Strike! The first in the world! Why, I see the whole thing!" (189).

On Monday morning, May 19, Haywood introduced Reed to the striking silk workers in Paterson. Over the next nineteen days, Reed trained them to reenact scenes from their strike, collaborated with them on writing a script, and rehearsed them in songs from the IWW's "Little Red Songbook."[6] According to Granville Hicks's account of the rehearsals, "Responding to Reed's enthusiasm, the strikers evolved the details of each scene, lost their self-consciousness, and felt themselves re-enacting the stirring events of their own drama" (qtd. in Golin 52). In addition, a small group of New York journalists and writers, including Upton Sinclair and Ernest Poole, helped to publicize and arrange the logistics for the event (Golin 52–53).

In promoting the pageant, the New York press seized upon the novelty of strikers acting out their parts on a stage, with headlines such as "Paterson Strikers Now Become Actors," and "No Mere Mimic Fervor, That of Striker-Actors" (Luhan 209). The supposed authenticity associated with the homegrown production further appealed to its reviewers. For example, the reporter for *Survey* magazine was pleased to note how "the pageant was without staginess or apparent striving for theatrical effect. In fact, the offer of theatrical producers to help in 'putting it on' was declined by those who wanted the workers' own simple action to impress the crowd" ("Pageant as a Form" 214). Evidently, the less contrived it seemed to be, the more the performance would need to rely upon the "direct action" of the workers.

The pageant consisted of six "episodes," or scenes, which detailed the recent history of the strike. The program brochure contained brief descriptions of each episode, prefaced by a statement that explained to the audience what they were about to see, which read: "The Pageant represents a battle between the working class and the capitalist class conducted by the IWW, making use of the General Strike as the chief weapon. It is a conflict between two social forces—the force of labor and the force of capital." The program goes on to link these two opposing forces with the principles of life and death, respectively. Thus, we are told, while the workers' strike has shut down the mills, "No violence can make the mills alive—no legal process can resurrect them from the dead.... Only the return of the workers to the mills can give the dead things life." Throughout the various episodes, songs played a particularly important role to unite the worker-actors with the members of the audience. In episode 1, the program states, "The striking workers sing the Marseillaise, the entire audience being invited to join in the song of revolt," while in episode 4 "They also sing the International, the Marseillaise and the Red Flag, in which the audience is invited to join." Finally, near the end of the pageant in episode 5, IWW leaders Elizabeth Gurley Flynn and Bill Haywood delivered speeches they had previously made to the strikers, with Flynn especially "dwelling upon the solidarity of labor shown in this vividly human episode" ("Pageant of the Paterson" 210).

A standing-room-only crowd of fifteen thousand spectators packed into Madison Square Garden to witness this reenactment of the key events of the strike, presented in front of a two-hundred-foot backdrop of a silk mill, with smaller sets of silk mills on either side of the stage (Foner, *Industrial Workers* 366; Golin 53–54, 57). The reviewer for the *New York World* (similarly impressed by the meaningful inarticulateness of the "mass") described the whole series of episodes as being "little more than a repetition of a single scene. But need can speak without elocutionists, and unison of thought in a great mass of highly wrought-up people may swell emotion to the point of tears" (qtd. in "Pageant as a Form" 212).

Indeed, because emotions often did swell to the point of tears, eyewitnesses of the event underscored the melodramatic and sensational effect it had upon all who were present, performers and audience alike. Writing in the *New Review*, Grace Potter noted how "here and there, from the balcony, the boxes, and the great main floor, the sound of sobbing that was drowned in singing, proved that the audience had 'got' Paterson" (qtd. in Foner, *Industrial Workers* 366). In a similar vein, the Paterson *Evening News* reported that "the entire audience was in sympathy with the movement which the Pageant portrayed, and joined in the applause, boos or cheers, as the occasion demanded" (Golin 58). The mixture of sobbing and singing reached a sort of climax in the third episode, which reenacted the funeral of Valentino Modestino, an onlooker to the strike and resident of Paterson who had been killed by police (Osborne 65–66). The reviewer for the *New York Tribune* described it as a scene that "worked the actors themselves and their thousands of sympathizers in the audience up to a high pitch of emotion, punctuated with moans and groans and sobs" ("Pageant as a Form" 213).

Of interest in these accounts is not so much the fact that they emphasize the generally emotional atmosphere of the event but that they describe the specific impact this emotion had on both the audience and the worker-performers. For those who attended the event, at some point in the evening it became either undesirable or impossible to maintain the distinction between the experience of watching the pageant and that of performing it. In her memoir recalling that evening, Mabel Dodge put it best: "For a few electric moments there was a terrible unity between all those people. They were one: the workers who had come to show their comrades what was happening across the river and the workers who had come to see it. I have never felt such a high pulsing vibration in any gathering before or since" (qtd. in Kornbluh, "Paterson: 1913" 202).

Dodge, however, was not alone in her impression of the event. In the words of the reviewer for the IWW newspaper *Solidarity*, the audience in the Garden that night experienced "the onrush of a stupendous force [that] seized the imagination with a grip that was expressed, after a short pause, in which its significance was grasped, in an outburst of cheers and applause that was prolonged and deafening." As a result of the "stupendous" impact of the performance, this reviewer concluded that "the audience was frequently as much a part of the Pageant as the strikers themselves," so that the funeral of Modestino, for example, "was enacted with a repressed intensity on the part of both players and audience." Phillips Russell, who reviewed the pageant for the *International Socialist Review* in an article entitled "The World's Greatest Labor Play," noted how "the people on the stage had long ago forgotten the audience. . . . The audience had long ago forgotten itself. It had become a part of the scene," and concluded that "no spectacle enacted in New York has ever made such an impression" (qtd. in Golin 58, 63). Likewise, the *New York Press* exclaimed, "At times they converged and actor became auditor and auditor turned suddenly into actor," while the *Independent* noted that "actors and audience were of one class and one hope" (qtd. in Golin 58, 63).

Instead of highlighting the opposition between performer and spectator, then, the pageant appeared to dissolve it and to replace it with a collective feeling of solidarity. The workers who performed their roles in the pageant, and the audience who joined in their songs and cried along with them, felt that they participated equally in a communal event that seemed to embody one of the key principles of industrial unionism (solidarity), at the same time defying the protocols of a traditional theatrical experience ("Pageant as a Form" 213).

In the socialist press, the pageant was praised for its apparent realism. The *New York Call* referred to it as "America's First Labor Play"—a label that, in their view, meant that it "showed the self-directing ability of the workers, and it manifests their great spirit of solidarity." The review in the *Independent* claimed that "no stage in the country had ever seen a more real dramatic expression of American life" (qtd. in Foner, *Industrial Workers* 365–366). Even Elizabeth Gurley Flynn, in a speech she made shortly after the failure of the Paterson strike, called it simply "a beautiful example of realistic art" and "splendid propaganda for the workers" (221).

However, the collaborative and communal experience of the pageant might explain why some critics went even further, celebrating it as an avant-garde work of art insofar as it seemed to transcend the formal limits of the various genres and media that it combined. The reviewer for the *New York Tribune* claimed that "there was a startling touch of ultra modernity—or rather of futurism—in the Paterson strike pageant in Madison Square Garden. Certainly nothing like it had been known before in the history of labor agitation. . . . Lesser geniuses might have hired a hall and exhibited moving pictures of the Paterson strike. Saturday night's pageant transported the strike itself bodily to New York" ("Pageant as a Form" 212). What most impressed this reviewer, and the reason she took the pageant to be an illustration of "ultra modernity," was that it appeared to substitute the "bodily" reality of the strike for mere pictures of it. In her view, the pageant was a uniquely modern representation because it seemed to overcome its status *as* a mere representation. Of course, the actual strike itself could not be transported to New York; but because over one thousand strikers were on the stage reenacting the same events in which they had originally participated, the reviewer could imagine that the strike had indeed been transported "bodily" to Madison Square Garden.

In short, because the actors who came to New York to represent the strike in the pageant were the actual strikers, it was easier for audience members to overlook the particular conventions of representation that underlay the artistic form of the pageant itself. During the performance, the workers were both the subject and the object, the representatives and the represented, of their own representation. In a show of their own making, the workers showed the audience in New York how they had made the strike back in Paterson. The actual workers were there on the stage, in flesh and blood, performing the act of re-presenting (or reenacting) their own previous acts of self-representation (the strike). Yet the pageant itself, a deliberate and calculated work of art, was also a representation of the strike (regardless of who performed in it), and therefore a type of picture—rather than the body—of what it was picturing. From the point of view of the audience, however, the aesthetic representation of the strike, in the form of the pageant, seemed, over the course of the performance, to transform the nature of representation itself and thus to turn it into an occasion for mass participation. As one historian of the event would later characterize it, "For the audience, class consciousness ceased to be an abstraction, and became a simple fact of experience" (Golin 59).[7]

From the standpoint of the publicity it generated for the strikers, the pageant was a resounding success. The day after the pageant, Bill Haywood told the strikers, "This was the biggest thing that the Industrial Workers of the World ever attempted. . . . We have obtained publicity what could not be bought at any price. That was the idea" (Golin 65). One reviewer, calling the pageant a "living drama," praised it for "having established a legitimate form of 'demonstration' before which all others must pale" and went so far as to predict that "in future we may well find strikers spending their best efforts to get their cause 'staged'" (Luhan 206).

All who were present that night also left with the feeling that the pageant had successfully bridged the gulf between economic and aesthetic forms of representation. But from a purely economic point of view, the grim reality of the situation was that—because of lower-than-expected ticket revenues—the pageant had not raised any money for the Paterson strikers. In light of this fact, several months later, Elizabeth Gurley Flynn argued that the pageant had thereby contributed to the failure of the strike. In a speech entitled "The Truth about the Paterson Strike," Flynn stated that "the pageant marked the climax in the Paterson strike and started the decline in the Paterson strike, just for the reason that the pageant promised money for the Paterson strikers and it didn't give them a cent." Flynn was referring to the lack of money in the strike relief fund, which the earnings from the pageant (and the publicity it generated) were supposed to replenish. "Bread was the need of the hour, and bread was not forthcoming even from the most beautiful and realistic example of art that has been put on the stage in the last half century" (221–222).

Yet Flynn's speech introduces another, more compelling reason to hold the pageant partially responsible for the failure of the Paterson strike. That is, as she explains, the Paterson workers simply forgot that they could not be in two different places, striking and performing, at once:

> In preparation for the pageant the workers were distracted for weeks, turning to the stage of the hall, away from the field of life. They were playing pickets on the stage. They were neglecting the picketing around the mill. And the first scabs got into the Paterson mills while the workers were training for the pageant, because the best ones, the most active, the most energetic, the best, the strongest ones of them went into the pageant and they were the ones that were the best pickets around the mills. Distraction from their real work was the first danger in Paterson. And how many times we had to counteract that and work against it! (221)

Caught in a bind between two simultaneous commitments—picketing around the mill versus putting on a show to raise money for their strike—the Paterson workers assumed these were equally important and complementary, rather than potentially conflicting, tasks. Once the strike had been lost, with the benefit of hindsight, Flynn accused the workers of falling prey to a "distraction from their *real* work," implying that the work they put into the pageant would never have been sufficiently real (even if it had raised a lot of money) to justify their break from the work of picketing at the mill. As Flynn's personal friend at the time, the writer Mary Heaton Vorse, recalled, Flynn blamed the pageant for "diverting the workers' minds from the actual struggle to the pictured struggle" (Golin 66).

Flynn's criticism suggests, therefore, that because the Paterson strikers were so focused on putting on the show in New York, they had temporarily and mistakenly overlooked the critical fact that aesthetic representation (the pageant) and economic representation (the picketing) were not, in reality, one and the same thing. That is, they had forgotten that the "actual struggle" was qualitatively different from the "pictured struggle." Applying the IWW's general critique of electoral political representation to the pageant itself, Flynn could see it only as a sort of "epiphenomenon, which reflected the strength of real forces but could not affect them" (Golin 69). As much as the workers and audience members on the night of the pageant might have wanted to believe that "playing pickets on the stage" was just another way of "picketing around the mill," the fact was that each of these distinct modes of representation could not really accomplish what the other could. Singing and crying together could help a mass of workers to become (theoretically) conscious of the fact that they were a mass, but it could not take the place (practically) of an actual mass of human bodies on a picket line.

Although Mabel Dodge had sold Haywood on the idea of a pageant by suggesting to him, "Why don't you bring the strike to New York and *show* it to the workers?" and although afterward the reviewer for the *New York Tribune* could joyously proclaim that the pageant "transported the strike itself bodily to New York," Flynn's critique targets precisely this notion that the strike itself could be picked up and moved, to be shown to others who were not actually in Paterson. Whereas an aesthetic representation is easily portable (a show can always be "taken on the road"), an industrial strike, as a specific form of economic representation, is not.

Flynn's remark calls attention, finally, to the unique materiality of economic forms of representation, since this is what distinguishes them from aesthetic forms of representation. While singing and picketing are equally forms of representation—and, as such, are always tied to a diversity of material conditions—their difference lies in the manner in which they are able to call forth, channel, and exercise the power of a mass of workers. The economic power of industrial workers, unlike the power of their aesthetic representations, is essentially grounded in a specific, concrete environment—in this case, the silk mill of Paterson. The reality of the "real work" of picketing, as Flynn put it, consists of its roots in this particular location. For the Paterson workers to exploit the power that they have, as workers, to force concessions from their employer, they must use their bodies to block production in the silk mill. Their songs, poems, and cartoons may assist in the accomplishment of this goal by helping to organize them, boost their morale, or raise money and awareness for their cause, but they cannot of themselves shut down the operation of the mill. For this, actual bodies—and not just any bodies, but the bodies of workers—must be standing in front of the mill's gates in Paterson rather than in front of a painted set on the stage at Madison Square Garden (Flynn 226).

Each of the three IWW-era novels we will now examine—Leroy Scott's *The Walking Delegate* (1905), Arthur Bullard's *Comrade Yetta* (1913), and Ernest Poole's *The Harbor* (1915)—strives to make sense of the distinction, as well as the problematic relation, between economic and aesthetic forms of representation. That is, each in its own manner attempts to sort out and come to terms with the relative importance of these two forms of representation in the movement for industrial unionism; and, in particular, each seeks to determine the extent of the role that acts of aesthetic representation could play within this movement.

The formal and ideological structure of these narratives is further shaped by two conflicting perspectives, or positions, on the relationship between acts of representation in general and the exercise of working-class power. Each novel emphasizes the difference between what Flynn termed "playing pickets on the stage" and "picketing around the mill," and therefore each works to reinforce the conceptual distinction between these different modes of representing workers. The successful exercise of working-class power, from this perspective, depends upon a clear recognition of the distinction between artistic and economic forms of representation. But each novel also tries to reconcile these two modes of representing workers—even by proposing that the perceived difference between them, in some instances, is nothing but a temporary obstacle to the advancement of working-class interests. From this contrary perspective, then, the successful exercise of working-class power depends upon a complete synthesis of artistic and economic forms of representation. In the end, however, these novels reach sharply different conclusions with respect to the question of whether, and to what degree, the gap between them can ever be closed. For example, Leroy Scott's narrative, foreshadowing Flynn's critique of the Paterson Pageant, suggests that every attempt by workers to conflate aesthetic and economic forms of representation is not only misguided from the start but a serious threat to the power of the industrial working class. By contrast, Arthur Bullard's and Ernest Poole's narratives, much like the audience members of the pageant, try in various ways to undermine the distinction between these two forms of representation by appealing to the sublime aspects of the IWW's vision of industrial unionism. By attending closely to the shifting tensions between these two opposed perspectives, then, the aim of the following analyses of these novels is to show how they provide a series of protocols for determining the specific value that had been assigned to the distinction between aesthetic and economic forms of representation within the movement of industrial unionism in the United States during the first two decades of the twentieth century.

Democratizing the Business Union

Leroy Scott's novel about New York City ironworkers, *The Walking Delegate*, published in 1905—the year of the IWW's founding convention—directly confronts the problem of trade union democracy that the IWW was created to solve. The narrative recounts a power struggle between its two main characters: Buck Foley, the corrupt president and "walking delegate" of a New York ironworkers' local, and Tom Keating, a reform-minded union member.

Buck Foley, though once popular among the ironworkers for his capable leadership, has become a tyrant increasingly "jealous of his power" and "harsh in the methods used to guard it." A perfect example of the despotic control wielded by leaders of "business" unions, Foley regards the interests of the union's members only as a tool to be manipulated in his lucrative dealings with New York's building contractors. He imposes his will on the members with the help of an "Entertainment Committee," a group of his supporters and hired thugs who terrorize dissenting ironworkers, scabs, and employers as the occasion demands. The workers have no voice in the affairs of their union. Foley simply orders them to work or to strike according to the amount of graft he is offered (or can extort) from the city's contractors (Scott 36; cf. Foner, *Policies* 136–173).

Tom Keating, an ironworker set on reforming the union to make it truly democratic, decides to challenge Foley's exercise of absolute power. Running against him as an opposition candidate, Tom is initially certain that the vote of the union's members—which is to say, the principle of representative democracy itself—will suffice to oust Foley and put control of the union back in the hands of the workers. "There was but one thing to be done," Tom believes, namely, "to get to his men, organize them in some way, wait till their number had grown, and then march in a body to the ballot-box" (Scott 136).

This plan of course goes awry. Foley rigs the election by stuffing the ballot box. Tom thus realizes that his strategy cannot rely solely on the democratic principle of electoral representation. To achieve a democratic union, he now knows, requires the channeling of forces that lie beyond the procedural limits of electoral politics. This new awareness subsequently forms the basis of the novel's characterization of Tom. As the story progresses, he learns to work toward the goal of union democracy by focusing more and more on concrete situations rather than principles, since the latter can be so easily manipulated to serve the interests of those, like Foley, who are out to profit at the expense of the union's members. For example, on the issue of high initiation fees for new members—which strengthen the union by enlarging its treasury but prevent many from joining who cannot afford to pay, thus forcing them to find jobs as scabs—Tom comes to feel that "the union was right in principle, but what was mere correctness of principle in the presence of such a situation?" (Scott 95; cf. Industrial Workers of the World, "Manifesto" 8).

Having ruled out the possibility of a fair election, Tom next tries to unseat Foley by organizing a strike among the rank and file of the ironworkers. He knows that Foley, who would normally oppose such an idea if it did not benefit him personally, is also eager to maintain his standing and control over the union. If the ironworkers were to strike, Foley would thereby be forced to either break off his profitable relations with the contractors by supporting the strike or oppose the strike and further alienate himself from his constituents. Hence, as Tom explains to his fellow ironworkers, "If we win the strike, with Foley against it, it'll be the end of him" (Scott 155).

Yet with or without Foley's support, Tom and the workers know that the success of their strike is virtually guaranteed by the strategic position of the ironworkers in relation to the other building trades. Indeed, Foley's original rise to power was itself a direct result of the critical role played by the ironworkers in the building industry. Before he became the union local's president and walking delegate, Foley had already recognized an opportunity for enormous personal gain in the potential strength of the ironworkers' bargaining power: "He foresaw the extent to which the erection of steel-frame buildings, then in its beginning, was certain to develop. His trade was bound to become the 'fundamental trade'; until his union had put up the steel frames the contractors could do nothing—the other workmen could do nothing. A strongly organized union holding this power—there was no limit to the concessions it might demand and secure" (Scott 33). If the ironworkers were to strike for even a short period, therefore, the building industry of the entire city would be quickly paralyzed. Tom, in organizing his fellow workers, is well aware of this fact, and soon after the strike begins he predicts that it will lead to "a general strike in all the building trades" (244). The ironworkers thus learn the extent of their power when, barely a month into the strike, "a great part of the building in the city was practically at a standstill; the other building trades had caught up with the ironworkers on many of the jobs, and so had to lay down their tools. The contractors in these trades were all checked more or less in their work" (254). Because of the privileged position they occupy in the building industry—a privilege derived not from the pure principles regulating their value in the labor market but from their concrete situation at the point of production—Tom and the ironworkers know that their strike is certain to end in victory for the union. Nothing, they feel, can weaken the advantage they possess in their struggle with the otherwise powerful alliance of the city's building contractors.

However, there is no such thing as a guarantee in a union run by someone as corrupt as Buck Foley. Surprising as it seems, the workers almost give up their fight after Foley accepts a bribe from the contractors, who have paid him to convince the members of his own union that the strike is hopeless. He does this by appearing gradually to lose confidence in their ability to win and by secretly coaching the contractors on the weak points of the union's bargaining strategy. Thus Foley preserves the appearance—for the sake of the union's members and their negotiating committee—of militantly supporting the strike, even while they feel they are steadily losing ground in their negotiations with the contractors.

Structural Power versus Theatrical Representation

What all this amounts to, then, is an apparent conflict between a structural power (Tom and the strikers) and a representational power (Foley): specifically, a conflict between a material force of position and the relatively immaterial mechanism of symbolic representation. The narrative of *The Walking Delegate* allegorizes the familiar struggle between capital and labor by juxtaposing alongside it a parallel struggle between the material force of the mass of ironworkers, who initially (and correctly) are sure they will win, and the strength of illusion mustered by Foley, their leader and representative, who "seems" more and more convinced that they will lose. In this manner, Scott's novel suggests that leaders who represent workers are apt, when the occasion demands, to misrepresent the concrete situation and interests of their constituents. To do so, they rely on other forms of representation that are essentially mimetic and theatrical, used to deceive or dissemble. At times, therefore, it becomes nearly impossible for the rank-and-file ironworkers in the novel to draw a line between two different and opposing modes of representation: Foley as the leader of the union (economic) and Foley as the deceiver of the union (aesthetic).

Nevertheless, Tom, the staunch champion of trade union democracy, knows better than to trust anything Foley says or does. Even when the outcome looks most promising for the strikers, Tom suspects Foley is working behind the scenes either to derail the strike or to exploit it for personal gain: "The negotiations seemed all open and above board; he could not lay his finger on a single flaw in them. But yet the strike seemed to him to have been on too solid a basis to have thus collapsed without apparent cause.... [Tom's] mind could not give up the suspicion that there was trickery, even though he could not see it" (Scott 291). Tom is trying to sort out two contradictory appearances: how the negotiations *seemed* to be going, on the one hand, and how the strike *seemed* to be on a "solid basis," on the other. Because he has learned to trust only concrete situations, he ignores his doubts and takes his stand on the "solid" material base of the strike—the strategic (structural) advantage of the rank and file. From this point on, his plan to win the strike and reform the union boils down to the task of unmasking the histrionics by means of which Foley seeks to influence the views of its members. That is, Tom's democratic distrust of Foley is tied to his instinctive distrust of theatricality in general—making a show, an appearance, in order to guide or control the beliefs of others. By portraying Foley to be just as much an accomplished actor as he is a tyrannical leader, the narrative further implies that Tom's antitheatrical struggle is a logical outgrowth of his democratic politics. Or, to put it differently, Tom's innate democratic impulse manifests itself as a politics of antitheatricality—a politics that in turn shapes much of the novel's (aesthetic) representation of class conflict.

The character of Foley might be dismissed as a run-of-the-mill villain, but his highly ambiguous status throughout the novel makes him the most interesting, if not sympathetic, figure of *The Walking Delegate*. While Foley signifies the archetypical labor traitor for some readers of the novel (Rideout 29), in the context of the narrative it is never quite clear what or whom he represents in his role as the representative of the union, its "walking delegate." We learn, for instance, that according to Foley's "theory of government" it was a "principle that [the workers] should feel an absolute confidence in him" (Scott 121) and while leading the strike he is shown "fairly hurling into others a confidence in himself" (211). Though there would seem to be nothing wrong about inspiring confidence in others, the narrative describes Foley's skill in this regard as a calculated theatrical device that he uses to bolster the workers' faith in himself, while simultaneously destroying their faith in the positive outcome of the strike: "And so, day by day, Foley continued to undermine their confidence. So skillfully did he play his part, they never guessed that he was the insinuating cause of their failing courage" (285).

The fact that Foley is "playing a part" here, as elsewhere, implies that Scott is encouraging us to interpret his betrayal of the union in theatrical terms. Indeed his "acting," whether for or against the interests of the workers, always connotes that his true motives are disguised. Although we know at least what some of these motives are—in this case, we have seen him bribed by the contractors—all the workers in the novel apart from Tom are fooled by the show, believing that "if Foley, Foley the fighter, were losing confidence, then the situation must indeed be desperate." On this point, Scott's third-person narrator intervenes to observe that "the courage of a large body of men, especially of one loosely organized, is the courage of its leaders" (287). By contrast, we might then assume, a tightly organized body of men would be a body that did not allow its morale to be tied to (and represented by) others. The challenge Tom faces in tightening up the organization of the union, then, involves disabusing them of the notion that their courage bears any sort of mimetic relation to the courage of their leader. Evidently democracy will come to the union only after the theatrical behavior of its officials—suggesting, further, the very representational function of its representatives—has been thoroughly stamped out.

Beyond the internal affairs of the union, the capitalist class as a whole is characterized in the novel by its penchant for various forms of aesthetic and theatrical representation. Its members often view society itself as an artistic spectacle, highly aware of the roles they are playing within it. For instance, the city's contractors, "their elbows on the polished table, looked on as though spectators at a play" while they watch Foley being bribed in one of their secret meetings (271). Much as Foley plays a role to secure the absolute confidence of his men, Mr. Baxter, one of the city's leading contractors, panics at the thought that his wife, "who believed him nothing but honor," may someday learn of his corrupt dealings (334). These wealthy characters likewise strive to avoid coming into contact with the world inhabited by workers such as Tom, "with its easily imagined coarseness, with its ignorance of books and music and painting, and all the little refinements that were dear" to them (238). The narrative consistently highlights the building contractors' "aesthetic taste" and "irreproachable gentlemanliness . . . all the things Tom was not" (307).

Solid Workers and Fictitious Commodities

Scott ultimately links such bourgeois aesthetic and theatrical inclinations to a common source: the belief in what Karl Polanyi has termed "the commodity fiction" of human labor power. This is nowhere better illustrated than in the novel's description of Mr. Baxter, the powerful contractor and president of New York's "Iron Employers' Association": "He hated trade unionism for its arrogation of powers that he regarded as the natural right of the employer; it was his right, as the owner of a great business, and as the possessor of a superior intelligence, to run his affairs as he saw fit—to employ men on his own terms, work them such hours and under such conditions as he should decide" (Scott 172), and

"By reason of the rights which naturally belonged to property, he said, by reason of capital's greatly superior intelligence, it was the privilege of capital, nay even its duty, to arrange the uttermost detail of its affairs without any consultation whatever with labor, whose views were always selfish and necessarily always unintelligent" (253). Apart from its crude arrogance, Baxter's doctrine of the natural right of the employer to use human labor power however he desires—as though it were merely a commodity, a piece of inanimate ("necessarily unintelligent") property like any other—succinctly expresses one of the core tenets of the ideology of free-market industrial capitalism. What Baxter considers his natural right here is nothing more than a self-serving narrative, a useful but unacknowledged fiction, that he believes in because it promotes his interests. In fact, though, the alleged commodity of human labor power is inseparably tied to real human beings, who, for precisely this reason, are not (and can never be) commodities in the literal sense of the term. This is because, as Karl Polanyi observes, unlike other commodities, human labor power cannot be "shoved about, used indiscriminately, or even left unused, without affecting also the human individual who happens to be the bearer of this peculiar commodity" (73).

Baxter and the rest of the capitalist class are not the only characters of the novel who put their faith in this fiction. The leading player of *The Walking Delegate*, Buck Foley, is more than willing to treat himself and be treated by others as a commodity. Not only do the services he provides to the contractors have a price, but in the duties he performs as walking delegate (the union's "business agent") he mediates between the union and the contractors by representing the interests of each of these. He *shows* the contractors to the workers just as he *shows* the workers to the contractors, and in the process he is always available to be bought by the one side in order to sell out the other, as circumstances require. The theatrical qualities Scott associates with him are therefore a reflection of his troubling, indeterminate status as a kind of freewheeling commodity (similar to a complex financial derivative or "toxic asset"). Describing the prevalence of such business agents among organized labor in 1903, one corrupt union official of the period himself admitted: "That sort of unionism ... is only a burlesque" (Foner, *Policies* 142).

In addition, Foley, a character of this particular work of fiction, could be taken to represent the fictional character of commodified human labor power in general. Not only does he officially represent both sides of the labor-capital conflict within the specific framework of the narrative, but above and beyond this he exemplifies, by dramatically personifying,

Polanyi's concept of the commodity fiction. By symbolically representing the interests of both capital and labor in his fictional role as a walking delegate—which here means a commodity for sale on the market—"Foley," the character of the novel, is at the same time an indexical representation of the fictitious, representational basis of industrial capitalism.

In stark contrast to Foley and the rest of the capitalist class, *The Walking Delegate* portrays Tom, the strike, and the rank and file of ironworkers as variations of the "solid basis," a material force directed against the potential threat of fictionality and representation. The narrator informs us, for example, that the ironworkers are incapable of performing even the simplest acts of disguise: "to give a false name would never have occurred" to them (Scott 293). Opposed to this, the contractor Mr. Baxter has a private study in his lush mansion in which, "when the mood was on him, he sometimes slipped to write bits of verse, a few of which he had published in magazines under a pseudonym" (332). The workers also maintain a deep skepticism with respect to newspaper accounts of the strike. When Tom is concerned that journalists' distortions may undermine their confidence, one of the strikers reassures him, "I saw how the bosses' fairy story goes. But the boys ain't kids, an' they ain't goin' to swallow all that down" (353). Furthermore, Tom knows that the job of organizing a democratic union "could have no spectacular methods and no spectacular features. Hard, persistent work, night after night—that was all" (78). Hence, the novel indicates that such expressly unspectacular methods are an integral part of the solid basis that characterizes the rank and file on strike.

Overall, the antitheatricality of Scott's ironworkers is most clearly portrayed in the character of Tom Keating. As the leader of the strike, as well as the main source of democratic resistance to Foley's rule, Tom is the obvious focal point of the novel's ideological perspective. It is somewhat surprising, then, to learn that he is also a persuasive orator. When he talks with Ruth Arnold—the single member of the capitalist class to take a personal interest in him—the narrator describes the impact Tom's rhetorical style has upon her: "Tom spiritedly presented the union side of mooted questions of the day,—the open shop, the strike, the sympathetic strike, the boycott. The things Miss Arnold had read had dealt coldly with the moral and economic principles involved in these questions. Tom spoke in human terms; he showed how every point affected living men, and women, and children. The difference was the difference between a treatise and life.... And he spoke well, for his sentences, though not always grammatical, were always vital. He seemed to present the very heart of a thing, and let it throb before the eyes" (Scott

82). Again, Tom's character is associated here with the concrete, human, and "vital" core of workers' concerns, in contrast to the "grammatical" and abstract "economic principles" by means of which they are typically represented. The "difference between a treatise and life" evokes the more general distinction between representation, fiction, and theatricality on the one hand, and solidity, fact, and materiality on the other. The vital quality of Tom's speech suggests that he is the virtual mouthpiece of the strike's "solid basis."

This image of Tom—the living voice of the life of the union—carries a wealth of implications when it comes to the novel's representation of the striking ironworkers. Since we are told, for example, that Tom "had never written when he could avoid it" and that "his ideas . . . struggled against the unaccustomed confinement of written language" (Scott 112), it follows that we never see him working out the details of a labor contract, making appeals to the text of the union's constitution in his fight against Foley, or writing editorials to the newspapers to correct their inaccurate coverage of the strike. Nor do we see any of the other members of the rank and file grappling with the intricacies of written language. This is because, in the form of their union, they seem meant to be understood as an essentially concrete body of matter, existing on a level that is somewhere beneath (or above or before) the sphere of representation. Thus, in light of the conceptual organization of the narrative, Tom and the workers alone constitute the only legitimate "text" of the union's constitution. Their struggles for democracy and to win the strike are likewise to be taken as struggles against the "confinement of written language."

Yet at one point early in the novel, when he still believes he can defeat Foley in an election, Tom composes a statement of his democratic principles to be mailed to the union's members. For the highly literate Ruth Arnold, who volunteers to get it printed, the draft of the letter reads to her "as though his crudity had dissociated itself from his other qualities and laid itself, bare and unrelieved, before her eyes" (Scott 115). Because the written language of the text of the letter dissociates parts of Tom from himself, Scott is implying here that the business of writing—at least to the democratically minded ironworkers—is akin to theatrical display. That is to say, writing, too, produces a type of spectacle whenever it strives to represent anything by "laying it before" the eyes.

When, at the end of the novel, Tom finally exposes Foley and convinces the workers that they will win the strike, to his chagrin he finds that, to address the entire body of the workers en masse, he must temporarily dissociate himself from them by leaving their ranks and standing on top of a piano in the union hall: "Tom realized the theatricality of his position on the piano, but he also realized its advantage, and did not get down" (Scott 326). It might appear that Tom at this moment has joined the ranks of Foley and the capitalist class, since he is putting on a sort of show to persuade the members of the union that only he can represent their true interests. That is, he must make a brief walk-on appearance to denounce the theatricality of the walking delegate. However, though he may seem duplicitous here, the fact that Tom realizes the advantage of his position on the piano also suggests that his action may have more in common with the strategic position of the striking workers than it does with the antics of Foley and Mr. Baxter. According to Tom's homespun dramaturgical tenets, this particular kind of theatrics may very well count as democratic because its representational power is completely contingent upon the *positional* advantage he holds, which in turn is backed by the material force of the evidence he has gathered against Foley. Tom's speech may then signal the "point of production" of union democracy, much as the workers' strike draws attention to the point of production of the building industry.

The narrative arc of *The Walking Delegate* would seem, therefore, to have come full circle. From denouncing theatricality by associating it with corrupt leadership, tyrannical rule, and capitalist deception, the story finally illustrates what it might be like to see the ideal of union democracy incarnated, and then placed on display, in the person of Tom Keating. We can now assume that the ironworkers' union will belong to its members, since Tom has assured them that, as president and walking delegate, he will play it straight with them. Apart from his single (but effective) lapse on top of the piano, Tom has presumably freed himself from the risk of misrepresenting the workers in the act of representing them. Nevertheless, how can he be sure? How can he be certain that, in the process of fulfilling his duties to the union, he does not find himself taking advantage of other positions of power beyond those that the rank and file already possesses? One thing at least is certain: if he does not allow himself to be "bought," he will never have to disguise his intentions behind the mask of the commodity fiction. Thus he will never have to resort to the theatrics on the basis of which Foley propped up his own control of the union. In Tom's union, by contrast, the power of its leaders is always supposed to spring directly from the solid basis of the workers themselves—their material and positional advantage at the point of production.

The Mass Worker Sublime (I)

How does a novel, or any work of fiction, represent a character, such as Tom, who openly contests all forms of representation and fiction? This question did not seem so pressing in the case of Buck Foley, whose motives and actions appeared to be complicit with the effects of the medium (fictional narrative) in which they were portrayed. But from the standpoint of Tom's democratic distrust of representation, it is not at all clear how one is ultimately to grasp the mechanics of representing the figure of the mass worker in the context of either a union or a novel. *The Walking Delegate* does not provide any definite solutions to this problem, but over the course of its narrative it reveals some of the difficulties involved in any attempt to come to terms with its complexity.

Perhaps the closest Scott comes to including the figure of a writer in his novel is in the character of Ruth Arnold. A prototypical "fellow traveler," she is at once literate and sympathetic to Tom's cause, as well as sincerely interested in the general struggles of industrial workers. From Ruth's relatively more educated (wealthy, mannered, and conventional) point of view, Scott offers us glimpses of how a hypothetical writer might choose to represent a mass worker such as Tom in the context of a fictional narrative. Initially, "She had been struck only by a vague bigness—a bigness that was not so much of figure as of bearing" (82). Later, assessing him again, she "looked [at Tom],—and felt herself growing small, and the men of her acquaintance growing small. And thought. . . . Yes, that was it; it was his purpose that made him big" (106). And on another occasion she concludes that "his purposeful power . . . dwarfed his crudity to insignificance" (119). These fleeting impressions give a sense of the wonder Ruth feels in Tom's presence. Although Scott probably intended Ruth's thoughts to convey only the first hints of a budding romance, it is also likely—particularly given the novel's focus on the problem of representing the industrial workforce—that her perspective offers a veiled commentary on his own practice as a writer.

Tom's "vague bigness" in Ruth's eyes signals a classic illustration of a sublime encounter, complete with its indeterminate moral connotations (a vaguely "purposeful power"). If an experience of the sublime is defined as the attempt to represent the unrepresentable (whether of size or force, "figure" or "bearing"), then it is an appropriate figure to suggest the dilemma of a novelist trying to represent a character who actively resists being represented by others. Scott finds a way out of this dilemma by thematizing it as such within his narrative. That is to say, he displaces and relocates the technical problem he confronts as a writer by turning it into a problem his characters (namely Ruth) must face. Tom, then, can indeed be fictionally represented as a character who resists all forms of representation, while Ruth is left to carry the burden—which has now become an entirely fictitious problem—of figuring out how to represent him. The fact, however, that it is now a fictitious problem—both a fictionalized problem and a problem concerning the state of fictionality—implies that its solution will be found in a certain practice of fictional representation.

Spontaneous Revolts

The attempt to capture and represent the intractable quality of the mass worker through an appeal to sublime experience is a recurring leitmotif of several IWW-era labor novels. With regard to Yetta Rayefsky, the young protagonist of *Comrade Yetta*, Arthur Bullard's 1913 novel about Jewish garment workers in New York's Lower East Side, we are told that whenever she tries to teach others about the true meaning of industrial unionism "she felt herself very small and the thing she wanted to say very big" (208). Thus Yetta, an organizer and labor journalist (unlike the character of Ruth Arnold), is directly faced with the challenge of finding a way to represent, in writing, the dynamic and incalculable force of mass industrial workers.

For Yetta, who is a mass worker herself, the problem of representation has a compelling personal significance. A vest maker in a sweatshop, she plays a leading role in organizing her Vest-Makers' Union. Alongside her work as an organizer, she takes a second job as a writer for a socialist daily newspaper. Over the course of the novel, she focuses more and more energy on her writing, appearing gradually to abandon her duties as an organizer. In fact, though, we learn that she has channeled her union work directly into her writing, thereby reconceiving it as the material basis of her work as a journalist. The "Labor Page" Yetta writes thus comes to play a critical role in the garment workers' movement to establish an industrial union. In this manner, Bullard's novel implies, journalistic representation has the power not only to advocate on behalf of mass workers but effectively to support—by portraying and making articulate—a labor movement that in part defines itself by its militant rejection of all existing economic and political forms of representation. Consequently, according to Bullard, where there is a push for industrial unionism, questions normally thought to belong to the realm of "pure" aesthetics are not lagging far behind.

A considerable part of *Comrade Yetta* is devoted to explaining the tenets of three explicitly ideological positions on the so-called "Labor Question," as it was debated by labor progressives circa 1913. The novel, through Yetta's perspective, casts comparative judgment on the philosophy and tactics of the socialists, the syndicalists, and the established trade unions. Bullard associates the views of these groups, respectively, with the official platforms of the Socialist Party, the IWW, and the AFL. The novel's omniscient narrator, however, leaves no doubt that it favors the syndicalist (IWW) position. Like the narrator of Upton Sinclair's *The Jungle*, Bullard's narrator frequently makes didactic statements directed at the reader. Invoking the idea of mass workers' "irrational" spontaneity, which had a particularly strong influence on French versions of revolutionary syndicalism (via Georges Sorel), the narrator teaches us, for example, that the "Industrial Conflict is not logical": "At least it does not follow any laws of logic known to the so-called 'labor leaders.' It is connected with, actuated by, a vague something, which for want of a better term we call 'human nature.' And labor leaders are just as uncertain what 'human nature' will do next as the rest of us. They will spend patient years on end organizing a trade, collecting bit by bit a 'strike fund,' preparing for a battle which never comes off or miserably fizzles out. In the midst of such discouragement, an unprepared strike in an unorganized trade will break out and with no prospect of success will sweep to an inspiring victory" (Bullard 123–124). This statement on the part of Bullard's narrator defines a key conceptual distinction in relation to which the novel as a whole is organized. If the distinction between theatrical representation and material force provided the basis for *The Walking Delegate*'s general narrative strategy, the narrative development of *Comrade Yetta* is based on a similar distinction, expressed in the form of an opposition between logic and spontaneity, the views of "labor leaders" in contrast to the forces of "human nature."[8] Thus, much as the ironworkers of Scott's novel learn that the power they derive from the solid basis of their strike can never be adequately represented by their so-called leaders, Yetta is frequently reminded by one of her mentors, the syndicalist Walter Longman, that "you can't crowd life into a definition" (Bullard 236; cf. Flynn 220; Nielsen 124).

It seems likely that such didactic observations on the part of *Comrade Yetta*'s narrator were designed to be read as a running commentary on the stages of Yetta's development as a character, for they usually appear just before or after some significant event or turning point in the novel's account of her life. For example, right before the passage (quoted above) where the narrator defined the illogical, spontaneous quality of the Industrial Conflict, this same idea had been illustrated by a concrete event—namely, a wildcat strike initiated by Yetta. In the following excerpt, Yetta is at work on a sewing-machine assembly line in a sweatshop that produces vests. When she discovers that her high level of productivity has unwittingly made of her an ideal pace-setter to speed up and increase the output of the other workers (who are all women), Yetta's spontaneous reaction is simply to turn off her machine:

> Yetta, feeling that she had helped to kill the woman [working next to her], stopped her machine. Jake [the factory's owner] rushed out into the shop.
> "*Wos hat da passiert?*" he demanded of Yetta, nervous and angry. "Did your thread break again?"
> "No." Yetta stood up. "I stopped."
> "Stopped?" he repeated in amazement.
> "Yes. I stopped. It's a shame. Mrs. Cohen is sick and can't keep up. . . ."
> "You come vid me to my office. I vant to talk vid you. . . . Vell—Yetta, you be a good girl and not make no trouble in the shop. Und ven de rush season is over, Yetta—I'll, yes, Yetta, I luf you. I'll marry you. You be a good girl and not make trouble, Yetta, and I'll marry you. . . ."
> He grabbed one of her hands and tried to kiss her. The slap he received dizzied him.
> "You come out into the shop, Jake Goldfogle," she cried, pulling open the door. "You tell them what you told me. What do you think the pig said to me?" she asked the surprised women. . . .
> Giving tongue to an incoherent burst of rage and filth, he rushed at Yetta. She thought he was going to strike her. But she was too angry herself to be afraid.
> "Don't you hit me, you brute," she screamed at him, shaking her own fists in his face. "I ain't working for you no more, Jake Goldfogle. See? I ain't one of your slaves any more. I'm a free woman. . . . You see what kind of a boss we've been working for," Yetta said to the other women. "He ain't a man. He's a pig! Wanted me to marry him—after the rush season. I've quit him and you ought to quit too."

"Shut up," Jake shrieked.

"I won't shut up. See what you've done to Mrs. Cohen. You've killed her, and now you want to throw her out. We ought to strike."

"Don't you talk strike in my shop, you—"

"Yes. We ought to strike. You know the dirty deal we're getting. Rotten wages and speed. It's because we ain't got no union and don't fight. We ought to strike like the skirt-finishers...."

"I'll strike vid you, Yetta," the girl said who had been to the ball. "My sister's a skirt-finisher. But the strike ain't no good unless everybody quits."

"I'll strike," another voice chimed in.

"All right," Mrs. Weinstein said. "We'll all strike...."

Yetta started uptown to the office of the Woman's Trade Union League. And all the long walk her heart was chanting a glad hosanna. She wasn't a speeder any more. She could look people free in the face. (Bullard 116–121)

When Bullard's narrator teaches us that human nature is responsible for the unpredictable and illogical character of the Industrial Conflict, we see it at work in just this kind of spontaneous, unplanned, spur-of-the-moment strike. Since this is a strike of unorganized workers, it does not originate with the vote of the members of a union. In other words, it is a strike that breaks out for no apparently logical reason, its sole cause being the women in the shop—who do not yet have the official endorsement or support of a union—and their shared sentiment regarding the speedup. Yetta herself does not initially think of it as a strike; but the fact that she stops working nevertheless produces a small-scale collective work stoppage, as the assembly line cannot continue to flow without every worker simultaneously doing her part. Her spontaneous individual act thereby reveals to her coworkers the conditions necessary for a much larger strike. In addition, Yetta here has no "labor leaders" giving her advice on strike strategy and tactics. Although she is the first worker to turn off her machine, and the first to suggest that the others turn off theirs as well, every woman in the shop is involved in the process of decision making that leads to the collective declaration of their strike. After all, it takes Mrs. Weinstein finally to proclaim, "We'll all strike," in response to another worker's comment that "the strike ain't no good unless everybody quits."

With this scene, as well as other similar examples of spontaneous rank-and-file action, Bullard illustrates the contrast between what he takes to be the rational character of the socialists' program versus the irrational character of the IWW's (syndicalist) vision of industrial unionism. To elaborate this distinction in a broader context, soon after provoking the strike in her shop, Yetta finds a new job as an organizer for the Vest-Makers' Union and helps to lead an industry-wide strike of all the garment workers in New York City. When she sees a hired thug trying to disrupt the strike by physically assaulting one of the women on a picket line, Yetta attacks the man by punching and kicking him. Prior to this incident she was learning to accept the rational principles of socialism, so she is now surprised by her sudden and violent reaction to the situation. On reflection, she concludes that "her act did not fit in with Socialism" (193). Yet instead of bringing her to reject the value of her spontaneous action for its supposed irrationality, her conclusion reinforces her belief in the efficacy of the improvised tactics industrial workers are often forced to adopt in their immediate struggles. Because she herself has successfully used such tactics when she did not have a more rational plan to guide her, Yetta comes to feel instinctively disposed to endorse the spirit and tactics promoted by the IWW: "They placed all their emphasis on the Spirit of Revolt. In a more specific way than the other factions they were out for the Revolution. They appealed strongly to that side of Yetta which was vividly touched by the manifold misery she saw about her, the side of her personality which had struck out blindly.... And she knew that the same thing was present in the hearts of all the down-trodden people" (250). Although she realizes that her motives in the effort to liberate herself and other members of her class have always reflected the IWW's "Spirit of Revolt," this moment signals only her acceptance of their tactics rather than their overall program and strategy. What is needed, then, is to show that "Comrade" Yetta is actually "Wobbly" Yetta.

"... Thus Making an Injury to One an Injury to All"

To this end, Bullard uses Yetta's character as a vehicle to illustrate the general principles of industrial unionism. Taking her individual perspective as a conceptual prism, the narrative first illustrates the interconnection of all the various trades engaged in mass industrial production:

> She began to realize that her "trade" was more than a routine of flying fingers, [it was a] complicated process of industry [involving cutters, weavers, shepherds, finishers, dealers, and

retailers].... And all these thousands of people, who were her coworkers, had to eat. Someone had to bake their bread. The bakers were really part of the vest-trade. And so were the cobblers who made shoes for the workers, and the coal miners who tore fuel for them from the bowels of the earth, and the steel workers who made their machines and their needles. It was hard to think of any worker who did not in some way contribute to the making of vests. (158)

Such a realization—that every worker she can possibly imagine is really her co-worker—is just the first step on the road to becoming an industrial unionist. The logical consequence and correlate of this notion is summed up in the Wobbly slogan "An injury to one is an injury to all," which Yetta once again discovers not in the form of a slogan but by way of a concrete experience. When she is thrown in jail for attacking the strikebreaker, the police and prison guards verbally abuse her: "And yet it was very little for herself that Yetta suffered. She was being sacrificed for a great host. What they did to her mattered very little, but in her they were striking at all the myriad 'people of the process'—the women of her trade, the cloth weavers, the wool-growers, those who grew wheat for their bread, who made beds for them to sleep in. She felt herself a delicate instrument for the transmission of sound. Those stinging, cruel words [the policemen directed at her] were going out to the remotest corners of the land, were bringing shame on all the lowly people of the earth" (177). Yetta, knowing that she stands in a synecdochic relation to every worker in her society, takes comfort in the fact that she is now no longer the individual worker whom the representatives of the law (mistakenly) think they are abusing. In this moment of realization, Yetta feels as though the entire labor movement had been distilled and incorporated into the form of her suffering body. Whatever the malicious police officers say to her they are saying to "all the lowly people of the earth" who are fighting for their rights. To be "a delicate instrument for the transmission of sound," as Yetta senses of herself, is therefore one of several figures Bullard uses to illustrate the IWW principle of synecdochic, working-class solidarity.

Staging the Social Drama

If Yetta's experience actually represents that of all workers everywhere, how can she bear such an enormous responsibility? If what happens to her happens to every member of the working class, and if every one of her actions reflects the actions of this entire class, how can she carry the burden of such knowledge and go on living day-to-day? The answer Yetta finds to this question is to identify herself, both intellectually and emotionally, with the notion of an irrational but all-consuming Industrial Conflict. By discovering and accepting the intimate ties that bind her to this conflict, Yetta learns to see herself as an actor in a vast social drama.

Consequently, she also comes to understand her work as a writer as being merely the synecdochic index of the work performed by those about whom she writes. In contrast to the repetitive tedium of her work in the sweatshop, her work as a labor journalist allows her to play a role in this drama that far surpasses anything she had previously known. Soon after she begins writing for the socialist newspaper, "Yetta learned a new meaning for the word 'work.' . . . In the new work there was no repetition, none of this dead monotony. Every act, every word she spoke, was the result of a consciousness vividly alive" (Bullard 243). Her consciousness here not only reflects a form of work in which she finds personal fulfillment but also signals a broader class consciousness that only the act of writing, apparently, can produce. Lest we have any doubts about the meaning of class consciousness and its origin in a certain fictitious (imaginary) representation of the working class, Bullard's narrator defines it for us through an extended theatrical analogy:

> It is a strange paradox of our life that, while no other social phenomenon touches us at so many intimate points as the organization of labor, while very few are of more importance, most of us know nothing at all about the details of this great industrial struggle. Our clothes bear the "union label" or are "scab." In either case they are an issue in the conflict. Heads have been broken over the question of whether this page, from which you are reading, should be printed in a "closed" or "open shop." . . . . From the human point of view there is no vaster, more passionate drama. Intense convictions, bitter, senseless prejudices, the dogged heroism of hunger, comfort-loving cynicism, black treachery, and whole-hearted idealism are among the motives which inspire the actors. The stage—which is our Fatherland—is crossed by hired thugs from the "detective agencies" and by dynamiters. In the troupe are such people as Jane Addams and Mr. Pinkerton, shedders of blood and preachers of peace. There are hardly any of us who do not at some time step upon the stage and act our parts. (Bullard 243–244)

In this description of the "stage" of the social drama, the notion of theatricality Bullard introduces to his novel differs in a few key respects from that which we encountered in Scott's *The Walking Delegate*. For one thing, Bullard's narrator asks us to recognize that even the most mundane aspects of our lives (such as commodities) are embedded in this drama, where they play significant roles. Just as every individual worker is tied to all other workers by virtue of the complex relations of production under capitalism, everything we buy or use in our day-to-day lives is "an issue in the conflict," including the book we are now reading (the novel *Comrade Yetta*). That is, for Bullard, the act of reading about labor struggles does not automatically place us at a distance from them, since books are themselves a product of the struggles that they are apparently only "about." Aesthetic representation, in the form of a novel, is thus explicitly linked here to its material and economic conditions of production.

In addition, this passage implies that our interest and participation in labor struggles are essentially theatrical before they are anything else. Since the narrator teaches us that society as a whole is simply one large stage, our conscious participation in the "great industrial struggle" is just a more deliberate manner of acting out roles that have always already been assigned to us. In sharp contrast to Scott, therefore, Bullard uses the theatrical analogy, not to suggest a manipulation of labor struggles from an outside (bourgeois) position of superiority, but to facilitate an understanding of every social conflict as being essentially a matter of role playing. All actors in this drama, as it were, are playing their "parts" more or less consciously.

From this perspective, the opposition that Scott wanted us to recognize between Buck Foley, the consummate actor, and Tom Keating, the militant worker, would no longer carry any weight in *Comrade Yetta*. This is made especially clear through the fact that Yetta, in addition to her labor journalism, has become the Vest-Makers' walking delegate or "business agent," a position that would easily allow her to put on a "show" for either the workers she represents or the firms that employ them. Bullard recognizes that these possibilities are inherent to the position when his narrator observes that "once in a while a 'business agent' sells out, betrays his constituents for a bribe, just as some of our political representatives have done." But unlike Buck Foley and other "representatives," Yetta, Bullard tells us, "has at heart the interest of the entire trade, men working in different places under varied conditions," as a result of her profound sense of solidarity with industrial workers everywhere (245).

The One Big Union of Marriage

Once Bullard, through Yetta, has spelled out the basic principles of the IWW ideal of industrial unionism—spontaneity (direct action), solidarity, and class consciousness—all that remains is to illustrate how these principles function on a practical basis and what the modern workforce might look like once it has been organized along industrial lines. The challenge he now faces is to find an adequate way to represent "One Big Union" in the context of a relatively conventional fictional narrative. It is at this point in the novel that the narrator's voice merges with Yetta's personal thoughts. As the Vest-Makers' walking delegate, as well as the labor journalist for a socialist daily newspaper, *The Clarion*, Yetta seems perfectly positioned to work toward the goal of industrial unionism on several fronts. The first obstacle on her path, however, is the marketplace bargaining power of certain groups of skilled craftsmen, which, as she sees it, hinders them from feeling ties of solidarity with the rest of the working class. As the narrator (now reflecting Yetta's own viewpoint) explains:

> In almost every industry there are small trades of highly skilled men who occupy a favorable strategic position. It is so with "the cutters" in the business of making clothes. . . . They could not be replaced by unskilled "scabs." They were in a position to insist that the bosses address them as "Mister." Why should they join forces with these new and penniless unions? What had they to gain by putting their treasury at the disposal of the struggling "buttonhole workers"? . . . Why should the opulent province of New York enter into a union with tiny Delaware or far-away Georgia? In the proposed Congress how could representation be justly distributed? The cutters would not listen to any proposal which did not give them an overwhelming voice in the Council. It was against such cold facts as these that the theory of Industrial Unionism, which had sounded so alluring to Yetta . . . has to make headway. (249)

Here Yetta recognizes the connection between the skills that some workers possess and their strategic position in the labor market. Although this connection is being broken every day—with the advent of new technologies and machinery that rapidly deskill large groups of workers—its economic value to skilled workers has not yet been made completely obsolete. In the meantime, however, it is precisely the belief such workers invest in the supposedly irreplaceable (timeless) value of their skills that prevents them from gaining anything like real class consciousness.

To break down these divisions, level craft distinctions, and promote working-class solidarity, the central question with which Yetta must grapple, therefore, comes back to the problem of representation—"How could representation be justly distributed?" That is, how can a program of equal class representation both account for and overcome the stubborn persistence, within this class, of unequal craft distinctions?

Bullard's novel translates this complex social and economic problem into the highly personal and romantic terms of a domestic marriage plot. Just as the narrator taught us that nothing else "touches us at so many intimate points as the organization of labor," so Yetta, in her search for the proper organization of labor (including the proper way to represent this organization in her work as a writer), is intimately touched in relation to two men in her life. The respective ideological commitments of these men—Walter, a syndicalist, and Isadore, an orthodox socialist—reflect two possible solutions to the problem of organizing labor along industrial lines. Faced with the choice of which one she should marry, Yetta chooses not simply between them as individuals but between the two main factions that, in 1913, were competing for the loyalty of the industrial working class in the United States. Even Walter himself explains to her how "it isn't a choice, Yetta, between me and Isadore. It's deeper than that, deeper than individuals" (339).

Much as the IWW ideal of class solidarity depends on viewing oneself and other workers as more than mere individuals, so Yetta's ideal of domestic solidarity involves seeing her future husband as more than an individual. The battle of ideological and political factions over the "organization of labor" is thus preserved intact, even though it now seems to be displaced and internalized, apparently to become only a question Yetta asks herself regarding the organization of domestic life: "Life as she had seen it was a ceaseless, desperate struggle, a constant clash of personalities, an unrelenting war of social classes. In an external, rather mechanical way she had been involved in this struggle. She looked forward to being 'a striker' all her life. But she had always thought of herself as a part of the conflict. Now—and this was the new viewpoint—it seemed that the fight was taking place within her. The strategic position, the key to the whole battlefield, the place where the fiercest blows were to be exchanged, was her own soul" (Bullard 347). Having arrived at this new viewpoint, Yetta realizes that her soul is nothing less than the syndicalists' cherished "point of production"; it has become "the strategic position" in labor's struggle with capital and the most effective site of spontaneous workers' revolts, since, from Yetta's perspective, it is "the key to the whole battlefield." This idea is confirmed by the first marriage proposition Yetta received, from Jake Goldfogle, her boss at the vest-making sweatshop. Recall how in this scene her refusal to marry Jake was expressed through the spontaneous work stoppage that she initiated. This strike at the point of production, then, originated with, and was articulated through, the question of marriage, as Yetta called out to the other women in the shop: "He ain't a man. He's a pig! Wanted me to marry him—after the rush season. I've quit him and you ought to quit too" (118).

While it is clear that Bullard's narrative does not apply the metaphor of an internalized "conflict" in more literal terms (in which case it would no longer be a metaphor), the romantic turn that *Comrade Yetta* takes at this point suggests that Bullard is using the convention of the domestic marriage plot to illustrate a political ideal that otherwise might not have accommodated itself to the representational strategies available in the political discourse of his day.[9] Once the principles of the IWW (spontaneity, solidarity, and class consciousness) have been metaphorically mapped onto a domestic marriage plot, these principles, based as they are on a rejection of conventional forms of political representation, reveal that the supposedly apolitical marriage plot may in fact be far more politically invested than its representations in novels have so far implied.

By 1913, the Socialist Party had become openly critical of the IWW, accusing them of abandoning the field of political struggle through their refusal to participate in local, state, and national elections. The party then used this issue to drive a wedge between those workers who supported both organizations. For instance, the IWW historian Melvin Dubofsky notes how, during the last days of the Paterson silk workers' strike in July 1913, "the old submerged grievances and conflicts separating IWW syndicalists from Socialist politicians soon rose to the surface.... The local Socialist paper [the *New York Call*] began to advise strikers: 'Industrial action has failed; now try political action.' ... As the strike weakened, the earlier Socialist support of IWW leadership turned to criticism. The New York *Call*, originally a leading advocate of the strikers' cause, became its most outspoken critic" (Dubofsky 282). Many Wobblies, however, maintained that their refusal to take part in electoral politics was a valid political act in its own right. They argued that it freed the industrial working class from its long-standing ties to corrupt political machines, allowing them to establish their own organizations with their own representative leaders.

The fictional representation of a politically charged marriage plot, then, suggests that Bullard's novel, on a more general level, is using this device to demonstrate the very real political achievements that had been made possible by the IWW's rejection of political (electoral) forms of representation. The fact that Yetta finally chooses to marry Isadore, a member of the Socialist Party, over Walter, a syndicalist, should therefore be read not as her abandonment of the IWW's Spirit of Revolt, but as her figurative wedding of these two rival factions to one another (a cause for which many members of both organizations were actually fighting at the time).[10] Hence, her feelings for the socialist, Isadore, are virtually interchangeable with the syndicalist Spirit of Revolt that she feels while helping to organize the industrial workforce. These two sets of feelings are "married" to one another, as well as united in the form of a representational medium par excellence—*The Clarion*, the socialist daily newspaper. It is no surprise, then, to learn that just after she marries Isadore "she transformed the labor page into a vital force in the trade-union world" (383). The following description of Yetta's feelings could likewise be read as applying to any one of three things at once: the fate of *The Clarion*, her recent marriage to Isadore, and the organization of the industrial working class: "The very uncertainty of *The Clarion*'s existence fitted into Yetta's mood. Any moment the flimsy structure might collapse. She thought of the future as little as possible.... She and the paper were struggling desperately to keep going until they found firmer ground underfoot" (Bullard 381–382).

Writing for the Workers, Socialism for the Babies

If *Comrade Yetta* has not entirely solved the problem of finding a way to represent an industrial workforce that refuses to be represented, the very lack of a viable solution is perhaps what led Bullard to use his protagonist, Yetta, as a means to figure this problem. On the one hand, he underscores Yetta's explicitly aesthetic relationship to the "drama" of labor struggles in order to imagine alternative modes of political representation for the mass industrial worker. The effects of her journalistic writing, then, allude to a potentially ideal form of revolutionary fiction. On the other hand, he invests her supposedly personal choices regarding marriage and motherhood with overt political significance to such a degree that it becomes virtually impossible to distinguish between the political themes of the narrative and those one would expect to find in a domestic romance. Her political activities are articulated through her romantic sentiments (the

Spirit of Revolt), and her romantic pursuits are shaped by her evolving political convictions (that extend "deeper than individuals").

Comrade Yetta therefore does not simply turn a political story into a story of domestic happiness, as one of its critics contends (Hapke 151–152, 165; cf. Conn 100–101). Rather, conversely, it ascribes Yetta's domestic happiness to the very workers she wants to represent. Specifically, she is working as a journalist and union leader to represent the industrial working class, while at the same time she is working as the fictional protagonist of a domestic romance narrative (wife and mother) to represent the joy of this class once it has found its proper form of organization, a "justly distributed" representation.

In the end, the novel places great faith in the power of a particular kind of aesthetic representation—newspaper stories—not only to represent industrial workers but also to help them to represent themselves more effectively. If the ideal of One Big Union has yet to be fully realized, the newspaper that prints Yetta's articles seems to serve as its prototype. For Bullard, *The Clarion* functions to articulate workers' demands and to organize their desires into a coherent program—satisfying both of these needs in lieu of an effective, mass industrial union. Thus the newspaper becomes a key site for imagining and instantiating the new rank-and-file form of democracy that the IWW had been calling for—one to take the place of the established and corrupt representative democracy from which workers had come to feel estranged. "Organized labor is fighting out the same problem in democracy which our larger community is facing. 'How shall elected delegates be made to represent their constituents?' The rank and file of workers cannot attend all the meetings of their central organizations any more than we can spend all our time in watching Congress. Labor bosses, like political crooks, love darkness. . . . Every day [Yetta] tried to run some story dealing with this issue of clean politics" (383–384). The narrator goes on to recount that

> as the months passed the sentiment for "One Big Union" grew steadily. At last, when Yetta had been about a year on *The Clarion*, a convention of all the garment trades was called to consider the matter. . . . Yetta and her friends saw at once that their only hope of success lay in appealing to the rank and file. So during the first days of the convention, while the official delegates were denouncing the principles of Industrial Unionism, Yetta spoke at noon factory meetings, two or three times each evening, and devoted almost all of *The Clarion*'s "Labor Page" to the same subject. This is the secret

of democratic politics. If the mass of the people can be stirred into watching and controlling their representatives, Democracy is safe. The mass of the garment workers believed in federation. They made their wishes heard even in the Convention Hall,—it is rare, indeed, that the will of the people control such assemblies,—and when the crucial vote was taken, the resolution of the industrial unionists was carried by an unexpectedly large majority. For close to five years, Yetta had been working towards this end. (386–387)

The specific function of the newspaper here is to serve as a watchdog over the political process within labor unions. More broadly, though, the passage suggests that Yetta's labor journalism is fighting to solve "the same problem in democracy which our larger community is facing." The implication is that, when democracy is finally achieved among working-class organizations—with the coming of true industrial unionism—then democracy on a broader, national scale will finally be possible. Nevertheless, this process must begin with vigilant journalists, such as Yetta, who are either literally or figuratively wedded to the interests of the working class.

The novel ends with Yetta realizing her goal of establishing One Big Union among all the garment workers. Bullard uses this achievement as an occasion to remind us again of those more "intimate" points of connection through which we are all touched by labor struggles. Yetta is now a happy wife, mother, writer, and industrial union leader. In a conversation with her former lover Walter Longman, the syndicalist who early in the novel encouraged her to reject romantic notions of "dream-love," Yetta, now older and wiser, confirms the correctness of his view; but in doing so, she reveals to him that she has replaced the sentiment of romance with one of sublime wonder:

> And that's the wonder of reality, it calls out something so immensely deeper than dream-love. . . . And then the babies! Think of it, Walter. I've got two of them. My very own! You said something like this once—that flesh and blood were more wonderful than any dream. . . . It's so wonderful a world! . . . And somehow it all seems to centre around the babies. They've given Socialism a new meaning to me, have brought it all nearer, made it more intimate and personal, more closely woven into myself. . . . The thought of all the millions of babies in the slums has become the very corner-stone of my thinking. It's for them. We've just got to win Socialism for the babies! I wish you could see mine. I'll send you a photograph. (444–445)

This peculiar passage may be taken to suggest that Yetta has renounced some of her more militant syndicalist and socialist principles, replacing them with an ideal of domesticity and motherhood. By now, however, it should be clear that Bullard's complex characterization of Yetta does not allow for such a reading. By having Yetta internalize her political principles, Bullard asks us to see her as more deeply embracing these principles rather than fleeing from them. Her babies are not a form of compensation for the loss of her political activism but a figurative extension of that activism. He thus preserves Yetta's sense of synecdochic identification with every worker, only now he has transposed this identification to another level. Instead of expanding her horizon of identification to include even more workers (since she earlier identified with all workers, this would not be possible), he is internalizing and deepening it, so that she now feels a corporeal bond with the entire industrial working class in and through the functions of her body.

In short, Bullard recycles and redefines the generic conventions of domestic fiction to portray a radical political and economic program—the IWW's brand of revolutionary syndicalism—which, to him, on account of its intractable and spontaneous character, cannot be adequately conveyed through the familiar narratives upon which the political and economic discourse of his day have relied. Likewise, he is trying to provide a new meaning for the concept of socialism, to bring it "nearer" to us by making its meaning "more intimate and personal, more closely woven" into the lives of his characters. According to Salvatore Salerno, the aesthetic productions of the IWW were characterized by "appeals to class feeling rather than formal ideology." The fact that Yetta's political decisions are informed by, and explicitly framed in, the language of sentiment can justly be read as illustrating Salerno's claim that "the IWW's philosophy of industrial unionism was a sensibility more than a doctrine or formal ideology" (*Red November* 147). For these reasons, therefore, Bullard's novel should be understood as an exemplary instance of Wobbly art. While it appears to stage the social "drama" in the space of an imaginary theater (the novel itself), it does this only to translate it into an aesthetic form of representation. And lest we forget to do the same once we put down the book, his narrator keeps discovering new ways to remind us that "there are hardly any of us who do not at some time step upon the stage and act our parts" (Bullard 244).

Recall how, earlier, Bullard's narrator asked us to see "this page, from which you are reading," as an instance of class struggle that is similarly "woven" into ourselves. Presumably, then, he wants his readers to feel the same sort of corporeal identification with the struggles of the industrial working class that Yetta feels. However, because he can accomplish this only through a fictional narrative, the goal he sets himself seems ultimately unrealizable. Just as Yetta tells Walter that "flesh and blood were more wonderful than any dream," Bullard seems to believe that an aesthetic representation, such as a novel, is capable of providing an encounter with flesh and blood, so that Yetta's wonder may actually be felt by others (readers). But since this would have to be a "wonderful" fiction and not merely a dream—a fiction that consisted of actual flesh and blood—his more or less conscious aim in writing *Comrade Yetta* may have been to transcend the formal limits of fiction itself. As odd as this idea may sound, one should recall that in 1913, the same year Bullard's novel was published, many of the audience members who attended the *Pageant of the Paterson Strike* at Madison Square Garden felt that it, too, had somehow managed to transcend the formal limits of theatrical representation. It would appear, then, that as a group Wobbly artists and writers sought to move "beyond formal political expressions to create a language and symbolism that made the IWW's principles meaningful" (Salerno, *Red November* 149–151).

Finally, if one individual's imagination has the capacity to identify with workers everywhere, as is the case with Yetta, then Bullard seems equally to believe that certain aesthetic representations—such as a novel or a newspaper—can potentially exceed their formal limitations. In doing so, these modes of writing may then be able to represent the modern industrial working class, which needs to see its interests represented in some trustworthy (albeit sublime) fashion in order to attain a more "intimate" sense of solidarity. The ideal IWW novel, from Bullard's perspective, must therefore undergo the same transformation that Yetta experienced in prison; namely, it should expand above and beyond its own narrative function to the point where it has engendered itself as "a delicate instrument for the transmission of sound" (177).

Living Books

Ernest Poole's 1915 novel, *The Harbor*, tells the story of one aspiring young writer's conversion to revolutionary syndicalism and his subsequent efforts to produce a novel according to the same principles that Yetta's "flesh and blood" labor journalism is supposed to embody. However, in part because of its self-conscious bildungsroman structure, *The Harbor* is less an example of syndicalist fiction in its own right and more a record of one writer's search to discover what exactly this new genre of fiction might look like.

Poole's narrative is told from the perspective of its protagonist, known only as "Bill." It exhaustively details his development as a writer, beginning with his childhood, when he was both fascinated and repelled by New York City's harbor, located directly next to his home in Brooklyn Heights. The story continues through Bill's education in college, where he befriends Joe Kramer, a bohemian radical who later becomes an IWW organizer during a mass strike of harbor workers. Bill first finds success as a journalist by writing profiles of rich and powerful corporate executives for popular newsmagazines. Over time, through his repeated encounters with Joe Kramer, who educates him about the general fate of the industrial workforce, Bill's curiosity about the struggles of the harbor workers leads him to write about their IWW-led strike.

To understand the workers' motives and interests, Bill begins by studying their movement as a detached observer. It does not take long, though, before he is swept up in the excitement of their strike and comes to believe in the radical potential of the mass worker. As this occurs, his ideas about writing undergo a parallel transformation. He learns to see books in themselves as "dry affairs," while the mass of workers, immersed in their strike, embody and dramatize the ideas that books can only describe abstractly: "I had read many radical books of late, in my groping for a foothold, and I had found most of them dry affairs. But now the crowd through its leaders had laid hold upon the thoughts in these books, had made them its own and so given them life. In the process the thoughts had been twisted and bent, some parts ignored and others brought out of all their nice proportions. Exaggeration, sentiment, all kinds of crudity were here. But it was crudity alive, a creed was here in action" (*Harbor* 323). In the same manner in which, as a writer, he initially assumed a detached point of view to observe the harbor workers' strike, the ideas printed in "radical books," separated from radical workers themselves, lack the "living" energy that only the actions of a mass movement of workers can give them. According to Bill, for the dry ideas of books to become "a creed in action," the working class needs to "lay hold" of the thoughts they contain and make them "its own." That is, workers are to treat the thoughts in books exactly as they treat the material means of production (factories and machines) when they are engaged in a strike: they are to seize, occupy, and possess them.

Mirroring a Mass

How then, Bill wonders, can he encourage workers to do this through his writing? What particular kind of writing will inspire workers to lay hold of his thoughts and make them their own, to turn his words into a creed in action? In sum, how can Bill lend strength to the workers' movement merely by writing about it?

The first lesson Bill learns is that modern industrial workers are routinely ignored by politicians in Washington, just as the harbor workers' demands are ignored by the corporate interests that own and operate the harbor. When Jim Marsh, the IWW leader of the harbor strike—a character modeled closely on William D. "Big Bill" Haywood—addresses these workers at a mass rally on the docks, he tells them bluntly that "sailors are men who have no votes" (*Harbor* 328).[11] Their voices, numerous as they may be, are not heard by those who have been elected (by others) to represent them. Lacking votes, the harbor workers lack officially sanctioned political representation.

However, by going on strike, the harbor workers discover a more immediate way to represent themselves. Once he has become personally involved in the strike, Bill begins to sense that the strike itself provides them with an alternative form of representation: "Caught up in the tide of democracy now sweeping all around the earth, they had wanted to feel themselves running themselves in all this work they were doing. So they had come out on strike and become a crowd, and in the crowd they had suddenly found such strength as they never dreamed could be theirs" (*Harbor* 350). This passage indicates that the value of democratic representation to workers is that it allows them to "feel themselves running themselves" in the work they perform. That is, democracy, to the industrial worker, means self-determination. In addition, it provides a kind of mirror reflection of these workers, directing their image back toward them so they can "feel" themselves (cf. Flynn 220).

In writing for and about workers, then, Bill's college-friend-turned-Wobbly, Joe Kramer, teaches him that "they've got to learn that they are a crowd.... But that's where you and me come in—we can help 'em get together faster than they would if left to themselves! You can help that way a lot—by writing to the tenements!" (*Harbor* 262–263). Although Joe here sounds like something of a Bolshevist—advocating a vanguard to organize workers and sharpen their class consciousness—his understanding of the purpose of writing assigns to it a more modest didactic function. Left to themselves, workers will inevitably sense that they are a "mass," for the conditions of modern mass production ensure this. Writers, however, can accelerate this process by representing a crowd of workers *as* a crowd, which subsequently allows these workers "to learn that they *are* a crowd." Writing for workers, according to Joe, should strive only to reflect these workers to themselves. By mirroring them, the writer simply helps to articulate and consolidate a mass identity that they have already claimed as their own.

"We were entering into an age of force . . ."

As straightforward as it may sound, one serious problem emerges from this notion of writing-as-reflection. Namely, how would any type of democracy (self-determination) be possible among workers who were looking for their reflection in texts that were written not by themselves but by others? Since their need for a mirror—or even their occasional use of one—implies a lack of self-determination, this would seem to make the project of writing "for" workers not only pointless but a dangerous influx of outside, nondemocratic authority at the very source of working-class democracy.

In spite of the encouragement he will later give to Bill to write "to the tenements," Joe Kramer's initial way of dealing with this problem is to give up writing entirely. As Bill puts it, "While I had gone up [in my career as a writer] he had gone down, until finally throwing up in disgust 'this whole fool game of putting words on paper,' he had made up his mind to throw in his life with the lives of the men at the bottom" (*Harbor* 240). For Joe, at this stage of the narrative, it is impossible both to write about workers and to lend effective support to their cause. One must choose to be either a writer or a fighter for the working class. There is no middle ground, since industrial mass workers can apparently derive no benefit from any form of representation they do not completely control. When Bill at one point tries to persuade Joe that his own journalistic writing could accomplish some good for the striking harbor workers, he recalls Joe's harsh reaction: "He had no use for such writing, or in fact for art of any kind. 'Propaganda' was all that he wanted. . . . The world had come to a time, he said, when talking and writing weren't going to count. We were entering into an age of force—of 'direct action'—strikes and the like—by prodigious masses of men. All I could do [as a writer] was worthless" (260). Because he is personally involved in the strike, Joe can picture it to himself only as a dramatic spectacle of brute forces, much as *The Pageant of the Paterson Strike* (in which Poole was personally involved) claimed to represent "a conflict between two social forces—the force of labor and the force of capital" ("Pageant of the Paterson" 210). As Joe sees it, the particular force required to win a modern strike—direct action at the point of production—has nothing to do with "talking and writing." Presumably, then, the "prodigious masses of men" he has in mind do not need to see their reflection in writing, since the efficacy of their collective action already reflects who they are (labor power incarnate). Joe implies here that Bill's writing, by contrast, is just another way to represent others by potentially *mis*representing their true interests—a job for politicians and business executives.

Joe's understanding of the nature of the industrial working class thus appears radical in its antihumanism. That is to say, his dismissal of writers and artists assumes that they rely on humanistic (and other suspect ideological) principles in their attempts to represent such a workforce. However, the single most important element of working-class power, the direct action of workers at the point of production—being a material force that exceeds the bounds of language—can never be represented as such. Writers and artists can therefore represent only the less significant aspects of a strike, such as the thoughts and biographies of individual workers. In themselves, however, these personal, humanizing details can never reflect the profoundly structural and material forms of power that industrial workers possess and exploit. Yet it is this very power that dictates the course of the strike. Specifically, the structural power they possess, manifested through their direct action, is the sole agent of the strike, from the workers' point of view. As individuals, they could never win the strike, since only the power they exercise en masse can determine the outcome of their struggles.

The challenge Bill faces, then, is to develop a style of narrative writing that can represent a uniquely modern, collective form of agency that transcends the individuals of which it is composed. The problem is that his training as a writer has led him to do exactly the opposite—namely, to focus his effort on portraying "great" individuals, such as wealthy executives and politicians. Up to this point, as he sees it, the notion of social agency applied only to these types of "representative" individuals: "For years I had labored to train myself to concentrate on one man at a time, to shut out all else for weeks on end, to feel this man so vividly that his self came into mine. Now with the same intensity I found myself striving day and night to feel not one but thousands of men, a blurred bewildering multitude" (*Harbor* 321). The fact that a large group of workers initially seems to Bill to be merely "a blurred bewildering multitude" indicates the difficulty he has imagining such a thing as a collective agent. He needs to be able to characterize this group of workers—which means, to forge a "character" out of them, to unify and distill many individuals into the form of a single entity—in anything he writes about them.[12]

Bill's task is made somewhat easier for him by the conditions of the modern industrial workplace. When his organizer friend, Joe Kramer, takes him down into the lower decks of a ship to become acquainted with the working conditions of the stokers in the engine room, he explains to Bill the origins of this new breed of mass worker: "The age of steam has sent the old-style sailors ashore and shipped these fellows in their places. And that makes all the difference. These chaps didn't grow up on ships and get used to being kicked and cowed and shot for mutiny if they struck. No, they're all grown up on land, in factories where they've been in strikes, and they bring their factory views along into these floating factories. And they don't like these stinking holes!" (*Harbor* 248). Factories, of course, produce profits for their owners, but they also produce militant workers who strike to have their demands met. These stokers, hidden away in the lower decks of the ship, exemplify the new mass workforce, one that is steadily infiltrating all sectors of industry and bringing with it a discipline acquired through its work with machinery.[13]

Because the smooth operation of a modern factory must convert large groups of individuals into an apparently homogeneous mass, Bill comes to see in this phenomenon a model for the literary representation of industrial workers. We even learn that Joe, who previously gave up writing, now edits a newspaper for these workers—an activity that he justifies as part of his work as an organizer. Like Yetta writing the Labor Page for her socialist daily newspaper, *The Clarion*, in *Comrade Yetta*, Joe sees his newspaper as a forum in which workers can speak for and to themselves: "The last issue of Joe's weekly paper, *War Sure* . . . was called 'Our Special Sabotage Number,' and in it various stokers and dockers . . . had crudely written their ideas upon just how the engines of a ship or the hoisting winches on a dock could be most effectively put out of order in time of strike" (*Harbor* 282). In contrast to Yetta's Labor Page, the purpose of this particular issue of *War Sure* is not simply to represent workers or to allow them to represent themselves but to serve as a sort of virtual meeting hall where workers can share ideas on the latest techniques of sabotage. It is also worth noting that *War Sure* does not print stories about individual workers, or varieties of human interest pieces, but rather "crude" descriptions of how the force of industrial machines can be used to fight against their owners. In an age of force, this is perhaps the only kind of talking and writing that counts for Joe.[14]

Since Bill, an aspiring novelist, has no desire to write for *War Sure*, much of the remainder of the story describes his effort to represent the ebb and flow of the strike in conventional narrative terms. To do this, he has to be able to portray acts of sabotage like these as the result of one single character, made up of the combined forces of the workers and the machinery they operate (or make inoperative). How, then, is he to endow all of this with a recognizable form of narrative agency, one constituted by a multitude of individual workers, as well as by ships, cranes, and other types of machinery?

Sticking with the technique of writing that is most familiar to him—to focus on representative individuals—Bill decides first to interview Jim Marsh, the IWW spokesman and lead organizer of the harbor strike, to see what he can learn about the workers' use of sabotage tactics. At a mass rally in the harbor, Marsh praises the huge group of strikers, reminding them of the unique type of power they possess: "They're scared because we've thrown over their laws—because they know that we now see our power—to stop all their ships and the trade of their land and send their stock market into a panic! . . . Look—and think—of what you *can* do—all you—and you—and you—and you—by just folding your arms! Think of all you *will* do! And laugh—laugh! Laugh! Laugh!" (*Harbor* 328-329). The speech is met with "wave on wave" of laughter from the crowd (329), and late that night, when Bill sits down with two strikers who are talking about the day's speeches, he sees that "from time to time they would glance up at the big ship they had paralyzed and chuckle softly to themselves" (330).[15]

One reason Jim Marsh tells the workers to laugh at what they have already done, and what they can still potentially do, is that it does not seem to conform to any established laws determining the nature of power. Marsh asserts that "we've thrown over their laws" because nothing in the current political, economic, or legislative discourse can logically account for what these workers have accomplished simply by folding their arms and refusing to work. The nation's laws (and dictionaries) take for granted that "workers," naturally, are always working. There is no meaningful concept in any given social discourse that corresponds to the simple phenomenon of a worker who stays on the job while refusing to work. In the case of the harbor strike, one particular group of commodities (workers) is not acting (working) like the commodities they are supposed to be. The absurdity of the idea echoes Marx's figure of the commodity that "speaks," yet this is precisely what has taken place in the harbor (Marx 176–177; cf. Kornbluh, "Paterson: 1913" 197). By folding their arms and shutting down the operations of the harbor, the workers, in a sense, have spoken through this act both as workers (commodities) and as something else—something that the discursive category of the commodity, much like certain categories of fictional narrative, cannot represent or otherwise comprehend.

Personifying the Strike

Bill, however, has no problem discerning what these strikers have accomplished. His problem rather is finding a way to represent it in a fictional narrative and, within this genre of writing, to make it recognizably the work of a single character or entity. The impulse to follow his training as a journalist and to focus his attention on individual workers no longer seems to be adequate to the task. Moreover, the extraordinary quality of the strike appears to Bill to render insignificant the very Wall Street executives about whom he once wrote his popular profiles. After he sees what the harbor workers en masse can accomplish, his estimate of them changes, for he now realizes the enormous power they possess: "I thought of the men I had seen that day. How crassly ignorant they seemed. And yet in a few brief hours they had paralyzed all that [Wall Street] had planned, reduced it all to silence, nothing" (*Harbor* 311).

To illustrate the change that the strike provokes in Bill's writing technique, consider his first impression of Jim Marsh, the IWW spokesman and strike leader: "The thing that struck me most at first was the cool effrontery of the man in undertaking such a struggle. The old type of labor leader had at least stuck to one industry, and had known by close experience what he had to face. But here was a mere outsider, a visitor strolling into a place and saying, 'I guess I'll stop all this'" (*Harbor* 270). At this stage, Bill is still trying to frame Jim Marsh as a "representative" individual—to make sense of his charismatic personality and the influence he wields over the harbor workers. In other words, he is again trying "to feel this man so vividly that his self came into mine" (321). This suggests that he has already sketched in his imagination the outline of a particular strike narrative and is simply looking for a way to include Marsh in this story as one of its central characters.

Yet Bill soon realizes that such a method of narrative construction will not suffice. Even to use Jim Marsh as a focal point of the story would go against Marsh's own conviction that, in a mass strike, there is no such point (or at least, there should not be any). In one of his speeches to the mass of assembled harbor workers, Marsh reiterates: "Even if I were a crook, or if I were dead, this strike would go on exactly the same—for think a minute and you'll see that whatever has been done in this struggle has been done each time by you. It's you who have decided each point. It's you who have been called here today to decide the one big question. Congress has said, 'Arbitrate.' It's for you all to decide on our answer. This is no one-man union, there is no one man they can fix, nor even a small committee. We're a committee of fifty thousand here to make our own laws for ourselves" (*Harbor* 336). Jim Marsh is assigning agency to every one of the strikers as a collective mass. In response, after he has heard this speech, Bill begins to shift the focus of his narrative away from Marsh and toward this same mass. However, because "there is no one man they can fix," as Marsh puts it ("they" referring to Congress, corporate executives, and assorted forces of law and order), Bill must also guard against fixing his narrative on particular individuals like Marsh.

Thus, once he reconsiders the actual mass of workers engaged in the strike, Bill discovers that collectives such as this one seem to have a will of their own: "Every plan of action, everything felt and thought and spoken, though it might start from a single man, was at once transformed by the feeling of all. . . . The crowd spoke its will through many voices, through men who sprang up and talked hard a few moments, then sat down and were lost to sight . . . they had simply been parts of the crowd, and the crowd had made them rise and speak" (*Harbor* 315). Note that Poole here is careful to depict the workers' collective will, not as a kind of mob rule, but as an ideal of industrial democracy actually put into practice (Den Tandt 242). This passage recalls the description of the rank and file of workers at the convention of the garment trades in *Comrade Yetta*, where the narrator happily exclaims, "It is rare, indeed, that the will of the people control such assemblies" (Bullard 387). What Yetta waited five years to experience, though, Bill witnesses immediately in the midst of an ongoing strike.

Soon after this moment Bill feels reinvigorated, filled with new creative energy, and he begins to develop a narrative style to represent what he is learning about the nature of industrial workers on strike: "And slowly in my striving I felt them fuse together into one great being, look at me with two great eyes, speak to me with one deep voice, pour into me with one tremendous burning passion for the freedom of mankind" (*Harbor* 321). What does this passage suggest about Bill's new technique for representing the harbor workers? In effect, that it is not quite so new as he thinks, for what he imagines here is nothing other than an individualized mass of workers. By "fusing" them into "one great being," and by giving them one will, one set of eyes, and one voice, Bill figuratively provides a human face for this collective—and not purely human—force. That is, he compresses all of its disparate aspects into the same figure of the "representative" individual that, up to this point, he has always tried to portray.

In one sense, Bill's personification of the strike marks a regression to an aesthetic model that, throughout the latter third of *The Harbor*, he is clearly trying to abandon (the profile). He knows that to represent the strike faithfully, the story he tells about it must not "fix" any individuals as being particularly significant. Therefore, he feels that by viewing the combined forces of workers and machines as a single, individual character he has solved the problem of representing the strikers' agency in his narrative. However, he has done so only by resurrecting and refitting the traditional (bourgeois) figure of the solitary, exemplary individual. He is still fixing an individual here, even if this consists of a mass of striking industrial workers. Thus he resorts to those very same conventions of narrative form that seem to have been rendered obsolete, or at least inadequate, by the nature of the strike itself.

In another sense, though, the recourse Bill has to the figure of the individual is perhaps not as regressive or seamless as this criticism suggests. Recall for a moment Bill's description of how he wrote profiles of famous individuals. His goal was "to feel this man so vividly that his self came into mine." It is already clear in this phrase that the genre of the profile, for Bill, seems to depend, not on his gaining aesthetic distance from his subject, but on the opposite. Instead of describing a process of objectification, he tells us that he required a kind of absorption, a complete identification between himself as a writer and the subject of his profile. Similarly, when writing about the mass of workers on strike, he claims that they "pour into me" in the form of an individual. As trite or sensational as it may sound, the apparent lack of aesthetic distance Bill feels toward the strike allows him to imagine new possibilities for representing it. For example, he tells us: "All around me as I marched I heard an unending torrent of voices speaking many languages, uniting in strange cheers and songs brought from all over the ocean world . . . for there was no separation of races, all walked together in dense crowds, the whole strike family was here. And listening and watching I felt myself a member now" (*Harbor* 337–338). This passage evokes a collective intimacy that any detached journalistic narrative would typically seek to avoid. In this regard, one might see Poole's novel as taking Yetta's desire to experience "Socialism for the babies!" and transposing it to the setting of a mass industrial strike. Yetta's children, she claims, have changed the meaning of socialism for her insofar as they "have brought it all nearer, made it more intimate and personal, more closely woven into myself" (Bullard 444). In part, the emergence of this new "intimate" form of socialism is due to her having figuratively overcome the separation of radical political factions (by marrying a socialist), just as the harbor workers, through their adherence to IWW principles, have momentarily overcome the separation of races. Hence, for Bill, who feels he is now a member of "the whole strike family," the experience of the strike is similarly "woven" or "poured" into himself. The result of such a deep level of identification, he admits, is that "exaggeration, sentiment, all kinds of crudity were here," but it nevertheless prompts him to speculate over the possible forms that representation in a narrative may take (*Harbor* 323).

The Mass Worker Sublime (II)

In this final phase of Bill's development as a writer, *The Harbor*—much like *The Walking Delegate* and *Comrade Yetta*—takes a slightly bizarre (but by now predictable) turn toward figures of the sublime. For all three of these novels, illustrations of sublime experience typically work to shore up their characters' fragile, tentative, and often vague aesthetic representations of mass industrial workers. Ruth Arnold and Yetta Rayefsky both experience feelings similar to those of Bill when they try to represent industrial workers in a particular discursive form that would be adequate to the vision these workers inspire in their imaginations. For instance, in another (typically fleeting) moment where he feels overwhelmed by the dynamic crowd of strikers, Bill gets a sense of the sublime wonder that drew his friend, Joe Kramer, to revolutionary syndicalism: "I thought of what Joe had said that day: 'When you see the crowd, in a strike like this, loosen up and show all it could be if it had the chance—that sight is so big it blots you out—you sink—you melt into the crowd.' Something like that happened to me. I had seen the multitudes 'loosen up,' I had felt myself melt into the crowd" (*Harbor* 311). Bill's sensation of melting into the crowd resembles the moment when he felt he had become a member of "the whole strike family" while he was marching alongside the workers. However, it is important to recognize that *feeling* as though he were melting into the crowd does not imply that he is actually *in* the crowd or that he is in any way a part of it. The feeling, rather, is premised on Bill's relatively detached point of view. Joe's comment refers only to a feeling that comes from observing the crowd ("When you *see* the crowd ... that *sight* is so big"), not from actually joining it. His sense of sublime wonder therefore presupposes an initial, classically aesthetic point of view.

While Bill's aesthetic detachment can easily be mistaken for a sign of his political alienation, as reflected in Peter Conn's and Christophe Den Tandt's readings of *The Harbor*, the novel suggests on the contrary that it is from just such a detached, objectifying, and aestheticizing point of view that the process of subjective identification with the working class truly begins (Conn 117; Den Tandt 242). When Joe explains to Bill how "that sight is so big it blots you out—you sink—you melt into the crowd," he could just as well be describing the forced obsolescence of a typical bourgeois writer; one whose thoughts, in the form of "dry" books, have been seized, taken over, and brought to life by the revolutionary mass: "Now the crowd through its leaders had laid hold upon the thoughts in these books, had made them its own and so given them life" (*Harbor* 323). Bill now also feels as though his individual thoughts—the thoughts of "great individuals"—had been seized by this crowd, which made them its own. It stands to reason, then, that Bill comes to see a reflection of his own thoughts in the collective actions of this crowd. Although they may be "twisted and bent, some parts ignored and others brought out of all their nice proportions," they still appear to him in the recognizable figure of a powerful individual ("one great being").

It is necessary to juxtapose these various episodes from *The Harbor* in order to understand how the process of identification begins as an aesthetic relation. This type of relation assumes distance, reflection, and an objectifying point of view on the part of the beholder. However, in relation to certain large-scale social events, such as a mass strike of industrial workers, it can also produce an overwhelming jolt to one's imagination. (Recall, for instance, how one reviewer described the performance of the Paterson Pageant as "the onrush of a stupendous force [that] seized the imagination" [Golin 58]). The latter, in one form or another, is then usually expressed as a sense of sublime wonder that cannot be fully conveyed through language. Whenever this occurs in these three novels—though in different forms and in different contexts—the characters who experience it enter into a new relationship with the mass of industrial workers. They do not necessarily *become* such workers (as Joe Kramer believed they must), but, like Bill, Yetta, and Ruth, they feel as though they have somehow become members of "the whole strike family."

Thus, when Yetta's first lover, Walter (the syndicalist), teaches her that her choice of a husband goes "deeper than individuals," he is only preparing her for an insight that she will gain from her specifically aesthetic relation to the mass of industrial workers (Bullard 339). Bill acquires a similar insight when he admits, at the end of *The Harbor*, that the strike taught him to have "a deeper view of life. . . . I saw something in that strike so much bigger than Marsh or Joe or that crude organization of theirs—something deep down in the people themselves that rises up out of each one of them the minute they get together" (368). This insight—gained not by joining the industrial workforce but by observing it and allowing it to "pour into" himself—provides Bill with the imaginative resources he needs to represent it adequately in the form of a narrative.

It is only in the last seven pages of the novel, therefore, that Bill finally feels ready to begin writing his story of the harbor strike. To do so, he needs only to close his eyes and imagine that the mass of industrial workers is embarking on a revolutionary voyage of sorts. This image is inspired by an actual ocean liner that Bill hears leaving the harbor late at night. The ship is carrying his friend Joe Kramer off to Europe, where Joe has decided to go in order to convince soldiers fighting the Great War to desert the military and join the One Big Union of the industrial working class:

> I shut my eyes and saw the huge liner on which Joe was sailing moving slowly out of its slip. Down at its bottom men shoveling coal to the clang of its gong. On the decks above them, hundreds of cabins and suites de luxe—. . . it seemed to be saying:
>
> "Make way for me. Make way, all you little men. Make way, all you habits and all you institutions, all you little creeds and gods. For I am the start of the voyage—over the ocean to heathen lands! And I am always starting out and always bearing you along! For I am your molder, I am strong—I am a surprise, I am a shock—I am a dazzling passion of hope—I am a grim executioner! I am reality—I am life! I am the book that has no end!" (*Harbor* 387)

These are the very last words of *The Harbor*. Bill's aesthetic relation to the mass of industrial workers has now reached its apex; with the strike ended and Joe leaving town, Bill, alone in his bed, is inventing a host of imaginary figures through which to represent them in his story.

In spite of the words he imagines the ocean liner speaking to the world—"I am a surprise, I am a shock"—Bill's rather fantastic personification of the ocean liner should not come as a surprise by now. To represent what he takes to be the almost mystical power and creative energies of the industrial workers' movement, Bill repeatedly and methodically projects the imaginative excess it inspires within himself into various figures of a "great being" that lies somewhere outside himself, which he then describes as a social force that is alive and speaking with one voice. This last figure of the ocean liner with its cargo of workers—a sort of Nietzschean force embarking on a revolutionary transvaluation of values—should therefore be understood as expressing the core ambition that has informed Bill's attempts to write about the strikers throughout the whole last third of the novel. Like Yetta, Bill wants his writing not simply to represent the members of the industrial working class but to stage and enact the new form of life that he feels this class is bringing into the world ("I am reality—I am life!"). Bill's imaginary ocean liner, like his "one great being" earlier, is designed to figure this obscure force of life and thus make it legible as the hero of his narrative, just as Yetta's newspaper and family figuratively serve to concretize and embody the life of the industrial working class. So where the liner tells these workers "I am your molder," Yetta could have similarly told them, "I am your mother."

Because *The Harbor* is told from a first-person perspective, its ending is all the more remarkable for Poole's suppression of the narratorial "I" to replace it with the "I" of the personified ocean liner, which thus fictionalizes his narrator's voice to the second degree. By choosing to end his novel with this voice that proclaims, "I am the book that has no end!" Poole, again like Bullard, seems to want to transcend the formal limits of narrative fiction itself. Of course, this particular book Poole wrote does have an end, but it is an end that alludes to the fictional beginning of a new story: namely, the beginning of Bill's (doubly fictional) book about the industrial working class. Bill's imaginary book, as opposed to Poole's, ideally should not have any ending, just as the imagined power of the mass workers should not find its end, its limit, or even a specifically defined purpose in any real aesthetic representation of it. Nevertheless, to provide even a glimpse of the economic and political power of these workers, Bill's fantasy book would eventually require the same kind of end that Poole supplies for his actual book.

Finally, by ending his novel in this manner, Poole implies that, in relation to the economic demands of the mass of industrial workers, the function of any aesthetic representation is simply to provide a real vehicle for figuring and articulating an imaginary power that the movement of industrial unionism (the IWW) has already ascribed to itself. In the specific case of *The Harbor*, the imaginary potential of this movement is figured in the (appropriately vehicular and moving) character of the ocean liner, which apostrophizes its cargo of mass workers: "I am always starting out and always bearing you along!" The imagined potential of industrial unionism to overthrow capitalism and liberate the modern working class is thus supplied with a determinate aesthetic articulation, which in turn may help to make its ideals legible, discursive, and finally representable in both economic and political terms.

Suppression and Recovery

After the massive campaign by the U.S. federal government, lasting from 1917 to roughly 1922, to arrest or deport the leaders and members of the IWW and to suppress the workers' movement as a whole, official organizations for radical workers barely managed to survive (Adamic, *Dynamite* 392). However, as noted by one acute observer of the era, Louis Adamic, the systematic suppression of workers' organizations did little or nothing to dampen the impulse to direct action that had taken hold of industrial workers. "The workers' radicalism," Adamic claimed, "now found individual, personal expression in doing as little as possible for the wages they received and in wasting as much material as possible" (*Dynamite* 393). With the brief but severe postwar recession of 1920–1921, large U.S. industrial concerns laid off many workers; and, to increase the productivity of the workforce that they retained, they instituted even harsher disciplinary measures (particularly increasing the speedup). As a result, over the course of the decade from 1921 to 1931, Adamic came to be convinced that "sabotage and 'striking on the job' have become part of the psychology and behavior of millions of American workers who would [otherwise] resent being called wobblies or Communists" (*Dynamite* 382; see also Hallgren 105–112).

With the coming of the Great Depression in 1929, the situation of industrial workers only worsened further. Throughout the following decade, they regularly faced large rounds of layoffs, periodic and unpredictable spells of unemployment, arbitrary and severe discipline by plant managers, and the overall intensification of production with the speedup. The widespread feeling of unrest among industrial workers inspired progressive labor leaders to renew the push to establish industrial unions, beginning in the fall of 1935 with the formation of the Committee for Industrial Organizations—which soon broke away from the AFL to become the CIO—and the UAW.

The substantive links between the IWW and the CIO were more than simply coincidental. Many of those involved in the late 1930s CIO campaigns had once been active Wobblies, bringing with them from their earlier experience a recognition of the need to organize mass workers along industrial lines. The views of Wobblies themselves lend further support to the notion that the more progressive of the industrial labor organizers of the 1930s were direct descendants of the IWW (Bird, Georgakas, and Shaffer 80; De Caux 8).

The novels examined in the next and final chapter detail the efforts of mass workers to use direct action tactics in order to organize themselves into their own grassroots industrial unions, sponsored by the CIO. These narratives of factory occupations and sitdown strikes from the 1930s depict a modern, technologically advanced workforce demanding its own kind of union, its own uniquely "mass" forms of economic representation, to realize itself as an agent of social power.

4 / The Powerful Worker and the Demand for Economic Representation: "They planned to use their flesh, their bones, as a barricade"

Workers in U.S. mass production industries learned a great deal from the legacy of the IWW. Most importantly, they learned that to make their voices heard in the modern workplace, there was nothing more effective than direct action at the point of production. This is nowhere better illustrated than by the workers of Ruth McKenney's 1939 novel about the wave of sitdown strikes that swept Akron's rubber industry in 1936, *Industrial Valley*. McKenney's workers understood perfectly that by sitting down at their jobs they could use the commodified mass of their own bodies to block production in the tire factories, thus hastening the recognition of their union by the large rubber companies. Instead of having to rely on union representatives to negotiate with the companies on their behalf, Akron's rubber workers—like their Wobbly predecessors—knew that they could literally "use their flesh, their bones," to take a stand against company policies. And, by doing so, they would be adding even more leverage to the workplace bargaining power they had acquired on the Fordist assembly line.

The novels examined in this fourth and final chapter reveal the process by which the demand of the IWW for the *aesthetic* representation of the industrial workforce became transformed into the demand of the CIO for its *economic* representation. By the 1930s, U.S. mass workers were learning to exploit the advances that industrial capitalism had made in the two decades between 1915 and 1935—advances such as the large-scale implementation of Fordist production methods, corporate centralization, and vertical integration. Reflecting this development of the industrial workforce, the figure of the mass worker one encounters in the present group of Depression-era novels is shown as truly *powerful*: a worker who not only makes economic demands but can ensure that they are fully met.

While certain aspects of this figure of the mass worker resemble those of its Wobbly counterpart from three decades earlier, there are significant differences between these two literary treatments of the mass worker. Where IWW-era novels included sympathetic portraits of mass workers who advocated doing away with capitalist forms of production altogether, the mass worker portrayed in CIO-era novels is typically shown demanding just a larger piece of the capitalist pie. The former, then, is characterized primarily through its *refusals* (to work, to be represented), while the latter is characterized primarily through its *demands* (for a raise, for representation by a union).

The novels examined in the present chapter also differ in important ways from those of their Depression-era contemporaries that we have analyzed in previous chapters. Recall how other novelists from this same period—such as Dalton Trumbo, Clara Weatherwax, Thomas Bell, Robert Cruden, and William Rollins—could represent the figure of the mass worker in only one of two ways. In their narratives, the mass worker was always either destroyed, silenced, and degraded by the forces of industrial capitalism (Trumbo, Weatherwax) or strengthened, ennobled, and rendered heroic by the machine technology of the modern factory (Bell, Cruden, Rollins). In the present group of novels, the figure of the mass worker possesses the same sort of strength that characterized the heroic mechanized worker in the novels of Cruden and Rollins. However, in the present case, the strength of the "powerful" worker is coupled with the syndicalist "spirit of revolt" that is more frequently seen among characters in IWW-era novels, such as *Comrade Yetta* and *The Harbor*.

The chapter begins with a general historical overview of the problems associated with attempts to organize mass industrial workers in the 1930s. This opening section considers the impact on industrial workers of New Deal legislation (the National Industrial Recovery Act [NIRA]), the rise of the CIO, and the revolutionary effects of the popularity of the sitdown strike tactic among diverse quarters of the mass industrial workforce. The chapter then shifts its focus to explore the complexities attached to the concept of representation in Depression-era workers' movements. To this end, it juxtaposes a close reading of a single scene from Thomas Bell's 1941 novel, *Out of This Furnace*, with an analysis of the debates that were common among the Left literary establishment of the 1930s. In both cases, it becomes clear that—for workers as well as creative writers—debates over the nature of, and the complex relationship between, economic and aesthetic forms of representation often took place in the guise of heated political battles.

After studying the core theoretical questions that were at stake in these debates, the chapter embarks on a close examination of four Depression-era novels about mass industrial workers. This portion of the chapter begins with a reading of Robert Cantwell's strike novel *The Land of Plenty* (1934), which is set among lumber mill workers in the Pacific Northwest. Cantwell's novel deserves attention in the present context for two reasons. First, it is the earliest novel published in the United States to contain a fictionalized narrative of a factory occupation by mass industrial workers. The novel appeared to critical acclaim in 1934, barely two years before the wave of sitdown strikes and plant occupations that would sweep through the rubber and auto industries. Second, *The Land of Plenty* was highly regarded by the intelligentsia of the Left as a prototype of "proletarian" fiction—a newly defined genre of revolutionary writing, for which Cantwell's novel was seen as setting the standard. Thus, in hindsight, it also provides a standard by which to judge the goals and aspirations of the Depression-era Left's literary movement more generally.

To gain a fuller sense of the development of the proletarian novel throughout the latter half of the 1930s, the chapter moves next to offer a close reading of Ruth McKenney's 1939 novel, *Industrial Valley*. McKenney's communist and Wobbly-inspired narrative affords a unique perspective on the ambivalent reactions of the organized Left toward the spontaneous sitdown strikes of mass workers. Finally, the chapter concludes by briefly comparing two further Depression-era narratives about sitdown strikers: Josephine Herbst's novel *Rope of Gold* (1939), and Paul Gallico's novella *Sit-Down Strike* (1938). These works are of particular interest here not only because they provide additional perspectives on the wave of sitdown strikes but because they both saw in this surge of workers' unrest a messianic possibility for the future of industrial capitalism.

Organizing the Mass Worker in the 1930s

At the outset of the Great Depression in late 1929, workers in mass production industries had been subjected to almost ten years of continuous deskilling, mechanization, and speedup in the workplace. The new mass worker identified with Fordist production methods could thus no longer be categorized according to the traditional distinction between skilled and unskilled labor power. In large part, this was due to the leveling of wages and job classifications that followed the introduction of new technologies at the point of production.

In addition to the sweeping technological changes that were affecting the nature and experience of work itself, as well as the environment of the workplace, throughout the 1920s and 1930s mass workers were subjected to a constantly increasing rate of production. Although speedup policies had become routine practice at most large industrial firms in the wake of the brief recession of 1920–1921, with the sudden drop in demand a decade later, companies often made up their losses by a combination of layoffs and a sharp increase in their rates of output. Those workers who were fortunate enough to preserve their jobs were expected to work two and three times as hard for the same pay.[1]

In the midst of such pressures, the first Roosevelt administration passed the NIRA, which created a legal framework for collective bargaining as well as a bureaucratic process to settle conflicts between labor and management. In large industrial centers like Flint, workers responded with instant enthusiasm, joining their AFL-affiliated unions by the thousands. In turn, to gain control over this new organizing movement, and to thwart the union drives that were making headway among their workers, many companies created their own "Employee Representation Plans" (ERPs) or revived their existing company unions that, under recent speedup policies, had grown dormant. Over the next two years, the majority of those workers who joined an ERP or an AFL union came to sense that these organizations, which promised to represent the interests of the rank and file, were just so many "cautionary measures" to keep genuine unions out of the mass production industries: they seemed designed only to undermine more serious efforts by workers to have a say in their working conditions. Nevertheless, because it sparked a popular interest in joining unions early in the decade, it was evident that the NIRA had provided the impetus for the rebirth of the industrial union movement, which culminated in a string of victorious CIO organizing campaigns between 1936 and 1940 in mass production industries such as steel, autos, and rubber.[2]

In addition to the outdated tactics and organizational principles of the AFL in the 1930s (outdated as far as mass industrial workers were concerned), the efforts of industrial workers to organize were also severely hampered by company spies who infiltrated and dominated the ranks of both the AFL unions and the company-controlled ERPs.[3] Moreover, in many hard-fought organizing drives the AFL leaders sided with the company against a workforce whose interests they claimed to represent (Kraus 10; Wechsler 227).

Such was the situation of mass industrial workers at the time of the creation of the CIO, in October of 1935. With respect to the automobile industry, to organize its workforce the AFL had created the UAW in August 1935. Shortly after this, in October of 1935, a group of eight dissenting unions within the AFL, under the leadership of John L. Lewis, formed their own organization to advocate for industrial unions in mass production industries. Originally calling itself the Committee for Industrial Organization, the dissenting group changed its name to the Congress for Industrial Organization after its unions were suspended from the AFL. By May of 1936, at the first convention of the UAW, the autoworkers voted to join the CIO and launch an organizing drive at GM. In response, GM promptly hired a small army of Pinkertons to counter these fledgling efforts to organize its workforce. At Ford, on the other hand, the company relied on its own "service" men to spy on workers and thwart the efforts of the UAW organizers.

In spite of the various kinds of illegal measures that were routinely taken by the automakers to block unionization drives, in late December 1936 the GM sitdown strike began, launching a series of UAW organizing drives in the auto industry that would culminate in a string of victories for the young industrial union. The GM strike started unexpectedly with a sitdown on December 28, 1936, at the Cleveland Fisher body plant. This was followed by another sitdown on December 30 at Fisher Body Plant 1 in Flint, and a third sitdown on December 31 at Flint's Fisher Body Plant 2. Although it was mainly a spontaneous movement onto which the UAW had not yet "securely attached" itself, the union was able to use these large-scale, rank-and-file actions to swell its membership quickly. Forty-four days after it began, on February 11, the UAW claimed a definitive victory in the GM strike, and a contract was signed covering workers at twenty GM plants on March 12, 1937, which recognized the UAW as the autoworkers' sole national bargaining agent. The UAW then went on to achieve organizing victories at Chrysler and, finally, at Ford—which did not sign a contract with the union until as late as June 1941.[4]

A New Tactic: The Sitdown Strike

Because of the relative speed with which the CIO campaigns were able to organize entire industries made up of thousands of mass workers—in large part thanks to the efficacy of the sitdown strike tactic—the CIO acquired an almost mythical image in the eyes of industrial workers (Kraus 293; Torigian 344). This image stemmed in part from the publicity the CIO received during the first major industrial strike that it supported, among the rubber workers in Akron, Ohio. In fact, John L. Lewis made his very first speech as the leader of the CIO for these workers on January 19, 1936, while on a visit to Akron to boost their morale (McKenney 250–251; Vorse 5). Ten days after hearing Lewis's speech, the rubber workers of Akron engaged in their first extended sitdown strike. It was started by workers at the Firestone tire plant, on January 29, 1936. During a fairly common and petty shop-floor dispute, a dozen workers in the department of truck tire builders abruptly sat down and refused to work until management had addressed their grievance. Louis Adamic relates what happened next:

> In a few minutes several other departments of the extremely complex and delicately organized production process in the factory, which employed seven thousand men, were in a mess. What had happened?
>
> Hundred of workers who did not know what the sitdown was about but who belonged more or less to the rank-and-file element experienced a thrill. A sitdown in the plant! Well, what do you know! In no time the most important departments of the factory were at a standstill. Thousands of workers sat down. Some because they wanted to, more because everything stopped anyhow.
>
> And sitting by their machines, caldrons, boilers, and work benches, they talked. Some realized *for the first time how important they were in the process of rubber production.* Twelve men had practically stopped the works! Almost any dozen or score of them could do it! In some departments six could do it! The active rank-and-filers, scattered through the various sections of the plant, took the initiative in saying, "We've got to stick with 'em!" And they stuck with them, union and non-union men alike. Most of them were non-union. . . . Superintendents, foremen, and straw bosses were dashing about. . . . Telephones were ringing all over the plant. This sudden suspension of production was costing the company many hundreds of dollars every minute. . . . In less than an hour the dispute which had led to the sitdown was settled—full victory for the men! (*My America* 406)

Adamic's account of the outbreak of this brief but prophetic strike underscores one of the more notable features of the sitdown strike tactic:

its pedagogic function, which allows the workers in mass production industries to realize the enormous amount of power they possess. That a mere dozen workers (or sometimes fewer) are able to cripple the operations of an entire plant employing thousands of workers proves how vital each and every worker is to the complex process of mass production. As degrading and dehumanizing as the experience of highly mechanized labor may be, the power that even a brief work stoppage has to force concessions from management demonstrates how precisely this *kind* of labor invests individual workers with the potential to disrupt the technologically linked process of production in the factory. In short, the degree of workplace bargaining power that workers possess seems, at least in this case, to be directly proportional to the degree of degradation—monotony, mechanization, deskilling, and alienation—they must endure on the job. Ultimately, the success of the Firestone workers' strike made the use of the sitdown tactic a standard policy in all the rubber strikes that were to follow over the course of 1936, in addition to inspiring the autoworkers, whose own sitdown strikes made headlines throughout much of the following year (Kraus 46; Vorse 7, 11).

Regarding the GM sitdown strike, which began a year after that of the rubber workers in late December 1936, the autoworkers and UAW organizers took the structure of the plants themselves into account as a crucial element in their strike strategy. For instance, they calculated that they could virtually paralyze GM's national operations by targeting the Fisher body plants in Flint, Michigan. Likewise, the Chevrolet no. 4 plant (one of nine major factories in Flint), where all the engines for every Chevrolet produced in the country were made, was for this reason "a unit destined to play a most significant role in the final phases of the strike" (Kraus 57, 78–79). On a national level, GM's operations in Flint were fed by, and in turn supplied, numerous parts manufacturers and auto assembly plants. The strike thus idled thousands of additional workers and machines, every day costing GM millions of dollars in lost revenue. While weekly sales at Ford and Chrysler during the strike were rising, GM's fell sharply, from their usual thirty-two thousand to a mere fifteen hundred units. As the strike was nearing its end in the first week of February 1937, GM's output had shrunk from fifty thousand cars per month to only 125.[5]

Inside the occupied GM plants, the sitdowners were the focus of national attention for two reasons. First, soon after the strike began, a fierce debate broke out on a national scale over the legality of the sitdown strike tactic. The GM sitdowns—as well as a host of similar strikes that they inspired—brought with them "a furor of discussion about their significance, their origin, and their economic and social morality" (Levinson 223).[6] Second, the autoworkers were praised in the national press for their overall discipline and restraint and for the "basic democratic society" they seemed to have created over the course of their six-week strike (Fine 156–177; Kraus 93). A regular feature of daily life in the occupied plants were the town hall meetings where individual workers could criticize or debate the strategy of the strike on equal terms with those whom they had elected as their leaders. In many of the plants the workers even devised their own judicial system, made up of "kangaroo" courts, in which judges and attorneys drawn from their ranks dealt with strikers who broke the rules of the community (Fine 159–160).

Beyond these headline-making features of the GM strike, however, there was something about the idea of thousands of assembly-line hands spontaneously occupying the huge factories in which they worked that inspired imaginations throughout the country. In Henry Kraus's words, it was as though the rest of the country suddenly "had a flash of the truly profound significance to the workers' cause" of this new weapon, the sit-down strike (Kraus 181). At last, it seemed, the resources of mass workers had proven to be "superior to those of their opponents," and who could tell where this new phase of the labor movement would lead?

Among the striking workers themselves, the long-drawn-out nature of the sitdowns, combined with their generally inspirational character, provided the perfect stimulus for new forms of creative expression. Henry Kraus relates how, at the victory celebration during the closing days of the GM strike, the autoworkers gathered at Pengelly Auditorium to represent the major events of their strike in the form of a play, co-written by the novelist Josephine Herbst and the labor journalist Mary Heaton Vorse. Kraus's description of the event—much in the spirit of the reviews of the IWW's *Pageant of the Paterson Strike* in 1913—concluded with the assertion that this theatrical spectacle signaled a "class awakening," specifically that of "a mass soul in birth" (292).

The Sitdown Strike Wave

In hindsight, one of the most significant aspects of the sitdown strikes in both the rubber and the auto industries was the way in which these mass actions brought to a head a long-standing debate within the U.S. labor movement over the relative value of two types of strike tactics: spontaneous, dramatic, rank-and-file actions that come as a surprise to both managers and union leaders, as opposed to more disciplined and carefully planned actions that respect the basic chain of command of the union's leadership structure.[7] The conflict boiled down to the fact that, once a labor dispute had been resolved and a contract successfully negotiated, the union, in Jeremy Brecher's words, was forced to become "the agency for limiting workers' direct action" on the job (222). At the same time, however, it was equally clear that no contract with management, however favorable its terms, would be "enough to control workers who had just discovered their own power" (223).[8]

As soon as workers in mass production industries realized how much pressure they could exert simply by sitting down for a few minutes in the middle of a shift, they began regularly resorting to this device to settle even the most minor of grievances. A tactic that was drawn directly from the worker's experience at the point of production, the sitdown strike thus proved to be inherently uncontrollable by managers and union leaders alike. Plus, as a tactic, it was both inspiring and contagious to other workers, for not only was it easy to carry out, but it was almost always guaranteed as a quick, effective means for workers to settle grievances in their favor (Adamic, *My America* 411). It would not take long for workers in other mass production industries to realize the enormous amount of power that they, too, could exercise—directly from their position on the assembly line in the Fordist factories where they worked.

From the very start of the GM sitdown strike, workers in other industries responded with enthusiastic support for the innovative tactics of the autoworkers, immediately embracing the sitdown tactic and testing it out in their own places of employment. Consequently, in the month of January 1937 there were no fewer than 25 sitdown strikes, affecting 74,479 workers across the country. In February there were 47 such strikes, affecting 31,236 workers. The sitdown strike wave finally reached its peak in the next month (March 1937), just as the GM workers were declaring their definitive victory, with 170 sitdown strikes, involving 167,210 workers in various occupations. The historian Sidney Fine relates how the city of Detroit "was at the center of the sit-down strike storm in that month, and the tactic had become so ubiquitous that a Detroit *News* reporter remarked, 'Sitting down has replaced baseball as a national pastime, and sitter-downers clutter up the landscape in every direction'" (331).

In the aftermath of the autoworkers' victory at GM, the wave of sitdown strikes continued to sweep across the country. At GM alone, between March and June of 1937, the company reported 170 sitdown strikes in their various plants. On a typical day in May, for example, a news service reported 24 strikes, of which 16 were sitdowns (Brecher 223; Levinson 223). Overnight, it seemed, the tactic had become popular with workers in every imaginable industry and occupation. Whereas there were 48 recorded sitdown strikes in 1936 (out of a total of 2,712 strikes) involving about eighty-eight thousand workers, in 1937 there were 477 recorded sitdown strikes (out of a total of 4,740 strikes), involving roughly four hundred thousand workers (Fine 331).

A Battle over Representation

The last third of Thomas Bell's 1941 novel, *Out of This Furnace*, tells the story of western Pennsylvania steelworkers in the 1930s and their efforts to organize the steel industry through the support of the first Roosevelt administration's NIRA, of which Section 7 (a) provided a legal framework for the expansion of industrial unions. As Bell sees it, the struggle to organize steelworkers amounts to a contest over the right to represent these workers. Who has the authority to represent? Of what does this authority consist? What is the aim of representation? How are "representatives" both formally and functionally determined in relation to those who are represented by them?

To outflank or suppress the growth of legitimate unions that the NIRA sought to facilitate, many of the large steel companies at this time created (or reactivated) their so-called "Employee Representation Plans" (ERPs). The purpose of any given ERP was simple: to offer workers a system of representation in the workplace that could be entirely controlled by the management of a firm. Management believed that to the extent that workers felt they had some say in their working conditions, and some channel through which their grievances could be redressed, they would be less eager to form unions of their own—unions that were not under the control, or subject to the immediate needs, of management.

The youngest of the three steelworker-protagonists of Bell's novel, Dobie, sees through the charade of the company's newly formed ERP. Sensing that the sole purpose of the ERP is to contain workers' unrest, he refuses to vote in an election of worker "representatives" at the behest of management (Bell 288). Shortly after the election, once the ERP is up and running, it quickly becomes obvious to Dobie and his coworkers what such a company union is actually designed to accomplish: "It was almost, but not quite, funny. As a labor union the E.R.P. was a joke. . . . Its purpose clearly was to circumvent the law and to hamstring genuine organization by splitting the men, supplying an approved refuge for the timid and the servile, isolating the recalcitrant" (292).

The logical option for Dobie and the rest of the steelworkers is to seek the assistance of the AFL's Amalgamated Association of Iron, Steel, and Tin Workers union. Incited by the support that the federal government's NIRA legislation promised to give them, steelworkers swelled the ranks of the Amalgamated in 1933, expecting that the union would carry out a national organizing drive throughout the industry. However, the steelworkers in *Out of This Furnace* soon learn that every one of their requests for aid is met with the same response from the leadership of the Amalgamated: namely, be patient, and let your leaders decide when and where to apply pressure on the companies. As Bell describes it, "There was a growing demand from within the ranks that the union seek recognition. Warnings by the union's executives—each one more like a rebuke than the last—that the time wasn't propitious only added to the rising discontent" (306).

One of the steelworkers in the novel, Gralji, finally confronts the local representative of the Amalgamated, an organizer named Walsh: "The men keep asking me when is the union going to ask for recognition.... They say if we get recognition, good. If we don't, they say we ought to go on strike. But as long as we don't have recognition we can't do anything" (Bell 306). To Gralji's warning, Walsh simply replies that if the workers in his local "knew a little more about it they wouldn't be so impatient. Rome ... wasn't built in a day" (307). Much like any scientific manager in an industrial workplace, Walsh relies on the knowledge and experience that he is presumed to have as a seasoned organizer to hold in check the demands of the workers he represents. "It might be a good idea," Walsh continues, "if they let Pittsburgh run the union. They've been doing it for a long time.... Pittsburgh knows what it's doing ... and the sooner a lot of the men around here realize it the better it'll be for all concerned" (307).

The style of union bureaucracy illustrated by the figure of Walsh is a direct outgrowth and reflection of the corporate managerial bureaucracies that had been created in the wake of scientific management. The hierarchical division between an unskilled labor force and a host of "expert" managers who define and oversee the tasks they perform, Bell's novel implies, is literally reproduced in the relationship between workers and their union leaders. In this case, a presumably ignorant and naive membership needs to be guided by an expert and select group of manager-organizers. As Dobie admits to his fellow steelworkers,

"It makes me sore to think how much a guy like Walsh knows that we could use. As it is, we've got to take his word for everything. . . . I even went to the library but they ain't got anything. For that matter, I don't even know if there is such a book."

"They probably wouldn't carry it if there was."

"The only trouble with books," Gralji said, "is they're written by writers." (Bell 308)

Gralji's final remark suggests that Walsh's knowledge as an organizer is analogous to the kind of book knowledge that specifically writers—not workers—possess. Because there are different types of knowledge, the kind that Walsh possesses and controls may turn out to be unrelated to the kind that the workers actually require. That is to say, as workers, rather than union officials, the steelworkers may in fact possess a kind of knowledge that is nowhere to be found in books: a non- or prediscursive form of knowledge that is a function of their experience in the material environment of the steel mill.

The latent tension between the members and the officials of the Amalgamated union over questions of strategy and authority—a variation of earlier "craft" disputes—soon developed into an all-out war. Beset with louder and more insistent demands from the steelworkers, Mike Tighe, the national president of the Amalgamated, started to withdraw organizers from the union's locals in the Pittsburgh region, thus "letting the rebellious lodges shift for themselves" (Bell 314). When workers responded by establishing their own rank-and-file campaigns to organize the industry, Tighe, seeing in this grassroots movement "a Bolshevik plot to destroy the AFL," revoked their union charters, finally expelling 75 percent of the members from the union. "Then, like a steel plant manager threatened with collective bargaining," Bell's narrator caustically remarks, "he summoned police to protect Amalgamated headquarters" (342).

Once they discover that both the steel companies and the AFL unions are pitted against them, the workers come to view the support that the NIRA seemed to offer them as simply another means to contain rank-and-file labor unrest: "It was something workers all over the country learned that crowded summer [of 1934]. While a great drought turned whole states into dusty wastelands, the hundreds of thousands to whom Section 7 (A) had been quite literally a promise of freedom learned the true value of that promise. The San Francisco longshoremen, the Minneapolis truckmen, the Milwaukee utility workers, the Kohler workers, the textile workers—strike after strike was systematically sabotaged by Government officials or broken by troops" (Bell 324–325). Left to their own devices, the steelworkers in Bell's novel assess their situation to determine what, exactly, they are up against. They conclude that the most serious obstacle standing in the way of their attempts to organize is the administrative bureaucracy that pervades both the steel mills and the union. As Dobie puts it in one of his final confrontations with Walsh, the Amalgamated's professional organizer: "You've been around unions so long maybe you've forgotten what they're for. But we haven't. And we ain't going to stand for what's going on much longer, whether it's in the mill or in the union" (311).

Dobie's realization—that industrial workers who seek reliable forms of representation must develop strategies to confront the power of administrative bureaucracies, wherever they may be found—marks a critical turning point in *Out of This Furnace*. For it is at this point that Bell's fictional steelworkers learn that their struggle to organize is in fact a struggle over the right to define the terms of their own representation in the workplace. The conflict between steelworkers and management is thus articulated through a discursive battle over the meaning of concepts such as "representation" and "recognition" in the context of the industrial workplace. In the following excerpt from the novel, the character of Burke is a steelworker who wants to discuss the grievances and demands of his fellow workers with the heads of the company. After waiting months during which their requests for a meeting are routinely ignored, Burke, Dobie, and a few of the other steelworkers finally manage to meet with Flack, their plant manager, and Mr. Forbes, a company executive who is described as "a representative of the City Office, with full authority." From the very start of the conversation, with Mr. Forbes's initial question to Burke, it is clear what the stakes of the conflict involve:

> "You claim to represent a number of our employees?"
> "The ones that are in the union. Yessir."
> Mr. Forbes leaned back and clasped his hands and bent his head toward them thoughtfully. "Now as you probably know," he said, "it is the policy of the management to recognize any individual or organization as the spokesman for the employees they represent.... However... I think you will agree that we must exercise a little discrimination. In other words, we must have proof that the spokesmen really do represent the employees they say they do and that those employees have authorized the spokesmen to speak for

them. Otherwise anyone could walk in here and claim they represented so many of our employees and we'd have nothing but confusion.... Have you any proof that you represent a number of our employees?"

"We've got our membership list and dues book. That ought to be proof enough."

"Can you arrange to let us examine it and check the names with our payroll?"

"I don't see how. The membership list is supposed to be confidential."

Mr. Forbes glanced at Flack and shrugged ever so slightly. "Then what proof have we," he asked, "that you do actually represent the employees you claim to?"

"We've got proof. We know how many men we've got in the union."

"But we don't. We don't know how many employees you represent or which ones, and until we have figures and proof there's not much that we can do...."

"When it comes to proof, what the hell proof have we got that you have the right to ask us questions?..."

"Mr. Forbes," Flack said coldly, "is here as a representative of the City Office, with full authority...."

"We came here to discuss matters that affected the men we represent. That's what we asked for a conference for, not to argue whether we have a right to be here or not."

"Very well. What are the matters which affect the men you say you represent?"

"We don't just say we represent them. We do. We've been instructed by our membership to ask that the company recognize their union, the Amalgamated Association, and to confer with you about signing a contract covering wages, hours, vacations with pay, and seniority."

"I'm afraid you're laboring under a misapprehension.... Even if Mr. Flack or I wanted to, we have no authority to sign a contract. That's something you'll have to take up with the City Office. As for recognizing your organization, I told you before that it is the policy of the company to recognize any group or individual—"

"I know. I heard you before."

Mr. Forbes's lips thinned. "Then I have no more to say...."

"So the answer is No?"

Mr. Forbes's eyebrows rose. "What was the question?"

"No recognition, no contract?"

"We've recognized you, haven't we, in granting this conference? And I repeat, neither Mr. Flack nor I has the authority to sign a contract. As you probably know, it's been the consistent policy of the corporation not to—"

"All right, all right. I guess there's no use keeping this up." He rose. "Let's go, boys." (Bell 317–320)

As fruitless as this meeting may seem in light of the steelworkers' broader efforts to achieve union recognition, within the context of the novel a scene such as this concisely illustrates two important aspects of the contest between labor and management in the mass industrial workplace.

To begin with, at stake here is the extent to which a certain kind of knowledge—of union membership and union-oriented activities—is recognized as belonging to the collective body of workers as their exclusive property. To be able to recognize a small number of workers as the official representatives of the others, Mr. Forbes claims that he needs to know what Burke and Dobie already know. Without having access to information that the workers themselves control, Forbes insists that his only option is to treat Burke and Dobie merely *as if* they represented the rest of the steelworkers, in a purely hypothetical sense.[9]

Managerial power, in Forbes's view, is therefore a matter of gaining access to a kind of knowledge that workers alone possess. Just as Frederick Taylor thirty years earlier proved that managerial control over the labor process required a transfer of intellectual property rights—namely, a transfer of knowledge from individual skilled workers to a small army of so-called scientific experts, who analyzed and reformulated this knowledge, thus claiming ownership over it—so here Mr. Forbes is attempting to wrest the knowledge of the union's affairs from those very workers who lay claim to it as their own. Much as the skills of previous generations of industrial workers gave them a degree of control over how their labor power was employed at the point of production, the steelworkers' exclusive knowledge of union affairs gives them (as well as other, recently deskilled mass workers) a measure of bargaining power in their dealings with management.

Closely linked to this struggle over knowledge as property is the question of representational authority: the problem of determining who has the authority to speak for whom. Because he does not know what the workers know (the details of union membership), Mr. Forbes, exercising the "full authority" that has been granted him by the City Office, is not willing to grant a similar type of representational authority to Burke and Dobie. As Forbes sees it, then, the authority of workers to represent themselves is premised on *his* ability to gain access to precisely that kind of knowledge that would allow him to control—and significantly undermine—their authority as representatives. In other words, he is willing to grant representational authority only to those whom he is able to deprive of the power to exercise this very authority. From the standpoint of the steelworkers, on the other hand, the authority to represent is strictly a function of the particular type of knowledge they possess, which they are withholding from Forbes. Hence, whatever authority they have to represent their fellow steelworkers is premised on their retaining control over this knowledge.

Underlying the question of representation in *Out of This Furnace* is, finally, a more basic struggle over the right to possess and exercise knowledge, power, and authority in the workplace. This is made clear by the fact that Mr. Forbes's power as "a representative of the City Office, with full authority," is still, oddly enough, "no authority to sign a contract." By refusing to discuss the terms of a labor contract, Forbes is disavowing the very authority that he invoked when he demanded access to the union's membership records. He instead tells the steelworkers that if they want to discuss the terms of a labor contract this is something they will "have to take up with the City Office." Yet who else if not a representative of the City Office "with full authority"—namely, Forbes himself—could be vested with the authority to sign a contract with the workers? If Forbes represents the City Office with full authority, why does he insist that the workers have to take up the problem of a contract with the City Office? Would the staff at the City Office have an even fuller form of authority? If so, then how could they, too, be seen as the representatives of their own authority, since they are presumably the "thing itself" that Forbes, the individual, is representing?

Forbes refuses to discuss the terms of a labor contract because, on some level, he is aware of the difference between saying that he represents the power of the City Office and actually having the right to exercise this power. Similarly, Forbes's question to Burke, "What are the matters which affect the men *you say* you represent?" implies that, in the eyes of the City Office, steelworkers who claim to represent their coworkers are simply speaking on behalf of an imaginary power (that of the rank and file) whose very existence the company refuses to accept as a reality. Hence the tactic of Burke's reply: "We don't just say we represent them.

We do." Burke underscores here that the fact of workers' acts of self-representation, in spite of Forbes's insinuations to the contrary, is not itself a representation but a material force, one that cannot be reduced to an abstract claim (which would make it verifiable as either a truth or a lie). Instead, the reality of workers representing the interests of their fellow workers, in the eyes of Burke and Dobie, is in no way subject to dispute. It is thus a kind of truth in its own right. But because it is also an action—something these workers are actually doing and not just talking about doing—it will never be reducible to the form of a logical statement that could be demonstrably "true" according to the terms of the categorical distinction between true and false. The fact that they *say* they are doing it will therefore never be enough to suggest that the rank-and-file workers' movement is a kind of lie, as Forbes seems to think. That is, where Forbes sees a basic falsehood of the steelworkers' movement in the fact that it relies on linguistic modes of expression (which expose it to the inherent ambiguities of representation), the workers see its truth as being a function of its ontological state, which changes from one moment to the next because it expresses an active and dynamic force.

Thus the steelworkers pit the material force of their grassroots activism against the abstract representational authority of the company, of which the primary example is the management-controlled "Employee Representation Plan," or ERP. Dobie conceives a way to hijack this organization by first encouraging the steelworkers to join it en masse, in order, then, to see how far they can use its bureaucratic structure to apply pressure to the company. "We could take over the whole E.R.P.," he tells his coworkers, "and by the time we were through I'll bet the company would be wishing to God it'd never thought of it.... Act as though the E.R.P. was an honest-to-God union. Make a stink every time a foreman looks at a man cross-eyed. And never let up" (Bell 344–345). With this suggestion, Dobie is proposing a kind of "unslacking guerilla warfare inside the E.R.P.," as Bell's narrator put it; a rank-and-file takeover of a representational authority that was meant to be under the exclusive control of the company managers. The goal, according to Dobie, is to test the bureaucratic limits of this organization by "passing resolutions for their publicity value in the minutes, belaboring the City Office with protests, straining the structure of the E.R.P. until it gave at the joints" (384).

Dobie's plan to act "as though" the ERP were designed to facilitate a genuine form of worker representation is simply a way of using the company's own tactics against them. After all, from the moment of its inception, the ERP was never anything more than a hoax, a thinly disguised ruse of the company to suppress potential unrest among its workforce. By way of response, Dobie's idea of hijacking the organization suggests the workers' own counterhoax: by appearing to take seriously and literally the expressed aims of the ERP, the steelworkers will retroactively prove that, from the start, it was never meant to function as an actual union (one that effectively represented their interests).

While it sounds like a potentially subversive idea, the goal of "straining the structure of the E.R.P. until it gave at the joints" finally teaches Bell's steelworkers that nothing is to be gained by playing on the company's terms. Prior to this moment in the novel, when disappointed steelworkers are first beginning to abandon the Amalgamated union in droves, Dobie is still convinced that "the company is our best organizer" (Bell 332). In his view, ultimately, it will be the absurd policies of the company, rather than the efforts of professional organizers, that will motivate the steelworkers to return to the union. However, just after they try unsuccessfully to use the ERP to fight the company, Dobie loses faith in this tactic of "unslacking guerilla warfare" from within the organizational structures of the company. He remarks: "I don't see how we can do much more from the inside than we've already done. Not with the set-up they've got now. What we need is some outside help, and I only hope Lewis means what he says about organizing the steel mills" (353). Dobie's reference to John L. Lewis is revealing insofar as it suggests that "outside help," according to Bell's characters, consists primarily of the influence of charismatic labor leaders—as opposed to, say, new methods of organizing workers at the point of production.

In fact, when such outside help finally arrives, it appears, not in the person of Lewis, but by way of the national media who have been "driven to hysteria by the Detroit sit-down strikers" (Bell 404). The success of the sitdown strikes in Flint and Detroit effectively scared the steel companies into complying with the demands of Lewis, Philip Murray, and the rest of the CIO organizers in the steel industry (the Steel Workers Organizing Committee, or SWOC). The rank-and-file steelworkers themselves—at least judging from Bell's novel—have practically nothing to do with the victory that the CIO celebrated by signing a contract with the major steel corporations. Yet Dobie, proud of the role that he believes he and his fellow workers played in the CIO campaign to organize the industry, explains to his wife that "the company signed because they had to, because we were licking the pants off of them" (405). Certainly, from a historical standpoint, it would have been far more accurate—and less self-serving—for Dobie to state that the new *tactic* of the sitdown strike in the auto industry was indirectly licking the pants off of the company by frightening them. Instead, he ascribes this victory directly to the efforts of steelworkers like himself.[10]

Writing and the Question of Representation: Debates on the Depression-Era Left

Leftist authors in the United States during the early 1930s took as a given the Marxian base/superstructure model of society as a concise guide for their theoretical and practical goals. The fact that its abuse (both potential and actual) as a substitute for more nuanced forms of analysis at times fostered a less-than-democratic organizational environment for their activities was acknowledged by them as a necessary stage in the world revolutionary process. Thus a certain measure of vanguard authoritarianism was not only justified but encouraged among many writers and political activists on the left during the so-called Third Period (1928–1935), especially since this was an era of geopolitical crisis marked by the combined threats of fascism and a world war that was presumed to be imminent.

If there were any doubts among radicals at the time as to the usefulness of orthodox Leninist theory for making sense of U.S. capitalism, these could be dispelled by invoking the mimetic structure of the U.S. Communist Party's vanguard program: by reflecting the real structures of managerial control in capitalist enterprises, vanguardist strategy seemed to guarantee a real program of revolutionary social change, even within the relatively limited sphere of cultural production (Seaver, "Proletarian Novel" 102). Thus, by defining their social and political functions in literal accordance with the dualistic schema of base/superstructure, the members of the revolutionary superstructure (the vanguard) could consider themselves "brain" workers, coordinators, or organizers, whose task it was to relay strategies to the "muscle" workers at the level of the base.

Translated into categories of literary analysis, the role of the radical writer and critic was inferred, then, to be a kind of mimetic reflection of the role of the professional revolutionary organizer, whose job was to make sense out of the words on the page in much the same way that the organizer made strikes out of the workers of a given factory. In the words of Michael Gold, the communist critic and esteemed founder of U.S. "proletarian" literature, "Literature is one of the products of a civilization like steel or textiles. It is not a child of eternity, but of time. It is always the mirror of its age. It is not any more mystic in its origin than a ham sandwich" (186). By positing this sort of direct material correspondence between literary and socioeconomic forms of production, radical writers such as Gold and Edwin Seaver were able to assert that "the growth of the proletarian novel in the United States can be measured accurately by the growth of the American proletariat and the growing recognition among our writers of the existence and historical significance of this proletariat" ("What Is" 6). Furthermore, because leftist critics at the time imagined the revolutionary proletariat as the direct offshoot of modern industrial production processes, they were convinced that these processes (and the changes they were undergoing) would have to be mimetically reflected in their own theoretical models of literary and aesthetic representation. Only in this way, they believed, could the figure of the revolutionary mass worker be drawn by them in an accurate and politically effective manner (Gold 205–206).

Such a mimetic imperative soon generated a heated conflict among leftist writers over the definition of the activity of writing, and, more generally, over the criteria for determining the revolutionary status of any given work of art. On the one hand, writers such as John Dos Passos who identified with the modernist avant-garde saw writing as a type of highly skilled technical work akin to that of an engineer. His speech for the American Writers' Congress in April 1935, "The Writer as Technician," was deliberately intended to counter the opposite view of writing that was espoused by figures such as Jack Conroy and Michael Gold. Dos Passos saw himself restoring dignity to the act of writing as an essentially independent, creative process. The professional "technician" of writing, as he described it, was a direct descendant of the romantic figure of the solitary genius: "The importance of a writer, as of a scientist, depends upon his ability to influence subsequent thought. In his relation to society a professional writer is a technician just as much as an electrical engineer is" (Dos Passos 79; cf. Kant 168–183, 212).

Opposed to Dos Passos's view—which suggested the "type" of the writer-technician that could fill the managerial position in a Taylorized system of production—Jack Conroy's speech at the same congress, "The Worker as Writer," argued that writers ought to identify so closely with the working class that it would no longer be possible to distinguish their words from the everyday language of miners, steel workers, or strike pamphleteers: "To me a strike bulletin or an impassioned leaflet are of more moment than three hundred prettily and faultlessly written pages about the private woes of a gigolo or the biological ferment of a society dame" (83). Conroy's disparaging remarks about the supposed decadence inherent to the form, content, and self-conscious representationality—or fixation on language—of professional bourgeois writers echoed Michael Gold's description, in his 1929 manifesto "Go Left, Young Writers!," of the ideal (male) proletarian writer:

> When I say "go leftward," I don't mean the temperamental bohemian left, the stale old Paris posing, the professional poetizing, etc. No, the real thing; a knowledge of working-class life in America gained from first-hand contacts, and a hard precise philosophy of 1929 based on economics, not verbalisms. . . . [The revolutionary writer] goes after a kind of flesh and blood reality, however crude, instead of the smooth perfect thing that is found in books. . . . He is a Red but has few theories. It is all instinct with him. His writing is no conscious straining after proletarian art, but the natural flower of his environment. He writes that way because it is the only way for him. His "spiritual" attitudes are all mixed up with tenements, factories, lumber camps and steel mills, because that is his life. ("Go Left" 188–189)

On one side of the debate over the nature of writing and the role of the revolutionary writer, then, were a group of authors—including Dos Passos, James T. Farrell, Josephine Herbst, and Henry Roth—who maintained that the purpose of creative writing resembled that of the social engineer: by rearranging or reorganizing the representational elements that constituted the discursive basis of the modern world, the writer produced a new representation, which could more accurately reflect the socioeconomic forces underlying working-class experience. In contrast to this view of writing (which would be more firmly consolidated in the politico-aesthetic doctrine of the reorganized *Partisan Review* after 1937), writers such as Joseph North, Jack Conroy, and Michael Gold maintained that the purpose of creative writing was analogous to that of the factory hand: by refusing to acknowledge, much less exploit, the (necessarily) representational aspect of writing, the writer pledged to produce concrete things rather than mere representations of things—"a kind of flesh and blood reality, however crude, instead of the smooth perfect thing that is found in books." This was made possible only through a redefinition of the act of writing such that it was seen, no longer to represent, but actually to produce, real things in the world, much as a steel worker produces real beams of steel.[11]

Although both these groups of writers were equally committed to the goal of socialist revolution, and both were equally convinced of the validity of Leninist theory for understanding U.S. capitalism and the crises that resulted from it, they located themselves at opposite ends of the spectrum with regard to the representational character of their work. The members of the vanguardist group were comfortable adapting themselves to the presumably bourgeois notion of the writer-as-technician, while the members of the second group wanted to do away with this notion and thereby align the activity of writing with other kinds of brute physical labor. Regardless of their differences, however, both groups thought of themselves as workers—either "brain" workers or "muscle" workers—and both, therefore, also claimed the right to be recognized as members of the working class.[12]

However, neither of these groups was comfortable with the idea that their work as writers placed them at a remove from the actual day-to-day struggles of the working class. The concept of the "worker-writer" was thus created precisely to overcome the perceived gulf between writing and working, just as it had presumably done in the case of the ex-bourgeois intellectual John Reed, who, as Gold eulogized him, "identified himself so completely with the working class, he undertook every danger for the revolution; he forgot his Harvard education, his genius, his popularity, his gifted body and mind so completely that no one else remembered them any more; there was no gap between Jack Reed and the workers any longer" ("John Reed" 153–154).

Power at the Point of Production

Robert Cantwell's 1934 novel about lumber mill workers in the Pacific Northwest, *The Land of Plenty*, was later acclaimed for foreshadowing the sitdown strikes and factory occupations that marked the second half of the 1930s. More than any of its predecessors, this novel established the point of production inside the modern factory as the most important site of workers' acts of resistance. Looking back on the legacy of radical literature in the 1930s, Jack Conroy, the influential proletarian novelist and editor, noted how "the sit-down strikes in Detroit were in the future, but the abortive seizure of the factory in *The Land of Plenty* plainly was a portent of things to come" ("Robert Cantwell's *Land*" 83). Conroy's assessment of the novel's historical significance reflects Robert Cantwell's own statements in the July 3, 1934, issue of the *New Masses*, shortly after the novel was published: "I tried to imagine what would actually happen, in the sort of community I pictured, when the workers entered the factory, what new factors entered a strike situation, what advantages were gained, what hazards encountered." However, perhaps because, for Cantwell, this imagined scenario of workers taking possession of industrial factories still seemed inconceivable, he admitted that he "couldn't imagine clearly what would happen" in such an uprising and that "the novel suffers as a result" (qtd. in Conroy, "Robert Cantwell's *Land*" 83).

Much like Jack Conroy—author of radical novels such as *The Disinherited* (1933) and *A World to Win* (1935), and editor of the workers' literary journal *The Anvil*—Robert Cantwell was regularly praised by his contemporaries on the radical literary scene of the 1930s for being an authentic "proletarian" writer: that is, in Michael Gold's terms, one who possesses a concrete knowledge of the life of the working class from firsthand experience as an actual member of that class (as opposed to a bourgeois interloper). For instance, in his review of *The Land of Plenty*, Conroy makes a point of reminding readers that Cantwell's "four years in the plywood factory gave him ample grist for the novel" ("Robert Cantwell's *Land*" 77). Hence, the plywood factory represented in the novel is not merely the product of the writer's fancy but has tangible and lived ties to actual factories, which are filled with workers like Cantwell himself. As Conroy sees it, then, the fictitious working conditions elaborated in the novel accurately reflect the conditions of real workers in the industry. "In the years that have elapsed since publication of *The Land of Plenty*," he concludes his review, "it has had no close rival for authenticity and accuracy" (83).[13]

One of the more remarkable features of this novel is its depiction of the modern lumber mill as a complex network of integrated operations. Cantwell presents the environment of the factory in strictly technological terms—a structure in which every element is designed to meet the needs of mass production. Although the workforce here is made up of relatively isolated individuals who do not interact directly with one another, the structure of the plant itself facilitates communication between them, even while they are busy attending its various machines. For example, because the isolated workers are technologically connected to one another through integrated machine processes, the news of special events or visitors spreads automatically throughout the entire plant. Cantwell's narrator tells us how "when the manager or some of the investigators from the Eastern office came to the factory it was known almost before they had stepped inside by the people in the most distant parts of the building. The spreading of a warning in these cases was a responsibility which almost everyone accepted" (16). While such a simple form of communication may not seem to imply any potential for worker resistance—being, as it were, the serendipitous result of spatial relations that had been planned for other purposes—Cantwell's description of the effects of the modern factory on its workforce goes one step further. He suggests that workers' internalized sense of familiarity with this environment can itself serve as a medium for acts of communication among members of the industrial working class:

> Then there was another way in which the knowledge of anything unusual spread among the workers. Working there eight or ten or twelve hours a day they came to be as familiar with the factory as with their own homes, and so they became aware of minute differences that no one else could detect, and learned to recognize the fine shadings, the nuances of sounds that were only confused or terrifying to anyone who came in for the first time. They became aware too of the variations in what their experience had led them to expect; they became aware of the absence of usual impressions and this absence too had its meaning, and again without knowing why, they became restless and uncertain, the restlessness and uncertainty also communicating itself to others who did not know where it came from or why they felt it. Each worker was aware of the men on both sides of him, and when the drain of the workers toward the tideflat and the head end of the mill began, those who were left responded by being conscious of the absence of those who were ordinarily near them. (17)

Cantwell's description in this passage—a catalog of the "fine shadings" and "nuances" of activity in the factory—attaches significance to every aspect of the worker's day-to-day experience on the job. Even the sounds that are missing from the repertoire of machine noise acquire significance for the workers, since they indicate that something has shifted in the existential conditions at the point of production. When, later in the novel, a small number of workers begin to shut down the machines and occupy the interior of the plant, the character of Johnny, along with the rest of the workers standing outside the factory on the picket line, knows exactly what is happening through the change he detects in the sound of the machinery: "Then he heard a sound that the police did not recognize: the motors stopping inside the main part of the factory.... The saws were still running and the transfer chains, but Johnny heard and recognized the gradual loss of sound, the others heard it too, and knew that their own men were moving through the plant, cutting off the motors" (321).

This type of knowledge is the result not of rational calculation on the part of the mill workers but of their concrete, lived experience on the shop floor, surrounded by an elaborate web of machines that have been carefully coordinated with one another. As such, no other forms of knowledge can substitute for this firsthand acquaintance with the sights and sounds of the factory. Thus, Cantwell hints, the rank and file of mill workers possess a knowledge that only they have the power to control, a knowledge that cannot be taken away from them at the whim of the factory's managers because it permeates, and is closely interwoven with, their everyday experience as mass industrial workers.

At the start of the novel, just after an electrical power failure shuts off the lights in the factory while the machines are still running, Hagen, a popular leader among the plant's workers, makes a round of visits to the other men in the plant. With a certain measure of pride he reflects how, as soon as the lights in the plant went out, "A hundred men moved without orders, checking the thousands of dangers, the thousands of dangers no foreman could ever see, had ever heard of, could not even imagine." The workers have learned to interact with this highly mechanized environment through a series of mechanical responses and gestures. To Hagen, this fact alone proves that the mill workers possess a distinct form of knowledge that "no foreman could ever see" or "even imagine." Cantwell tells us how Hagen, in surveying the factory and consulting with the other millworkers, "walked, the flashlight swinging loosely at his side, the gray light washing across the floor. He did not need it. He knew the factory; he could find his way around it in the dark. The minute rises in the floor were blue-printed in his mind, and the narrow trails between the machines were so much a part of his way of thinking that he could not have forgotten them, even if he had wanted to" (49).

The second chapter of this study explored how several other novelists—Cruden, Sinclair, Conrad, and Rollins—depicted mass workers as though they had become fused with the material structures of the modern industrial workplace. Cantwell's novelistic technique in *The Land of Plenty* deploys a similar set of representational strategies, but his purpose for doing so seems markedly different. For Hagen, as for the rest of the mill's workers, the machinery of the mill is "so much a part of his way of thinking" that it has come to define him as an individual. Far from exerting a simply negative or dehumanizing effect on Hagen, this image of machine-consciousness reflects the emergence of a new type of humanity. Without trying to demonstrate that mass workers are basically degraded through their mechanization (à la Sinclair and Conrad), or that their identification with modern machinery has turned them into heroic models of efficiency (à la Cruden and Bell), Cantwell's novel, like that of Rollins, instead tries to show that mechanization is a necessary precondition for revolutionary acts of resistance on the part of mass industrial workers.

Hence, the mechanization of an entire workforce, in Cantwell's view, is not an inherently oppressive phenomenon. That which in other novels served either to condemn or to glorify the process of mechanized dehumanization has now come, in *The Land of Plenty*, to signify a uniquely technological environment that enables workers' acts of resistance. At stake here is no longer the humanity of the workers but the degree of workplace bargaining power they do or do not possess. Conversely, their gain or loss of such bargaining power does not imply, as a corollary, their gain or loss of presumably humanizing characteristics. Rather, from the perspective of Cantwell's narrative, it is precisely the mutual sense of familiarity between individual workers and their machines—and between the mass of workers and the mechanized environment of the modern factory—that allows them to fight against the various forces of industrial oppression.[14]

If in *The Land of Plenty* the technological environment of the modern lumber mill is characterized literally as a medium of communication between mass workers, then, by contrast, actual spoken language exists here only in the form of disembodied words. Spoken language thus becomes a medium of signification in relation to which the workers—by virtue of the physical and mechanized quality of their labor—feel deeply estranged. On the one hand, as Cantwell represents it, their experience as mass workers expresses itself only in a kind of "murmur" made up of "slow patient sentences," much like Clara Weatherwax's description, in *Marching! Marching!*, of workers' speech that is saturated with the materiality of their bodies. Similarly, in *The Land of Plenty*, workers who converse with each other are depicted as uttering "those tiny distilled drops of experience given in words so rich and so varied and inadequate" (Cantwell 50). On the other hand, more frequently there are simply "no words that could get down deep enough to say" what these workers feel about their experience in the lumber mill. For instance, Cantwell tells us that, when trying to discuss their feelings about Carl, the "efficiency" expert who has recently been hired as a plant supervisor, the workers "fell back on savage monotonous curses, never describing him except in terms of filth, of excrement, as though his very name suggested only some nauseating mess" (89). Likewise, when Johnny, one of the younger and less experienced workers in the mill, takes a short break from the monotony of his job, Cantwell tells us how he "relaxed from weariness, although he did not know it was weariness, for he had as yet found no name for the curious hunger to lie down which attacked him at this hour every night" (101). In light of these reminders of the inadequacy of language—in addition to many similar remarks found throughout the rest of the novel—it would appear that, if words fail these workers, it is not only because they have not yet learned or invented the right words to convey their experiences (as in Johnny's case) but because the lived quality of their experience cannot be symbolized as such. Their words cannot be made commensurate with their experience because their experience itself does not function as an object in a system of linguistic reference.

Although their relationship to conventional language has been thus attenuated—reduced to a minimal use of sounds and gestures—the workers treat the machines in the factory as their personal means of expression. Consequently, when the power lines of the plant are cut off, it is as if the workers' only source of communication were cut off as well: "The factory was quiet. Only now and then some sort of commotion spluttered meaninglessly like the chatter and blur of sparks leaping across a live wire. When the voices rose they were disembodied and unreal; the words drained off into the dark as though they did not care whether they were heard or not" (Cantwell 24). With the silencing of their machines, it would be reasonable to assume that Cantwell's workers have regained the ability to speak to one another. Yet this passage suggests that just the opposite is the case: once the factory operations grind to a halt, acts of linguistic communication between workers "splutter meaninglessly" in the empty and "unreal" form of "chatter."

Judging from these passages, then, it seems likely that Cantwell was deliberately trying to represent the means of production in the plant as if they were the most appropriate means of expression for the mass worker. Instead of figuring the modern machinery of the factory as the emblem of the worker's degradation through technology, Cantwell assigns a series of positive values to his images of the mechanized mass worker. In his novel, workers who do not depend on the language of conventional speech to communicate among themselves are clearly superior to the management, who can exercise their power over the workers only through verbal commands. Because the managers of the lumber mill, such as Carl, depend on acts of linguistic exchange to regulate and account for the workforce under their command, the rank-and-file workers in the factory equate the familiar activity of mute, machine-driven labor—for which words are not necessary—with the possibility of a certain type of shop-floor resistance. For example, to find alternative forms of light after the power outage in the factory, the militant worker Hagen "felt too tired to go through all the explanations that Carl would require; it would be easier to scrape up a crew somehow and get it done with no talking" (184).

In this manner, Cantwell illustrates how Hagen and the rest of the workers are able to operate the factory's machines more efficiently once they are given the opportunity to work on their own terms, free from the "expert" supervision of management. Likewise, we can infer, to be truly productive, these workers—in contrast to their managers—do not need to communicate with one another through conventional spoken language. In the same way that Robert Cruden described the character of Jim Brogan, the protagonist of *Conveyor*, as a "perfect unit" of productivity when he worked with his machine at a feverish pace, the machines in Cantwell's lumber mill represent simply an extension of these workers' own bodies and minds. Much as Jim Brogan felt himself "a perfect unit in the machine-filled building as it throbbed ... with the feverish heat of production" (*Conveyor* 155), the workers depicted in *The Land of Plenty* are rendered heroic insofar as they and their machines constitute individual, self-sufficient, and smoothly flowing units of production. Words—exactly like so-called expert managers—can only hamper their productivity by potentially interfering with the harmonious, mechanized flow of the factory.[15]

Oddly enough, however, Cantwell's identification of mass workers with mute (pre- or extralinguistic) forms of mechanized production leads him to imply that the ultimate purpose of a strike is to allow the workers simply to work better and more efficiently. Again echoing Cruden's portrait of Jim Brogan, workers like Hagen are convinced that a strike will allow them to work even more productively, since it will free them from the tyrannical and counterproductive whims of management. From the millworkers' standpoint, the company managers cannot even comprehend the basic elements of mass production, primarily because they do not have firsthand knowledge of the experience of working with modern machinery. Ironically, therefore, for both Cantwell and Cruden, the implicit goal of workers' revolts against management is not to cease working entirely but to get *back* to work, and to be allowed to work more quickly and productively, without managerial interference. Traces of this idea—that workers go on strike in order to go back to work—are evident in the praise that Jack Conroy gave *The Land of Plenty* over thirty years after it was first published. "Most important of all," Conroy observed, Cantwell's "workers walk and talk with a dignity few of the other proletarian writers gave them. Too often they were like galley slaves chained to a machine they hated and yearned to be away from. Cantwell's workers are proud of their work and their ability to perform it" ("Robert Cantwell's *Land*" 84).

It is one thing to take pride in the work one performs, but quite another to fight for the opportunity to perform that work at an even faster pace. In the peculiar sort of praise he bestows on *The Land of Plenty*, Conroy interprets Cantwell's strike novel, correctly, as a story about the inherent dignity of mechanized work in mass production industries. To Conroy, that is, Cantwell demonstrates his superiority over the other proletarian writers of the 1930s precisely by *not* condemning the degrading and dehumanizing aspects of the labor associated with mass production. In this novel, rather, it is the arbitrary rule of ignorant and wasteful managers—and not the structural forms of oppression attached to processes of mass production under a system of monopoly capitalism—that the workers' revolution is called upon to destroy.

The character of Carl is portrayed in the novel as a stubborn obstacle to efficient production. A Taylorist efficiency expert who has recently been brought to the lumber mill to oversee and speed up production on the shop floor, Carl—like the "service" men in Robert Cruden's fictional version of Ford's River Rouge plant, *Conveyor*—only interrupts the smooth flow of factory production by his presence. Accordingly, Cantwell tells us, the bulk of the veteran lumber mill workers "hated Carl because he interfered with their work, because the factory could only run when they disregarded what he told them to do. But the rest of them hated him because he drove them, drove them endlessly and senselessly even when there was nothing to do—or most of all when there was nothing to do—drove them in a fever of activity to do something that would have to be done over again tomorrow, or drove them like mad on some insane job they would have to spend the rest of the week, at the same sweating pace, undoing" (89).

The speedup Carl seeks to impose on the workers is figured here as just one of many senseless schemes on the part of management to control the method and pace of the production process. In the context of Cantwell's novel, such managerial schemes lead to only one end: inefficiency and waste. Their final aim, from the workers' point of view, is simply to produce ever more counterproductive methods of employing labor. In the words of Winters, one of the other millworkers who complains about Carl: "You got to drive that guy out of here. You can't *work* as long as he's here. You got to fight him off" (202). The following passage further elaborates Winters's thinking along these lines—a solidly prowork, antiwaste attitude that is shared by the rest of the rank-and-file mill workers in the novel:

> He [Winters] remembered Hagen saying bitterly, "We can't work as long as he's here." It was true. He [Carl] was tearing it down, he was wrecking the whole factory, letting the machines go to pieces and demoralizing the crew so that no one could get anything done. It had been bad in the old days, it had always been bad, but there had been moments, at least, when it had run smoothly, when the whole factory hummed like a single, intricate machine, smooth and beautiful, perfectly coordinated, perfectly timed. Then for a few moments, even for an hour, they would all be refreshed with pride at the way they worked, each man in his place, each tiny act fitting in perfect time with the swing and drive of the factory. Now he saw what Carl was doing, now he understood why they could not endure having him in the road. He was wrecking something that had been built up out of years of practice and labor, and even though they were not conscious of it they sensed what he was doing and they were horrified and outraged as they would have been at any wanton destruction, responding as they would if they should see food being destroyed while people were starving, or clothing being burnt while people needed it. (279–280)

Note how Winters, echoing the thoughts of the other millworkers, is accusing Carl here of "wrecking something that had been built up out of years of practice and labor." This "something" could be taken to refer to the skills that seasoned millworkers have acquired over the years. It more likely refers to the entire system of mass production, with its complex technological structures and highly coordinated labor processes. Indeed, there is no doubt that "years of practice and labor" were taken into account in the sophisticated design of modern lumber mills. According to Winters, Carl must therefore be removed from his position of authority within the process of mass production, for his impracticable efforts to increase the output of the factory, combined with the incessant and unreasonable demands he makes upon the workers, are needlessly (hence, wastefully) lowering the plant's production levels. By contrast, the novel implies, if the workers were given the chance to run the factory in the best way they saw fit, mass production could achieve hitherto unknown levels of productivity.

The productivism that characterizes Cantwell's novel resembles similar idealizations of productivity that one finds among a broad spectrum of communist theoreticians of the era. It echoes, for example, the glorification of productivity that is evident in Gramsci's view of Fordism, or in Lenin's praise of Taylorism, or in the hyperproductivist cults that dominated Stalinist Russia during the 1930s (Braverman 12–13; Gramsci 298–312). The radical political and cultural theorist C.L.R. James provided a brilliant critique of this unique brand of leftist productivism. As James saw it, "The kernel of all [Stalinist] philosophy is that the worker must work harder than he ever did before" (121). He explains how "the labor bureaucracy" that emerges out of any vanguardist communist party—most clearly exemplified by the administrators of the Soviet Union—will invariably see "the solution to the crisis of production in scientific progress, greater output." This type of labor bureaucracy "consciously seeks to plan and organize the division of labor as the means to further accumulation of capital. In ideology it is ready to expropriate those representatives of private property who stand in the way of this complete rationalization" (116). Viewed from a Stalinist/productivist perspective, therefore, socialism, according to James, is basically a matter of keeping "the proletariat at work while the leaders and organizers plan" (126); "The proletariat's role in the struggle for socialism is to work harder and harder, while the leadership and organization are left to the 'criticism and self-criticism' of the elite, the bureaucracy, the party" (125).

In sum, *The Land of Plenty*, as much as it deserves recognition as one of the first novels about workers taking over and occupying a modern factory, is limited in its ability to imagine viable alternatives to mass production along capitalist lines. The lesson to be learned from this narrative of rank-and-file unrest is that modern industrial workers, at the end of the day, belong in factories, working at their machines. Furthermore, ideally, they should be working at a pace that is growing faster all the time (because they alone determine it). The purpose of the factory occupation, at least as it is represented in this novel, is not to undermine capitalism as a specific mode of production but to strengthen it by putting its basic instruments in the hands of the workers, those who know best how to use the machinery of the plant to ensure that it functions in the most productive manner. The only trait that distinguishes *The Land of Plenty* from similar productivist novels of the period, such as Robert Cruden's *Conveyor* (1935), is the tone of rebellion that Cantwell's workers openly display. In this regard, the novel conveys an ultimately procapitalist message, yet one that is carefully disguised behind the rebellious attitude of its characters.

In addition, however, there is a second lesson to be learned from Cantwell's vision of the factory occupation, one that pushes against this more obvious discourse of production, creating friction in the seams of the novel's labor-centric vision of capitalism. Once the millworkers are fully committed to their strike, they realize where their power originates. At the same time, they develop a kind of consciousness—a consciousness of themselves, not exactly as a class, but as a mass of industrial workers, endowed with a certain type of power. "They were proud; they were excited; some of the kids began yelling as they ran toward the factory. They had their first sure knowledge of their strength" (Cantwell 204). The strength they realize they possess here is not solely a function of numbers. That is, the power of "mass" workers, they come to learn, does not stem from their sheer size in numerical terms. Instead, it is a function of the role they occupy in the process of mass production—their position within the integrated structures of the modern factory.

Early in the strike, when the worker-leader Hagen asks the character of Dwyer how many mill hands can be expected to cooperate in their plan to take over the factory, Dwyer replies, "Not more than thirty-five or forty . . . even if you get all of them." However, to this apparently dim assessment, Winters, the veteran labor radical, quickly responds, "Think where they are. The whole head end. The electrician and the drier crew and enough sawyers so the saws can't run. They won't be able to run" (Cantwell 257). Winters is teaching his coworkers that even a small number of mill hands possess the power to shut down the operations of the entire factory, provided they occupy key positions within the production process. Likewise, the character of Vin Garl, a millworker and former Wobbly, teaches Hagen, Winters, and the rest of the striking workers to see the strike within the larger context of the lumber industry as a whole. As Vin Garl explains, their own strike has the power to alter the production levels of the other lumber mills in the area; for, situated as they are within an integrated network of mills, the output of each individual mill is delicately coordinated with that of the others to regulate the mass production of lumber: "You think it don't mean anything to them to have five hundred men out here, a thousand out on the other side of town, five hundred out in the South End? You think that don't keep them on the jump? They don't know what's happening; they don't know but what *every* mill is going to walk out. But you notice as soon as we went out they eased up at Superior and they postponed their cut at Maloney's" (349). Because a strike or even a mild slowdown in one mill means a potential obstacle to production in all the other mills, the lumber workers realize that their power emanates not from a particular worldview, labor union, or political affiliation but from their material location in the broader network of operations. The actions of a mere thirty-five workers in one mill have the power to disrupt production in mills scattered throughout the region, thus potentially idling thousands of other lumber workers—again, not in spite of but precisely because of the fact that the labor processes at these different mills have been carefully brought into synch with one another to ensure the steady output of mass-produced lumber.

At the local level, concerning their specific strike, Vin Garl informs the millworkers that the power they hold over the company is directly proportional to the power they exercise over the machines in the factory. They cannot rely on the strength of a large number of dues-paying, organized lumber mill workers across the country to shut down the mill—and to keep it shut until their demands are met—since this would require an industrial union that does not yet (and may never) exist. But these workers know that their close personal acquaintance with the plant machinery has given them the technical knowledge and ability to take over the factory themselves, to run the machines as they see fit, and, in this manner, to gain recognition from the company as a collective body of workers.

Thus, even without a union to speak on their behalf, the millworkers discover that they can articulate their own demands to the company from a position of strength: at the point of production inside the factory. From this new perspective, Vin Garl, the militant syndicalist and Wobbly, continues his speech by explaining to the millworkers the basic principle of direct action:

> I say, *now* let's talk business with them. Now we're in their God-damned factory. We busted their scab crew. We're here where we can stop them from trying to work a hell of a lot easier than we could stop them by walking back and forth on that God-damned picket line, and yes, if we want to, if they make us, we can keep this factory from running for a hell of a long time. *Now* let's go to Digby. We can tell him this, we got some cards to play now that we didn't have before—take out your efficiency man, take back the men he canned, take back the cut, and we'll stay right here and start work tomorrow morning! (Cantwell 349–350)

Vin Garl's proposal—to begin negotiations with management while still occupying a position of strength—shows that the workers' bargaining power, the leverage they might use to guarantee that their demands are met, does not have to be derived from the membership base of a strong international union, or from the ability of their strike to turn public sentiment against the company. Indeed, now that the workers have taken control of the plant from the inside (instead of picketing it on the outside), they feel they can practically dictate to the company the terms of their future employment.

By sitting down at their machines and refusing to move, Cantwell's lumber mill workers have voluntarily reduced themselves to the mute condition of the machines that they operate; yet they have done so, paradoxically, to make their voices heard in negotiations with management. By remaining inside the plant at their machines, these workers have openly identified themselves with the material environment of the factory. It is as if they had *literally* become the very machines into which factory managers and industrial engineers had been trying figuratively to transform them, with little to no success, over the last forty years.

The New Unionism: Spontaneity, Blockage, and Sitdowns

Ruth McKenney's 1939 novel about the sitdown strikes in the huge rubber plants of Akron, Ohio, explores what exactly it might mean for workers to identify themselves with the actual materials that constitute the environment and means of mass production. Like the western Pennsylvania steelworkers in Thomas Bell's *Out of This Furnace*, the rubber workers presented in McKenney's narrative initially (and naively) place a great deal of faith in the ability of the established AFL unions to better their working conditions. For instance, with the advent of Roosevelt's NIRA in 1933, the rubber workers of Akron simply assume that the AFL will work with President Roosevelt to organize their industry, even though, as McKenney describes them, "they were completely innocent of formal trade union experience" and "knew nothing of union rules and regulations" (101). McKenney—who actually worked in the city as a journalist, covering labor issues and municipal politics—observes how, throughout working-class Akron during the summer of 1933, "Always the cry was 'Join up.' But nobody said what came after you joined. The rubberworkers believed, blindly, passionately, fiercely, that the union would cure all their troubles, end the speedup, make them rich with wages. They had no clear idea, and nobody told them, just how the union would accomplish these aims. Vaguely, they thought President Roosevelt might just order the rubber bosses to raise wages and quit the speedup. Some of them talked strike, but when they spoke about a strike, it was always something gay, like a picnic, a contest that you won right away without any trouble" (101). To capitalize on this enthusiasm for unions, and, most importantly, to channel it into relatively harmless directions (by appearing to give workers a voice in their negotiations with management), employers throughout the Akron region created their own company unions. "Every little machine shop and store suddenly sported a brand-new system of 'employee representation,'" McKenney sarcastically notes (106).

What distinguishes McKenney's account of the industrial union movement of the mid-1930s from that of Bell is that the rubber workers of Akron are not as slow to realize that institutions such as the NIRA, along with various company-controlled "Employee Representation Plans," are not designed to reflect their true interests. One reason Akron's workers are comparatively more savvy than Bell's steelworkers in this regard concerns the idiosyncrasies of their local traditions of labor activism. In Akron, in contrast to Pittsburgh, the workers are more apt to use their bodies to "speak" for themselves, effectively sidestepping the need for an official representative from a labor union. Hence, from the start, McKenney's workers have learned that they can do for themselves what others—the self-appointed labor leaders—have claimed the exclusive right and expertise to do for them.

For example, her novel highlights a series of spontaneous wildcat strikes that occurred throughout the region in the years preceding the large—and similarly spontaneous—sitdown strikes in the rubber industry. In her account of these earlier strikes, McKenney underscores that the workers used their own bodies on picket lines to form what she frequently refers to as "human barricades" or a "solid mass of men." McKenney tells us how, near Akron, at the Columbia Chemical strike in Barberton, Ohio, in April of 1934, "every gate was covered by hundreds of men. They stood and sat and squatted in a thick solid mass, a human barricade. The railroad gate itself was crowded twenty deep with rows of men. In front of this solid mass a gang worked swiftly, under the direction of a foreman, building a series of pyramids made of old ties and wood and stones on the railroad track. No engine would pass this way tonight" (151). Not only have these men—who are on the picket line outside the factory—formed themselves into a collective body, a group that resembles the dehumanized mass of workers that they were inside the factory, but they have done so specifically "under the direction of a foreman." In this manner, McKenney suggests, the rubber workers are doing precisely what the process of modern mass production has trained them to do: they are using their bodies to approximate the inhuman force of machinery. Even though their ultimate aims may be directly opposed to those of the company, the nature of their tactical choices on the picket line in the street reflects the very process of mechanized labor to which they have had to adapt themselves at the point of production.

Similarly, McKenney explains how during the strike at the General Tire and Rubber Company in Akron in June 1934, soon after the ranks of workers picketing in the street were temporarily broken and disordered, they managed to reconstruct themselves as a uniquely corporeal mass: "The parade re-formed instantly, only now men stood close together, shoulder to shoulder, packed tightly, toe on the next man's heel, covering the streetcar tracks with a solid mass of men.... [A] roar of laughter went through the human barricade" (170). An even clearer illustration of this method of representing workers en masse is found in McKenney's description of the strike at the Ohio Insulator plant in Barberton, which occurred in November 1935, just prior to the wave of sitdown strikes in the rubber factories. McKenney tells us how these workers "lined up quickly, arm linked in arm, before the main gates. In this silent dawn, the strikers clasped hands. They had no weapons. They had nothing but the physical weight of their bodies to use against the danger that awaited them in the fog. But they planned to use their flesh, their bones, as a barricade" (228).

Through these and other similar depictions of the bodies of striking workers gathered together en masse, McKenney implies that the corporeal solidarity of the rank and file forms the true material basis of their class consciousness. Thus it would seem that, on its own, the imposing mass of their bodies linked together to create a collective force is sufficient to speak on their behalf, to articulate their needs and desires (cf. Vorse 8). In her extended descriptions of sitdown strikers later in the novel, McKenney stresses how these same kinds of bodily tactics both effectively produce and reflect the ideological and material strength of the rubber workers. For instance, we learn that at the height of the Goodyear strike in Akron, in February 1936, "the pickets marched in two ovals, very close together, a moving wall of human beings.... The pickets stood still in their tracks, arms locked in arms" (293). Lest we read this image in merely figurative terms—as connoting the abstract "wall" of the strength of workers' class consciousness, their resolve, or an unwavering commitment to their cause—one must account for the dominant presence of their bodies within it. The primary reason they are a "moving wall" is that they have self-consciously formed themselves into a mass of actual bodies: "The picket line walked in a kind of lockstep, so close together that one man could feel the frosty breath of the marcher behind him on his neck. The howling wind drowned out their cheers. Pickets learned to keep time, so that one man's legs could touch another's and still not stumble" (290).

In the last of these images of rank-and-file solidarity, McKenney gestures toward the possibility that class consciousness is in part produced through acts of literal, physical touching between workers. In the course of a strike—whether marching together as pickets in the street or sitting alongside each other by the machines inside the factory—the rubber workers become aware of the fact that they belong, collectively, to a uniquely modern class of labor power, one that is defined primarily by the material qualities of workers' bodies. Moreover, this realization of theirs is a result of the dramatic changes to the labor process that have been occurring over the last fifty years. Recall how, for management theorists such Horace Arnold and Frederick Taylor, one of the key principles of mass production was expressed by the persistent effort to speed up and intensify the labor process within the factory. Only by maintaining the fastest possible production rates could the increased expenditure on elements of fixed capital (machinery, plant structures, and raw materials) be justified. By increasing the productivity of the individual worker, and the output of the plant as a whole, the company could sharply reduce the costs of its products, thereby increasing its market share by gaining an edge over its competitors. The speedup, then, not only signified the general idea of mass production but also served as one of the most common techniques to realize production on a mass scale.

It is no accident that by 1933, from the point of view of rank-and-file industrial workers, the speedup had come to be seen as the most obviously inhuman practice of modern capitalism. McKenney reports how in Akron "the speedup in the mills was heartbreaking, mindbreaking. The cry, 'It ain't human!' came every day out of the rubber shops, echoed up and down the city streets" (96). This same cry quickly acquired the status of a "battle cry" among Akron's rubber workers (99). As with any kind of battle cry, general lines of conflict need to be drawn before a battle can be waged. Indeed, this is exactly what spontaneous work stoppages are good for: demarcating the battle lines between workers and management at the point of production. Or rather, for McKenney—who was openly affiliated with the Communist Party of the United States in the period of her life during which she was writing *Industrial Valley*—the battle lines are between the U.S. industrial proletariat, signified by the rubber workers of Akron, and the general interests of U.S. monopoly capitalism. Of all Depression-era radical writers, McKenney is above all distinguished by the fact that, like her IWW predecessors, she takes seriously the revolutionary political and social significance of spontaneous (independent, nonunion, nonpartisan) work stoppages among the rank and file of industrial workers.

The conflict between socioeconomic classes depicted in *Industrial Valley* therefore has its origin—its primal scene, as it were—in the wildcat strikes that break out among small numbers of workers inside the rubber plants: "Without any kind of formal meeting, without Mr. Claherty's knowledge or sanction, without announcement or consultation, without advice from William Green [president of the AFL] and other experienced trade union leaders, the rubberworkers at General Tire and Rubber Company struck. Going on strike is rather a formal way of putting what really happened. Tirebuilders simply stopped work and began yelling, 'The hell with the speedup! We're through'" (McKenney 166). In McKenney's account of the events that led up to the major sitdown strikes in Akron in 1936, spontaneous strikes such as this one are the direct result of three interrelated factors. First, they are made possible by the complex machinery in the factory, whose maximum degree of usefulness demands that workers perform a highly mechanized, monotonous, and repetitive type of labor. Second, the long-term effects of the speedup on the workforce bring these workers to rebel against the inhuman demands of these same machines, which, apparently independent of human will, drive them to keep up the pace of production. And last, a spontaneous work stoppage such as this can be effective as a kind of strike—however short-lived, on however small a scale—only because the machinery in the factory is so closely integrated and coordinated with the tasks that its workers perform. Whenever any of the workers stops doing anything that he is supposed to be doing, this can lead to a major crisis, potentially disrupting the entire production schedule of the plant.

The fact that McKenney's narrator hesitates even to call it a "strike" therefore draws attention to the wild, unruly nature of this variety of work stoppage—as though a more official type of strike would inevitably adhere to principles of organization and leadership that, at least in this case, are entirely lacking. Much like those machine-mediated forms of communication depicted in Cantwell's *The Land of Plenty*, by means of which workers who were spread out over a vast plant were able to convey messages to each another almost instantly, the alluring idea of stopping work wherever and whenever one chooses becomes contagious for the workers in the rubber factories, spreading from one worker to the next as a result of the close physical proximity and technical integration of their machines. For example, McKenney's narrator explains how, at the start of the brief strike in Akron's General Tire and Rubber Company in June of 1934, "the revolt spread up and down the tire machines. 'The goddamned speedup is working the guts out of me,' men growled, and suddenly, without any warning, a tirebuilder yelled, 'I ain't going to stand for it. Let's quit, boys!' They backed away from their machines. A frantic foreman shouted threats. The grapevine telegraph flashed the news instantly to other departments. The tirebuilders were quitting. . . . That was the way it began. A man in the truck tire department said he wouldn't stand for it any more, and out of that came the strike" (167). By emphasizing the seemingly individualistic character of the origins of this particular strike, McKenney dulls the force of the more explicitly ideological point her novel attempts to make about labor unrest in mass production industries: namely, that the conditions of production on a mass scale require a *collective* workforce, one that necessarily becomes a revolutionary (though naive and spontaneous) army of the industrial proletariat through its day-to-day experience of collective mechanization.

In spite of this oversight on McKenney's part, her narrative suggests that a certain measure of individualism definitely has its place in the movement for industrial unionism. The novel is filled with scenes of labor unrest, such as the one cited above, that flirt with the notion that each worker has within him or herself the power to cripple the vast system of industrial capitalism. This idea echoes the older Wobbly (revolutionary syndicalist) principle that "An Injury to One Is the Concern of All." It also reflects the common belief among Wobblies that there are no "leaders" in the labor movement, since, ideally, every worker is his or her own leader, and each is equally capable of leading others.

When John L. Lewis, the organizer and founder of the CIO, makes his first appearance in *Industrial Valley*, his speech to the rubber workers clearly reiterates aspects of these Wobbly principles. Lewis arrived in Akron in January of 1936 to boost the morale of the rubber workers, who had just recently begun a series of strikes against the rubber companies. Instead of speaking as their leader—whose role in labor disputes is to speak *for* them, to represent them to others—Lewis implies that the best thing any leader can do is to inspire workers to act independently of their officially designated leaders, to take matters into their own hands whenever and wherever they deem it necessary to do so. In stark contrast to the authoritarian, top-down, bureaucratic structure of the typical craft unions that were affiliated with the AFL (whose veteran organizers were known for their condescending attitudes toward rank-and-file industrial workers), the CIO, as McKenney portrays it here, is committed to the principles of direct democracy—principles that justify workers' direct action on the shop floor, with or without the sanction of an officially recognized union:

> Here was a man who put into words—what eloquent and educated and even elegant words—facts they knew to be true from their own experience. Here was a man who said things that made real sense to a guy who worked on a tire machine at Goodyear.... He evoked a dream in the minds of men, a dream of security, and a dream of freedom.
>
> Suddenly he stopped speaking. There was a long pause. Then he said quietly, and very earnestly, "I hope you will do something for yourselves...."
>
> His speech and his appearance was remembered in the valleys because he said what the people already knew. (250–251)

What the working people of Akron already knew—and what the emergent wildcat strike movement was teaching them every day—was that they did not need to rely on outside leaders to fight on their behalf; neither President Roosevelt nor William Green was about to come to Akron in order personally to ensure that the rubber companies met the demands of their employees. And besides, as one worker puts it, "A union leader ain't no tougher than the guys on strike, and usually not as tough.... He can't be" (331).

Not surprisingly, it is precisely at this moment in the narrative that the rubber workers discover the tactic of the sitdown strike. According to McKenney (whose account is based upon the actual historical record of events in Akron), the man who teaches them about this peculiar strike method is named Alex Eigenmacht. This man, McKenney's narrator tells us, "ran the union print shop out near the Firestone plant," and he was well liked among the rubber workers "because he was the best storyteller in town.... Alex—rubberworkers had difficulty pronouncing his last name, so he went simply by his first—had a real talent for reciting the stories of his improbably adventurous life" (251).

One should note here that Alex's name, translated out of German, means literally "the power of one's self," "own power," or "self-powered." Thus it is all the more fitting that he should be the person through whom the rubber workers learn about the principle of self-representation, which the tactic of the sitdown strike both displays and enacts. Once they have learned from Alex about the efficacy of the sitdown strikes that he witnessed in Europe, they acquire a new perspective on the resources available to them in their struggles with management. That is, they learn that they too possess their own power—their "Eigenmacht"—to fight the rubber companies. This power is grounded, not in the abstract representational function of a politician or union delegate, but in the concrete, physical structures of the rubber mills, the actual machines, which can be shut off and blocked by the bodies of the workers in the mills. Because they are well aware that the company values them solely for the potential labor power contained in their bodies—a lesson driven home by their recent experience of the speedup—they know that the act of sitting down on the job is, in the eyes of the company, just another way of shutting off the power of one's machine. Above all, neither of these requires the leadership or expertise of a veteran labor organizer in order to cripple production in the mill effectively. If even a small number of workers in a single department of the mill decide to sit down, they can, through their action, practically force all the other departments in that mill to cease work as well.

It is in this moment of collective realization, when the rubber workers finally understand the nature of the power they possess inside the plant, that McKenney's novel reaches a dramatic turning point. Once they are sure they can bring the company to its knees without having to rely on the assistance of the union or any other mediating third party, the rubber workers resolve to put the sitdown strike tactic—the principle of self-representation—into practice. Looking back on a time prior to their discovery of this tactic, when they still had faith in the power of the union to protect them from the company's inhuman labor practices, one worker observes, "We was all the time talkin' and didn't do nothin'," to which his coworker replies, "Yeah, and we let a lot of guys do the talkin' for us. This time we run it ourselves, and we don't tell nobody, and we don't ask nobody if it suits them either" (257). This last worker is referring to the course of the strike itself. In the phrase "we run it ourselves" McKenney reveals a newfound recognition on the part of the workers that they possess the necessary knowledge, as well as the means, to conduct their own strike and to represent themselves by themselves in their negotiations with management.

The rubber workers' first sitdown strike—carried out at the Firestone truck tire plant in late January 1936—dramatizes this first realization of the true source of their bargaining power. In the following excerpt from the novel, note the emphasis McKenney places on the workers' experience of their own, seemingly miraculous type of agency at the very moment that the machines in the plant grind to a halt. It is as if these workers only became aware of the highly mechanized nature of their productivity once they were able to step away from their machines; as though the act of shutting down the machines made them suddenly realize that they, too, had all along been treated by management as more or less "productive" appendages to these same machines—a condition that might very well have been obscured, rendered anonymous or unnoticeable, by the sheer cacophony of the mill's operations. McKenney describes this moment as follows:

> The tirebuilder at the end of the line gulped. His hands stopped their quick weaving motions. Every man on the line stiffened. All over the vast room, hands hesitated. The foreman saw the falter, felt it instantly. He jumped up, but he stood beside his desk, his eyes darting quickly from one line to another.
>
> This was it, then. But what was happening? Where was it starting? He stood perfectly still, his heart beating furiously, his throat feeling dry, watching the hesitating hands, watching the broken rhythm.
>
> Then the tirebuilder at the end of the line walked three steps to the master safety switch and, drawing a deep breath, he pulled up the heavy wooden handle. With this signal, in perfect synchronization, with the rhythm they had learned in a great mass-production industry, the tirebuilders stepped back from their machines.
>
> Instantly, the noise stopped. The whole room lay in perfect silence. The tirebuilders stood in long lines, touching each other, perfectly motionless, deafened by the silence. A moment ago there had been the weaving hand, the revolving wheels, the clanking belt, the moving hooks, the flashing tire tools. Now there was absolute stillness, no motion anywhere, no sound.
>
> Out of the terrifying quiet came the wondering voice of a big tirebuilder near the windows: "Jesus Christ, it's like the end of the world."
>
> He broke the spell, the magic moment of stillness. For now his awed words said the same thing to every man, "We done it! We stopped the belt! By God, we done it!" And men began to cheer hysterically, to shout and howl in the fresh silence. Men wrapped long sinewy arms around their neighbors' shoulders, screaming, "We done it! We done it!"
>
> For the first time in history, American mass-production workers

had stopped a conveyor belt and halted the inexorable movement of factory machinery.

"John Brown's body," somebody chanted above the cries. The others took it up. (261–262)

McKenney's vivid depiction of the start of the first sitdown strike emphasizes that it begins with the simple phenomenon of all the men in a single department stepping away from their machines, "in perfect synchronization, with the rhythm they had learned in a great mass-production industry." In other words, she implies, not only have the highly mechanized techniques of the labor process prepared the workers for taking this kind of action, but, on a more profound level, it is as if they had been designed with this vulnerability (to sabotage) built into them, as an immanent factor of mass production itself. Once the workers have stepped away from the machines, as a result of their acclimation over the years to the rigors of mechanized labor, they know they will be capable of cooperating with one another and acting in unison. Hence, McKenney adds, because they are "accustomed to order, to precise machinery, to a pattern of work-life in which every detail fitted and no second of time was lost through mismanagement, they set about applying this discipline to their own strike" (302).

In a scene describing how, "for the first time in history, American mass-production workers had stopped a conveyor belt and halted the inexorable movement of factory machinery," McKenney makes a point of reminding us that this dramatic action has been made possible by a uniquely corporeal sense of solidarity among the rubber workers. Recall that, in earlier strikes, these same workers used their bodies, "their flesh, their bones, as a barricade," and literally touched each other while marching in picket lines. Likewise, here in the factory, as soon as the machines are turned off, we learn how, in the first moments of the strike, "the tirebuilders stood in long lines, touching each other," thus holding their ground, not sure of what will come of their action. The point is, the workers become aware of their bodies in relation to one another, as well as in relation to the machinery of the factory, only at the moment that these machines cease to operate. By shutting down all the machines in the plant, the rubber workers discover that they constitute, collectively, a single body of homogeneous, mass labor power. Their simple action concretely illustrates—and literally embodies—a new concept of corporeal, mass industrial solidarity. Just as the "inexorable movement" of the machinery of mass production grinds to a halt, thereby becoming transformed into the inert material structures of the plant, the abstract idea of solidarity gets transubstantiated in this moment. No longer a mere ideological principle, it becomes a material reality, acquiring a bodily substance in the form of the workers sitting at their idle machines.

The effects of this type of small-scale strike, however, extend well beyond the individual department in which it originated. Because all the operations in the tire plant are carefully timed and coordinated to blend into a single, continuously flowing process—which is a necessary condition for the plant to realize the maximum possible output—when one stage of this process slows down or stops, the entire system is thrown into a state of disarray. Hence, as a result of the sitdown strike in the truck-tire department,

> Firestone Plant One gradually shut down completely. The departments that didn't actually sitdown and strike were paralyzed by lack of work or materials. The delicate mechanism of mass production was dealt a brutal fatal blow. Engineers had worked for years to synchronize every labor process in the great factory. The most remote departments were dependent on the flow of materials from some other faraway corner of the great plant. But once the line was broken, factory operations came to an uneven jerking halt.... There were 1,200 tirebuilders actually on strike and, as a matter of fact, most of the workers in the other departments were really striking too, only their departments had just closed down for lack of material. (McKenney 264–265)

As is evident from the far-reaching consequences of even a small sitdown strike, carried out by only a handful of workers, workers' power in this instance is rooted in the basic operation of blockage. Since every type of mass production is founded upon the principle of continuous flow, anything that possesses the capacity to interfere with, block, or rechannel such a flow can function as a potential weapon in the struggle between workers and management. Sensing their strength, and the newfound bargaining power it gives them in the factory, McKenney tells us that the strikers "were surprised and jubilant when they found so little resistance" on the part of the company. Since they were now living in the tire factory as a collective body, they felt that they legitimately "owned the factory. Nobody dared say them nay. So they used power carefully" (265).

The key to the success of this kind of strike is the workers' realization that they alone possess the power to render the plant idle—but only in the degree to which their labor power has become embodied and reduced to a part of the fixed capital within the structure of the plant. The plant's managers view the mass of workers collectively as one machine among others and thus factor their labor into the operations of the plant in a purely mechanical sense. However, in spite of this techno-managerial fiction, the workers know that they are human beings, not mere machines. Hence, unlike the rest of the actual machines in the plant, they can consciously *choose* to make themselves idle. Yet once they have chosen to do this, their decision forces the multitude of the plant's machines to embody, collectively, a state of willed and willful inertia—the exact opposite of the company's ideal of "continuous flow."

Recognizing the unique form of power they now possess, the rubber workers of *Industrial Valley* sense that it can serve as the organizational basis of a new kind of union: an *industrial* union, democratically run, because it is composed of mass production workers who know that each one of them, individually, has the power to cripple an entire plant's operations at will. Unlike the AFL craft unions, which ignored the desires of their rank-and-file members (while seeming all too eager to make compromises with the company), this new industrial union will respond directly to the needs of the workers because, for the most part, it will consist of workers who are intimately familiar with the operations of the plant, regardless of their trade or level of skill. As one rubber worker put it shortly after the start of the sitdown strike, "The union ain't the same one that sold out the boys last year. We threw [AFL president William] Green out on his ear, in case you haven't heard. The union belongs to us now" (McKenney 263–264).

Inspired by the success of the sitdown strike at the Firestone tire plant, by February 1936 the workers at Goodyear began to assert themselves in local meetings of the rubber workers' union, demanding a strike of their own. McKenney's portrayal of them celebrates their apparently spontaneous outbursts in these meetings. As she explains, "Men rose all over the room and in a confused din shouted, 'Let's strike! Strike! Strike!' . . . This time the rubberworkers were doing the talking. This time it was their union, their meeting" (288). Not only is the union "theirs" for the first time, but their control of it is due directly to their use of the sitdown strike, the most effective and democratic of strike methods. From this point through to the end of the novel, the speeches of the union members are remarkably "full of confidence," McKenney tells us, "for these workers had discovered a way out: the sitdown" (283). The workers all know that they have a voice in the union's affairs; they will be heard because there is no longer a discrepancy between the union's affairs and their own. In addition, every individual rubber worker has now become a kind of Alex Eigenmacht, the first character in the novel (apart from John L. Lewis) who promoted the principle of workers' self-representation, since he explained the sitdown strike tactic to his fellow workers: "East Akron, South Akron, Kenmore Hill, and Barberton did not depend on the newspaper stories of the great sitdown strike. The sitdowners themselves came home for shaves and clean underwear, and they spread the story with feverish excitement. Goodyear tirebuilders sat patiently downstairs in little frame houses for hours waiting for a Firestone sitdowner to wake up and tell them all about it. The Firestone local hall was jammed day and night, and men worked twenty hours of twenty-four signing up new members and explaining how the sitdown worked" (266–267). Such an unbridled manifestation of direct democracy is not only a constant threat to the company but also a potential threat to those union officials who seek to steer or lead this grassroots movement. For, in this radical form of workers' democracy, each worker has the authority to make his or her voice heard, solely because, by sitting down, each worker can effectively block the system of mass production.

Beyond the rubber workers' union, McKenney's novel suggests—in a rare departure from the historical record—that the Communist Party of the United States exercised a significant influence over the rubber workers in Akron. Yet for the CP or any labor union to gain control over these workers, it must grant itself the authority to dictate to them when and where the weapon of the sitdown strike is to be used, for both practical and strategic purposes. Moreover, to represent these workers—to speak on their behalf in negotiations with management—the workers' official representatives need to be able to preserve so-called "regular relations" between the workers and the company. That is, because each party to a signed labor contract is expected to hold up its end of the bargain, from the moment a contract is signed, it becomes the duty of the union officials to ensure for the company that the workers will fulfill their contractual promises to work—when, where, and how they have promised to work. In effect, then, this type of monitoring deprives the workers of a key weapon: the use of spontaneous and improvised forms of blockage, including the sitdown strike, as well as even less conspicuous types of on-the-job sabotage. Thus the very power that has given the workers the leverage they needed to negotiate a favorable contract is subsequently undermined by the perceived need to satisfy their contractual obligations.

In *Industrial Valley*, this dilemma expresses itself through the character of Jim Keller, a section organizer for the Communist Party local in Akron, who makes it clear to the rubber workers that their contractual obligations will have to be fulfilled, even if this means voluntarily renouncing the very tactic (the sitdown) that gave them bargaining power in the first place. "The sitdown is an extremely effective organizational weapon," Keller tells the workers, "but credit must go to Comrade Williamson for warning us against the danger of these surprise actions. The sitdowns came because the companies refused to bargain collectively with the union. Now we must work for regular relations between the union and the employers—and strict observance of union procedure on the part of the workers" (McKenney 340). In short, Keller—who expresses the strategic priorities of many U.S. Communist Party labor organizers in 1936—declares that the sitdown has done what it was supposedly intended to do: it has brought the company to the bargaining table. Now that the workers are finally able to have what he calls "regular relations" with the company, the sitdown tactic is to be retired, stored safely away in the annals of the union's institutional memory—along with all other spontaneous forms of direct action on the shop floor, even (potentially) direct democratic procedures within the union. Instead of relying on such proven tactics, Keller merely encourages the rubber workers to "take the picket line back to the tire machines and the mill room." In short, he tells them to preserve the mind-set but abandon the actual exercise of workplace bargaining power. Somehow, as odd as it sounds, and in spite of the workers' new plan to renounce the entire basis of their bargaining power, Keller insists that the "Goodyear strike will be America's new declaration of freedom" (369).

Messianism, Revolution

Clearly, the Communist Party labor organizers in McKenney's narrative do not recognize the extent to which their strategic goals undermine the leverage they have gained from the workers' own improvised tactics. Nevertheless, *Industrial Valley* continues to be of interest as one of the only novels from the period that devotes close and sustained attention to the phenomenon of the sitdown strike wave.

Soon after it first appeared in Akron, Ohio, the tactic of the sitdown strike had an especially profound impact on the automobile industry. In 1939, the same year that saw the publication of McKenney's novel, a writer who considered herself a fellow traveler of the U.S. Communist Party, Josephine Herbst, completed her semiautobiographical trilogy of historical novels by publishing the third and last novel in the series, *Rope of Gold*. No doubt reflecting the heightened level of national interest in the sitdown strike wave, Herbst chose to end *Rope of Gold* (and thus the trilogy as a whole) with a brief scene set in a Flint, Michigan, GM plant in early 1937, during the autoworkers' historic sitdown strike. Because Herbst does not offer a detailed account of the GM strike—devoting only the last ten out of the novel's 439 pages to the event—what little her novel does say about it is, for this reason, all the more telling.

Herbst's narrative explicitly frames the GM strike as a messianic portent of things to come. The character of Ed Thompson, the novel's fictitious stand-in for a typical GM plant manager, expresses a profound sense of anxiety over the issue of workplace control and the prospect that the workers will appropriate an ever-growing share of control over the system of mass production. Mistakenly attributing the sitdown phenomenon solely to the influence of John L. Lewis, Thompson exclaims: "Lewis. There's the rub. We managed it all right until he popped. Why, I had the plant in complete control. We busted things as fast as they happened. Pop goes the weasel, just like that. I don't see yet how he got started. For one thing he pulled a strike without more than a handful back of him. I'm trying to look at this reasonably and learn something. I don't want to just yell. It was successful, see. He got the fellows sitting down and the rest liked it. He worked out some wonderful tactics. I got to hand it to him. They can make forts out of a plant. That's another thing, and the thing works, see, so it spreads" (420). Although he is aware that Lewis did not single-handedly cause the workers to engage in their strike, Thompson, who goes on to blame "outside agitators" for leading the strike, is lamenting the fact that the machinery of mass production can be shut down by precisely that homogeneous mass of workers who are supposed to be an unconscious part of it. "I never thought I'd see the day when our own plant would be shut against us," he admits to his assistant, warning him of how, "when it's sabotaged long enough, then watch out. Before that comes we have to get control of the machinery again." Herbst deployed this character as a mouthpiece to give voice to the very real fears—as well as the future plans—of corporate managers who were faced with the possibility of perpetual unrest among the workforce at the point of production. An eminently modern and "scientific" manager such as Ed Thompson, Herbst's narrator wryly concludes, "had put everything he had ... into one basket. And that basket proved to have a hole in the bottom. It wasn't even his basket. A lot of brainless workers were grabbing it as if they had a right to it" (422).

Though one might expect the feelings of the autoworkers in Herbst's portrait of the GM strike to reflect the same unambiguously euphoric sense of emancipation that the rubber workers in Akron felt, they instead feel an ambivalent and ill-defined sense of hope for their future. Similarly, in light of the hitherto unimaginable effects of the sitdown tactic, the future of industrial capitalism in general seems, by the end of Herbst's novel, to be temporarily suspended. Looking toward a future of job security in mass production industries, the exemplary GM worker, as Herbst portrays him, justifies the sitdown tactic to himself by insisting that his job in the factory is a kind of personal property, a possession that belongs to him, since it constitutes his livelihood: "This is my job, he thought, and he seemed to see his job like a box that could be carried in his hand. . . . Not a fancy job, just the run of luck that most men had. A job at the bottom where a man had to feel a man if there was to be any sense to the world. A job belonged to a man, more than a wife or child or mother. He had to have it to live and the world, much as it might pretend he was nothing to it, had to have him" (428).[16]

One year before the publication of Herbst's novel, in 1938, the sports writer and novelist Paul Gallico—best remembered today for his 1940 story "The Snow Goose"—published his own idiosyncratic rendering of the GM sitdown strike. Set in a fictitious steel town named "Iron City," Gallico's short novel, *Sit-Down Strike*, is told from the perspective of a labor journalist who is covering the steelworkers' strike at the "State Steel" company. Because Gallico's novel appeared only once, in the April 1938 issue of the magazine *Cosmopolitan*, it has escaped the attention of virtually every cultural historian of the era, with the notable exception of Sidney Fine, who observes that, "although a work of fiction, [it] contains some shrewd insights into the Flint sit-down based on the author's own observations in the city during the strike" (423). While both Herbst and Gallico covered the GM sitdown strike as journalists in early 1937, only Gallico's account thematizes the writer's complex relationship to the events of the strike. Harking back to the challenges faced by writers who were affiliated with the IWW, Gallico's narrative openly wrestles with the problem of representing a group of workers who are skeptical of any individual or organization that claims to represent them. Yet in contrast to most IWW-era writers, for Gallico the modern entity known as "the media" now plays a much bigger role in the dynamics of the strike. From the standpoint of the reporters who cover it, according to Gallico's account, the sitdown strike is above all a media spectacle. In *Sit-Down Strike*, journalists who try to remain neutral in order to tell the "objective" truth of the strike inevitably get swept up in the action, only to be exploited (by both sides) as an ideological weapon in the battle between labor and management.

On the one hand, Gallico's focus on the problem of the journalistic representation of the sitdown strikers reflects the actual bewilderment on the part of press and public alike toward this supposedly new breed of militant worker. As Ruth McKenney reported in *Industrial Valley*, the managers of large corporations typically "were stunned by the news" of workers occupying their factories. "Here was something they had never heard of before, something frightening and queer. How did you deal with it? How did you break it up?" (266–267). Since the sitdown, as a particularly effective strike tactic for assembly-line factories, was still relatively unknown to many Americans, the novel *Sit-Down Strike* provides an explanation of it that underscores the importance of the physical environment of the factory, its location, and the technological integration of its various machines (Gallico 158). Similar in this regard to Robert Cruden's *The Land of Plenty*, one of the lead organizers in Gallico's novel explains to the strikers how, although the union president, Appleby, is at the state capitol meeting with the governor, "he's in a bad spot for bargaining now" because "we're here" in the plant itself. The workers here learn that they exercise real bargaining power only on the grounds of the actual factory, at the point of production, rather than in some backroom in the state capitol. This notion is driven home by another rank-and-file organizer, who confidently asserts that "there are enough of our men in town to knock off any plant. Once they get inside, they'll hold it, all right. Even if we had only fifty guys inside, the element of surprise would make up for what we lack in numbers" (176).

If this last striker's comments sound a bit cavalier (especially given the strength of the forces rallied against them), they also indicate the extent to which these workers, in Gallico's words, "were enjoying their power" (159). While the rubber workers of *Industrial Valley* are described as enjoying their power for only a brief moment at the start of their sitdown—before the Communist Party and union officials begin to take charge of their strike and enforce discipline—the steelworkers of *Sit-Down Strike*, in stark contrast, are shown reveling in their ability to convert the site of their exploitation into a powerful fortress, one that will effectively protect them in their struggle against the company. Gallico's protagonist-narrator—who, like Gallico himself, is a labor journalist covering the strike—visits one of the plants they have occupied and is particularly impressed by the confidence and joy of the workers he meets there: "It was astonishing how they had managed to create a home out of a factory. Nothing had been damaged or dirtied.... I felt a gaiety and excitement about these men. They were children playing at a new and fascinating game. They had made a palace out of what had been their prison. They were playing house in and about the property where formerly they had worked. The rest, the sleep, the unlimited food had soothed their nerves" (159). That these sitdown strikers take not only pride but genuine pleasure in their bold actions suggests a deep connection between enjoyment and the practice of willful idleness in the workplace. Such an identification between pleasure and idleness is potentially revolutionary, since it threatens the interests of unions and company managers in equal measure. It therefore receives very little attention in McKenney's Communist Party–oriented narrative, which is meant to promote the idea of a worker-controlled system of production and, conversely, to scorn any activity that seems nonproductive. By contrast, Gallico's novel, whose narrator tries hard to remain "neutral" throughout the strike, is relatively less hampered by political or ideological constraints and thus freer to examine notions of working-class desire and enjoyment for their own sake.

Gallico's narrative also distinguishes itself from those of McKenney and Herbst by detailing several of the conflicting (and confused) popular views of the sitdown strike. For instance, it examines the opinions of many who saw it—both positively and negatively—as a revolutionary force, one that had recently been placed at the disposal of the broad masses of working people everywhere. In one of the novel's climactic scenes, as soon as he perceives the true stakes of the conflict, Gallico's protagonist, a labor journalist named Alan, exclaims in a sudden outburst to one of the union's organizers: "You call it strike, but it isn't strike. It's revolution. You occupy private property and hold it for ransom" (166). As the narrative proceeds, Alan continues to write about the strike, but his reflections take on a distinctly messianic tone as he ponders what the possibility of this new tactic means for the future of capitalist society:

> There were bigger things at stake than wages and hours and speed-up and collective bargaining at State Steel. Iron City seemed to me like the laboratory chosen for a dangerous and daring experiment—for a revolution in thought as well as deed; the first attack in America upon private property and its inviolability.
>
> The men occupying Plant 7 were clearly outside the pale of all existing laws. The machinery of the law had proceeded against

them up to a point and there had bogged down. Therefore law was law no longer. Something higher had taken its place. In the name of emergency and humanity, the governor of a Democratic state had suspended the execution of laws he was sworn to uphold. He would not order troops to massacre unarmed citizens and workers. But in the meantime, there were no new laws to take the place of the old.

And deeply behind it were political moves . . . and a bitter fight and schism in the labor ranks over the revolutionary methods of the sit-down strikes. . . . It was still a part of the industrial revolution that had started back in the nineteenth century when machines began to replace men. (169)

The narrator's reflections in this passage reveal a critical perspective that looks far beyond the relatively more limited horizon of the other CIO-era strike novels we have been considering. For here the sitdown strike tactic is hailed not merely as one among many clever ideas that workers devised to gain power in the workplace but as a truly revolutionary force, something that cuts through the deadlock of existing laws by surpassing, and even transcending, their origins in social convention. Gallico's narrator thus invites us to ponder the messianic significance of the sitdown strike, when "law was law no longer" because "something higher had taken its place." A grassroots, more or less spontaneous tactic, based on the experience of rank-and-file mass workers in modern factories, the sitdown strike, the novel implies, can practically suspend the temporal meaning and relevance of established laws. At the same time, it also signals the need for new industrial laws that will be more fully commensurate with the conditions of collective, mechanized mass production.[17]

Represented Labor—Contracted Unrest

During the second half of the 1930s, the numerous victories of CIO-affiliated industrial unions such as the UAW were both profound and widespread. By the outbreak of World War II, mass workers in the United States found themselves in a position of strength unmatched by anything they had previously known. Yet oddly, their newfound bargaining power came with a set of severe limitations. On the one hand, workers' use of the sitdown strike tactic made it possible for a genuine form of industrial unionism in mass production industries finally to become a reality. On the other hand, as soon as companies began to grant official recognition to these unions, industrial workers found that they were being disciplined by the very same union organizers who had encouraged their previous acts of resistance. From this point on, the function of unions changed dramatically: instead of planning and coordinating acts of resistance among the rank and file, their new aim was to enforce the conditions of the contracts that they had fought so hard to procure for the workers they represented (Adamic, *My America* 415; Brecher 296).

In each of the novels considered in this chapter, a pattern emerges repeatedly in the relations between rank-and-file workers, the union officials who represent them, and the various managers of companies representing corporate interests. Initially (and typically), a company refuses to recognize any single union as the sole representative of its workforce. In response to this deadlocked situation, workers carry out spontaneous acts of on-the-job sabotage, wildcat strikes, and sitdown strikes. The union then quickly attaches itself to this spontaneous movement of worker resistance, seizing on the workers' own momentum to increase its membership. It assumes leadership over the strike wave—coordinating strike actions on a company-wide basis—and uses the leverage possessed by the workers at the point of production to negotiate with the company for union recognition and a favorable labor contract (Brecher 212).

However, once these goals have been met and a contract has been accepted, the stability of the union—and of the jobs of the union officials—depends upon enforcing it, first and foremost by preventing the outbreak of wildcat strikes. That is to say, the moment a labor contract has been negotiated and signed by both the management of a particular company and the union officials, the union, to fulfill its side of the bargain, must occasionally ignore the problems of workers at other companies in the same industry, a situation that undercuts its theoretical commitment to the idea of industry-wide solidarity. The union leaders must also be constantly on the lookout to curtail, check, and contain any form of spontaneous strike activity among the rank and file that would constitute a breach of the labor contract, thus jeopardizing the union's relationship with the company. From this standpoint, then, the ultimate aim of representation by a union appears to be, not the support of workplace democracy and rank-and-file acts of resistance, but rather the institutionalization—and mutually satisfactory resolution—of conflicts between labor and management (American Federation of Labor 201, 213; Brecher 297–299). A wildcat strike under these conditions is not only a threat to the company's profits but equally a threat to the existence of the union, since it undermines the very principle of union representation, which now functions primarily as a disciplinary tool (James 42). "By a remorseless logic, therefore, representation of the proletariat turns into its opposite, administration over the proletariat," observed C.L.R. James in 1950 (116). James's trenchant critique of institutionalized forms of collective bargaining—or what he called the "labor bureaucracy"—goes directly to the heart of one of the key problems associated with the nexus of power and representation in the mass industrial workplace.

By the late 1930s and early 1940s, once the initial round of labor contracts in mass production industries had been signed, the CIO-affiliated industrial unions were quite explicit about the fact that their main goal was to help businesses run smoothly and increase their productivity. In negotiations with corporate executives, they could now boast that they offered "union protection," or, more exactly, "a kind of plant policing by the union for the company" that openly aimed to suppress all manner of rank-and-file unrest (Wechsler 229). Union officials did this, for example, by signing contracts in which they pledged "no labor trouble" to the companies with which they were negotiating and by regularly opposing sympathy strikes between workers in the same industry.[18]

Oddly enough, then, at the same time that the CIO appeared to support the sitdown strike wave in mass production industries, it was actively trying to suppress it by making appeals to the common goal of "union recognition." But for those workers who had become impatient with the businesslike methods of their own union, as McKenney's novel underscores, the term *recognition* appeared so vague as to be practically meaningless. On the one hand, to mass workers who were being sped up and pushed to an extreme, recognition meant higher wages, shorter hours, seniority, benefits, and all-around better working conditions. On the other hand, to the company's managers, "recognition" of the union had come to mean a disciplined, docile workforce, steadily increasing rates of productivity, no strikes, and a reliable flow of profits (Brecher 235).

Union officials representing the interests of the workers were sometimes forced, therefore, to take extreme measures to keep their constituents in line, so as not to break the terms of their contract with the company. From denouncing communists and other militant agitators within their ranks to signing no-strike pledges and other kinds of "sweetheart" contracts with corporations, by 1940 the bulk of the leadership of the UAW and other CIO unions in mass production industries more often appeared to be working against the interests of the very workers they had rallied behind five years earlier (Brecher 225). Indeed, such a strained relationship between union leaders and workers in mass production industries led these workers to use sitdown strikes even more frequently, as a way of resisting the disciplinary measures imposed on them not only by the management of the company but by the union's officials as well.

In conclusion, the figure of the powerful worker that appears in these narratives—one who demands to be represented not only as an economic agent but as an essential element in the process of mass production—formulates and expresses this demand within a framework that has already been defined by the needs of modern capitalist production. That is, as C.L.R. James points out, the labor bureaucracy of CIO and UAW officials "inevitably must substitute the struggle over consumption, higher wages, pensions, education, etc., for a struggle in production. This is the basis of the welfare state, the attempt to appease the workers with the fruits of labor when they seek satisfaction in the work itself. The bureaucracy must raise a new social program in the realm of consumption because it cannot attack capitalism at the point of production without destroying capitalism itself" (41–42). To cite what is perhaps the clearest illustration of this tendency of industrial unions to formulate their demands in terms of consumption, when Tom Shutt, the autoworker and labor organizer depicted in Upton Sinclair's 1937 UAW-sponsored novel *The Flivver King*, rallies his fellow autoworkers, he does so primarily by reminding them of their economic rights as consumers rather than producers. "Make up your minds that you are going to demand and win your full share of the products of high-speed machinery," he exhorts. "Demand your share! Keep on demanding, over and over, until the just demand is granted!" (114).

Hence, the powerful worker depicted in these novels is ambiguously suspended between two possibilities of representation. This situation might further explain the ambiguous and at times apocalyptic character of the outcome of the various strikes presented in these narratives (particularly those by Cantwell, Herbst, and Gallico). By signing a labor contract with the company, following the dictates of the union's leaders, and pledging to behave on the job—to work productively without restricting the company's output in any way—the mass worker can be represented equally by unions and employers as an essential (and essentially pliable) element of capital itself. The worker who is seemingly content to work under contract would thus appear to offer positive proof of the notion that human labor power can in fact be treated as a commodity like any other. But by sitting down, questioning the prerogatives of management, and making further economic demands—in short, by breaking the terms of the labor contract that has been signed—this same worker can also challenge the basic ideological principles and techniques of economic representation in the workplace.

Looked at from a wider angle, therefore, it is clear that whenever mass workers act as "troublemakers" they call into question the legitimacy of even the most basic concepts and categories that have been used for representing human labor power in economic terms. Yet insofar as these workers continue to make economic demands—including the demand to be represented by a union *as workers*—it is also implied that the conflict at the heart of the question of economic representation in the modern industrial workplace can never be adequately resolved. This is because, in the final analysis, what is at stake in this question is simply the degree to which the mass worker in any given circumstance will allow him or herself to be represented (and thus treated) as a commodity like any other.

The sitdown strikes that marked the last years of the Great Depression posed this question in one of its most acute formulations. But for U.S. workers at least, the basic issue—the degree to which workers in mass production industries are to be treated as elements of fixed capital, like machines—would never be conclusively resolved. Moreover, as soon as large industrial enterprises (such as automakers) began moving their operations overseas in the postwar period, it seemed even to be forgotten *as* a question for U.S. workers. Instead, over the next sixty years, while Americans were gradually becoming acquainted with the bitter effects of deindustrialization, the concentrated wave of unrest among mass production workers that marked the growth of industrial unionism in North America reproduced itself throughout the rest of the world—in various locations, according to different circumstances, but always migrating to those sites where auto manufacturers chose to relocate their plants, together with the Fordist production methods these required. Appearing first in western Europe (the United Kingdom, France, Italy, Germany, and Spain) in the 1950s and 1960s, large-scale spontaneous strike movements among autoworkers surfaced next in Argentina, Brazil, and South Africa in the 1970s and early 1980s, and then in South Korea in the late 1980s and early 1990s.

Troublemaking, evidently, had gone global—once and for all.

Conclusion: Making Trouble on a Global Scale

Once the CIO had consolidated the gains it had made—due largely to the success of the sitdown strike tactic—Fordist production methods were exported from the United States to western Europe. This was done not only as part of an effort to rebuild Europe's war-torn economies but also as a way to stem the labor unrest that had resulted from the implementation of Fordist methods in the United States over the previous four decades. This concluding portion of *Troublemakers* first briefly sketches the labor unrest that erupted in U.S. industrial enterprises immediately following the end of World War II. It also explores several of the common effects that attended the globalization of U.S. mass production techniques. These included the formation of new mass industrial working classes in various regions of the world, combined with the structural forms of power these acquired in the process of their formation.

To illustrate the effects of industrial capital's migration beyond the borders of the United States, the bulk of this conclusion will be devoted to examining a specific case study: the Italian mass workers' movement of the late 1960s. It first provides a general overview of this movement, touching upon its causes as well as its substantive links to the CIO and UAW organizing drives of the 1930s. The remainder of the conclusion then analyzes a vivid fictional account of the Italian workers' movement: Nanni Balestrini's novel about striking Italian autoworkers, *Vogliamo tutto* (*We Want It All*), first published in 1971. Balestrini's novel details the wave of sitdown strikes and work stoppages that swept through the industrial centers of northern Italy in 1969. Much like previous generations of mass workers' struggles in the United States, the Italian mass workers' movement was based on a critique of traditional forms of representation by unions and political parties. Formally and thematically, therefore, *Vogliamo tutto* bears a resemblance to Ruth McKenney's CIO-inspired novel from 1939, *Industrial Valley*, even though it is set in a Fiat auto factory in Turin in 1969. In contrast to the U.S. industrial workers' movements during the 1930s, however, the goal of the Italian workers' movement in the 1960s was simply the "refusal of work."

The primary purpose of this conclusion, and the reason it deliberately shifts attention away from the U.S. context, is to demonstrate that structural forms of working-class power are not specific to one region or historical period. On the contrary, they are likely to appear wherever and whenever modern (Fordist) processes of mass production are flourishing. This concluding portion of *Troublemakers* thus studies how Italian novelists in the 1960s encountered the same set of problems that U.S. novelists faced when they tried to represent the figure of the mass industrial worker in a fictional narrative. If such different works as *Industrial Valley* and *Vogliamo tutto* nevertheless share certain features, it is because they are both attempts on the part of writers to represent workers who are struggling to resist being represented by others. When considered together, therefore, the novels of McKenney and Balestrini both illustrate (each in its own way) how twentieth-century authors of working-class novels must themselves struggle to perform the "work" of representing the figure of the mass industrial worker. For this is a figure whose power derives from the fact that it refuses to be represented on the basis of the work that it performs.

The Postwar Revolution of Industrial Workers in the United States

When the Ford Motor Company finally capitulated to the demands of its workforce by recognizing the UAW as the autoworkers' sole national bargaining agent in June 1941, it seemed to many in the U.S. business community that the CIO had acquired a virtual "stranglehold" on mass production industries (Wechsler 228). After the United States entered World War II, many other groups of unorganized industrial workers carried on the tradition of spontaneous work stoppages that had been established by the auto and rubber workers during the Great Depression. The last two years of the war saw a sharp rise in incidents of unrest in industrial workplaces; once the war ended, though, the frequency and scale of strike activity in mass production industries increased exponentially.

In the immediate aftermath of World War II, the major demand of U.S. mass industrial workers was to preserve the same level of wages to which they had become accustomed during the war years. To this end, in a united show of strength, workers throughout the country began walking off their jobs. By the fall of 1945, 43,000 oil workers, 200,000 coal miners, 44,000 Northwest lumber workers, and 70,000 truck drivers in the Midwest were out on strike. In addition, a walkout by 40,000 machinists was accompanied by strikes of longshoremen, flat glass workers, and textile workers in the San Francisco and Oakland areas. On November 21, 225,000 GM workers struck.

All of this strike activity, however, was just the beginning of an even greater wave of labor unrest. The system of wartime production had integrated the U.S. economy to an unprecedented degree, and this integration had the unintended effect of strengthening the ability of industrial workers to paralyze not only particular companies but also entire industries. Over the first six months of 1946, close to 3,000,000 workers took part in strikes that broke out simultaneously in several branches of the U.S. economy. Already by mid-January of 1946, there were 174,000 electrical workers, 93,000 meatpackers, and 750,000 steelworkers out on strike (the last of these setting a record as the largest strike in U.S. history). In early April, 340,000 soft-coal miners stopped work. Finally, May 23 marked the beginning of a nationwide railroad strike that almost put a complete halt to the nation's commerce (Brecher 245–246; Tronti 288–289). In its overall scale, the explosion of U.S. labor unrest in 1946 was comparable only to that which occurred in 1919, when there were 3,630 strikes involving 4.2 million workers, or roughly 20.2 percent of the entire employed workforce in the nation. In 1946, by comparison, there were close to five thousand strikes, amounting to 120 million lost workdays for 4.6 million workers, or 16.5 percent of the nation's workforce (Tronti 283). The U.S. Bureau of Labor Statistics therefore dubbed 1946 "the most concentrated period of labor-management strife in the country's history" (Brecher 246).

In some notorious instances, the federal government responded to this wave of labor unrest by taking advantage of a provision of its "wartime powers" that authorized its direct seizure of the means of production in key industries (oil refineries, packinghouses, railroads, and coal mines). For their part, the leadership of major industrial unions generally dealt with these strikes by making settlements with companies on a case-by-case basis, without taking account of other workers in the same industry who were still out on strike. Thus, as Jeremy Brecher explains, "the division of the working class that had been the source of so much criticism of craft unionism was reproduced on a larger scale by the new forms of industrial unionism.... Indeed, most union leaders would have preferred to avoid the strikes of 1946 altogether. They led them only because the rank and file were determined to strike anyway, and only by leading the strikes could the unions retain control of them" (246–247; cf. James xvii–xviii).

Large U.S. business concerns handled this sudden outburst of labor unrest in a number of different ways. Their first and most common response took the form of what Erik Olin Wright calls a "capital strike": a strategy of relocating their production facilities away from sites where unions had recently gained strength (990). As soon as the war ended and world markets were opened up, U.S. multinationals began shifting their operations and capital investments to western Europe. Two other common responses to the strike wave by U.S. employers were "process innovations (mainly automation), and 'political exchange' (the promotion of 'responsible' unionism and the repression of 'irresponsible' unionism)"—both of which, according to Beverly Silver, "progressively undermined the structural strength of U.S. labor in general, and autoworkers in particular" (48–49).

One reason the U.S. automobile industry was originally concentrated in and around Detroit, Michigan, was that the entire region had come to be known as a stronghold of antiunionism. The business-friendly reputation of the area was the result of an open-shop campaign led by the Employers' Association of Detroit in the early years of the twentieth century. In response to the militancy demonstrated by autoworkers in the 1937 sitdown strikes, however, GM quickly began diffusing and relocating its production facilities so its output would not depend so heavily upon its factories in Flint. In 1937, it acquired an engine plant in Buffalo, New York, and then started to move its operations to various rural and southern areas of the United States. U.S. automakers—as well as the rest of the world automobile industry—would repeat this basic pattern throughout the twentieth century. Beginning in the United States, the diffusion of automobile production around the world operated in direct relation to levels of labor militancy (Silver 41, 46–48).

In the late 1930s, labor unrest in the world automobile industry—in the form of sitdowns and spontaneous work stoppages by rank-and-file autoworkers, often without union authorization—was centered in the

United States and Canada. By the late 1950s, the main site of these militant and spontaneous forms of unrest among autoworkers had shifted to the United Kingdom. In the late 1960s, it shifted again to France and Italy, followed by Germany and Spain in the early 1970s. By the late 1970s, autoworkers in Argentina represented the core of militant labor unrest in the industry, followed by the movements of South African and Brazilian autoworkers in the early 1980s. Finally, by the late 1980s and early 1990s, South Korean autoworkers were carrying out the bulk of these types of strike actions (Silver 44). In light of this pattern, Silver adds, "The trajectory for the world automobile industry suggests that where capital goes, conflict goes.... The geographical relocation of production [in David Harvey's terms] is a 'spatial fix' that only 'reschedules crises'; it does not permanently resolve them" (41).

Italy's "Hot Autumn" of 1969

While the first major phase of expansion of the automobile industry occurred between the years 1910 and 1950 and was centered in the United States—a period and region upon which *Troublemakers* has exclusively focused its attention until now—the second phase of the industry's expansion took place in western Europe during the 1950s and 1960s. From 1950 to 1960, production of automobiles in western Europe increased fivefold, from 1.1 million to 5.1 million. In the 1960s, this number doubled to 10.4 million (Silver 50–51). The auto manufacturers located in the industrial cities of northern Italy were key sites of this expansion, with Fiat's giant Mirafiori plant in Turin symbolizing Italy's postwar mass industrial boom in much the same way as Ford's River Rouge plant was seen as an emblem of the wonders of mass production during the 1920s and 1930s. Paralleling the earlier experience of mass workers in the United States, workers in Italy's mass production industries during the 1960s likewise discovered that they, too, could take advantage of the integrated structure of the plants in which they worked to carry out successful acts of resistance in the workplace. Based in the northern industrial cities, the metal-trades workers formed the largest and most militant group of striking workers. Throughout the 1960s and early 1970s, the peak periods of Italian strike activity coincided with those years in which the metal workers' national contracts came up for renewal.

The postwar mass workers' movement in Italy began in the early 1960s when "articulated" strikes—brief, coordinated stoppages lasting only one or two hours—started occurring in some strongly unionized industrial factories in the North. According to observers of the Italian labor movement during this period, the effects of such strikes depended almost entirely upon the structural power mass industrial workers had acquired at the point of production in the integrated factory (Regalia, Regini, and Reyneri 112–113, 116). New forms of workers' organizations then began to appear, exemplified by the creation in 1966 of a rank-and-file strike committee during wage negotiations at Siemens in Milan. However, the mass workers' movement that culminated in what was dubbed the "Hot Autumn" of 1969 began to emerge on a wide scale in early 1968. At this time, a series of labor conflicts erupted in northern industrial plants, the intensity of which was inversely related to the level of union presence in each of the different plants. Because the primary aim of established industrial unions in Italy was to satisfy workers' demands and control their behavior, in strongly unionized plants the conflicts were typically brief and contained. However, in plants where the union's presence and authority were weaker, workplace disputes took on a more spontaneous and unpredictable character.

By the spring of 1968, Italian mass industrial workers had begun to form their own "base" committees (*comitati unitari di base*) to settle disputes that broke out on the level of the individual plant or shop. These committees were often formed independently of union organizations and acted without union authorization. In addition, at this time, a variety of radical intellectuals and activists chose Fiat's Mirafiori plant as the site to test out and generalize their theories about workers' innovative new forms of organization. In the words of two such activists and observers of the events that were unfolding in Turin, "In the spring of 1968, a battle commenced that would gradually encompass the entire Mirafiori plant, which had the goal (among others) of reducing the work week to forty-four hours. In this battle, the hostility of the workers was not directed simply against employers, or against certain aspects of exploitation; rather, it radically targeted the most basic conditions in the factory. 'Working at Fiat is hell for the workers; starting now, every day at Fiat is going to be hell for the management.'"[1] At the same time that mass industrial workers in northern Italy were beginning to receive serious attention from leftist intellectuals, Italian university students established the first support and information network for workers at Fiat's Mirafiori plant. Their network, called Lotta Continua, closely identified itself with the idea of the "spontaneous immediacy of [workers'] self-organization from below" (Balestrini and Moroni 205). As a result of the combined efforts of students, activists, and workers, from the spring of 1968 to the summer of 1969 industrial workers' struggles took on a new political quality, the originality of which was characterized by the integration of the student movement with that of the workers. A variety of student-worker coalitions, such as Lotta Continua, helped to convey information about, and strengthen the organization of, the emerging mass industrial workers' movement (199).

This unique period of Italian labor unrest—from the spring of 1968 to the summer of 1969—is often referred to as the "creeping May," since it was drawn out for over a year before reaching its peak in the "Hot Autumn" of 1969. In particular, from October to December of 1968, a strike at the Pirelli Settimo plant helped to launch a wave of labor struggles that took place exclusively inside Italian industrial factories. At first, this dramatic rise in plant-level conflicts only appeared in factories where unions were more active. But by the spring and summer of 1969, workers throughout northern Italy began replacing the conventional, union-sanctioned tactic of mass picketing outside the factory with actions that were designed to be executed inside the factory, where unions could not so easily control them (Regalia, Regini, and Reyneri 148). The basic dynamic of the Italian movement in these years, then, can be traced in the points of overlap and opposition between union strategy and the initiatives of independent workers' groups, which reflect an ongoing contest between two modes of generalizing workplace disputes.

By 1969, it had become clear to the bulk of Italy's mass industrial workforce that the established unions were focusing so much of their energy on organizing mass rallies only in order to suppress the influence that vanguard groups of workers were exerting within the actual factories (Balestrini and Moroni 210–211). Inside the factory walls, by contrast, industrial workers were busy inventing a variety of methods to resist the prerogatives of management, none of which depended upon union authorization or the prior approval of union officials. The numerous types of internal strikes they carried out included "spot," "checkerboard," "rolling," and "lightning" strikes, as well as a tactic known as the "go-slow" (Dubois 9; Regalia, Regini, and Reyneri 114). These various strike tactics were not tied to a centralized body of decision makers. Indeed, beginning in early 1968—but especially during the entire year of 1969—the most important characteristic of these labor conflicts was the decentralized nature of the workers' decision-making processes. Each individual factory, shop, and workplace became the primary site at which workers carried out their struggles, using radical direct action tactics that they devised and controlled themselves. To ensure that their demands were met, the rank and file of mass industrial workers knew that they did not have to wait for the union to negotiate the terms of a new contract. Instead, by relying on forms of direct action, they could "put their aims into practice" whenever they chose while still inside the factory, which meant that they did not have to forfeit any of their pay through a more traditional strike or walkout (Regalia, Regini, and Reyneri 118).

In the spring of 1969, the first spontaneous strikes broke out at the Fiat plant in Turin, initiated by a group of skilled workers from the North (a group that sought to hinder such strikes after 1970). By the summer of 1969, the industrial workers' movement had already begun to divide into two factions: on the one hand, the "spontaneists" represented by Lotta Continua, and, on the other hand, a Leninist group of "vanguardists," represented by an organization called Potere Operaio (and its official journal, *La Classe*).

Under these circumstances, the Hot Autumn more or less officially began when, on July 3, 1969, an alliance of industrial unions called for a general strike in Turin around the specific issue of housing reform. As soon as the rally in support of the strike got under way, however, its aims were radicalized and generalized to reflect the broader concerns of the independent organizations of workers and students. In the streets around the Mirafiori plant in Turin, Fiat autoworkers escalated the protests of the rallying workers and students, eventually hijacking an automobile trailer truck to use as a barricade against riot police. Later in the same month, from July 26 to 27, 1969, a national meeting of industrial workers' base committees took place in Turin, marking the first attempt to create a united front out of the various grassroots worker and student organizations.

In early September 1969, workers in Department 54 of Fiat's Mirafiori plant initiated a series of "checkerboard" strikes: a carefully coordinated type of articulated strike in which workers scattered throughout different locations inside the plant slow down or cease work, while others continue to perform their tasks. In retaliation for these brief but costly strikes, Fiat locked out thousands of its workers and refused to pay their wages. Then, on October 10, the workers associated with the Lotta Continua groups briefly occupied the auto body assembly department of the Mirafiori plant—an action followed by almost continuous strikes of one sort or another during the rest of October and November. One of the last major events of the Hot Autumn occurred on November 19, when another general strike for housing reform was called.

The response of the Italian state to this unprecedented wave of labor strife was a massive campaign of repression. In just three months, from September to November 1969, over thirteen thousand workers and activists were arrested. Finally, on December 12, four bombs exploded in a series of planned attacks on banks in the city of Milan. These events were widely seen as a state-controlled tactic to curb the momentum of the recent wave of strikes and to discredit the struggles of mass industrial workers throughout the country more generally (Balestrini and Moroni 204–213; Regalia, Regini, and Reyneri).

By the spring of 1970, the momentum of the mass workers' movement that had culminated in the Hot Autumn of the previous year was already being channeled in new directions. The Italian government passed what came to be known as the "Workers' Bill of Rights," the Statuo dei Lavoratori. This piece of legislation established guidelines and created a bureaucratic mechanism for the regulation of both industrial disputes and the process of trade union organization. Though it especially favored the interests of large federations of unions, such as the CGIL (the Confederazione Generale Italiana del Lavoro, or General Italian Confederation of Labor), it also offered significant legal protections for workers and activists (Regalia, Regini, and Reyneri 152).

However, as would be proved over and over again, the weakness of this new system of industrial relations "lay in the difficulty of controlling rank-and-file action" in the factory (Regalia, Regini, and Reyneri 148). As early as 1968, Italy's major industrial unions had already started to appropriate the innovative strike tactics devised by mass workers, for the purpose of regaining control of spontaneous revolts on the shop floor and to intensify ongoing conflicts in particular industries. When another series of wildcat strikes erupted between 1970 and 1972, union authorities and skilled workers joined forces to moderate this escalation of factory-level unrest, in some cases actively suppressing such grassroots strikes. This new wave of wildcat strikes was initiated by the youngest group of rank-and-file mass workers, who, over the course of the Hot Autumn, had lost whatever sense of deference they might have had toward veteran union leaders. By and large, then, between 1972 and 1976 Italy's industrial unions adopted a strategy of prudence, shifting to more defensive bargaining positions and scaling back their basic demands (Regalia, Regini, and Reyneri 117–118).

The Legacy of U.S. Mass Workers' Movements in Italy

The legacy of the sitdown strike wave in the United States—and, more generally, the unionization drives in U.S. mass production industries between 1933 and 1947—left an indelible mark on European mass industrial workers' movements three decades later. As Mario Tronti himself put it in 1970: "Yesterday's American political situation is the historical western European present. We must know that we are living events already lived. But without any preconstituted outcomes, without any sure conclusions" (311). Specifically, the grassroots campaigns to organize mass industrial workers in the United States during the 1930s served as concrete models of action for Italian workers and activists in the 1960s. Tronti goes on to explain, "If, within the class struggle, victory is measured by what and how much has been gained, then the European workers find before them, as the most advanced model of behavior for their present needs, the way of winning, or the way of defeating the adversary, adopted by American workers in the 1930s" (282, cf. 289, 310). Because the bulk of the workers involved in the uprisings of the Hot Autumn were non- and semiskilled assembly-line operatives who had little contact with established unions, the Italian mass workers—much like their U.S. predecessors—had to create their own tactics and representative organizations.

Despite all the differences between the Italian and U.S. waves of industrial labor unrest, it is important to note a few key similarities between these two movements. On the whole, both the U.S. and Italian movements to strengthen the bargaining power of mass industrial workers were informed by a general critique of economic and political practices of representation. This critique of representation often targeted the practices of existing unions, which claimed the right to represent the interests of new (and apparently intractable) workers in mass production factories. Thus the suspicion that characterized the stance of the IWW toward the institutions of representative democracy, for example, was expressed in almost exactly the same terms by members of the Italian mass workers' movement, who came to view parliamentary and representative democratic practices as inherently corrupt (Tronti 71, 95, 240). Similarly, underlying the Italian workers' critique of political and economic practices of representation was a profound rejection of the scientific discourse that saturated the modern industrial workplace. As in the United States fifty years earlier, the discourse of scientific management and rationalized production in Italy during the 1950s and 1960s defined the individual mass worker as simply one element of the plant's physical machinery, in order to account for the day-to-day, minute-to-minute output of the factory. To reject this discourse meant resisting the systematic attempts, on the part of an army of "expert" production engineers, to reduce assembly-line workers to so many cogs in the industrial mechanism.

Along with this critique of the scientific discourse that permeated the culture of the factory, Italian mass workers dwelt upon the fact that they felt no sense of personal satisfaction from the mechanized work they performed on the assembly line. As Tronti put it, "The only connection individuals have to the forces of production and to their own existence—namely, work—has lost every appearance of personal expression for them. Their enemy is therefore not only the capitalist but also work itself" (191; cf. Balestrini and Moroni 200). Rather than trying to compensate for this situation by providing the mass worker with alternative sources of personal satisfaction, however, the more militant groups within the Italian workers' movement instead emphasized the repulsive nature of every kind of work in the capitalist system, particularly the kind one is expected to perform in the modern factory. "The individual worker must become *indifferent* to his own labor," Tronti proclaimed, "so that the working class as a whole can come to *hate* it" (80).

Again echoing the prior experience of U.S. workers, by the mid-1960s Italian mass industrial workers realized that the site where they possessed the most power was the interior of the factory itself. The best place to organize, they now understood, was at the point of production, on the assembly line or on the shop floor, where they could decide for themselves what direction their various struggles would take. Because their actions at this site did not have to rely on the official mediation of union representatives, the point of production inside the factory was also, they believed, the primary source of mass workers' uniquely materialistic and nonideological sense of class consciousness. "What is generally known as 'class consciousness,'" Tronti explained, "is for us nothing other than the moment of organization" on the shop floor of a mass industrial factory (251; cf. 58, 215–216; Silver 52).

In Italy, just as in the United States, the non- or semiskilled "mass" worker (*operaio massa*) was seen as having definitively displaced the skilled "craft" worker (*operaio professionale*) of a previous era. This new type of worker inspired intellectuals and activists on the Italian left to develop a nuanced theory of "massification" to account for the structural and historical conditions of its emergence (Tronti 308–309). The term *mass worker*, according to these theorists, "was meant to designate a social and cultural mutation in the relationship to work; hence, also, an opposition to the institutions, to the whole field of work, to the surrounding world and the perception of oneself within it, both individually and collectively" (Balestrini and Moroni 201). The culture of sacrifice and career pride that had characterized earlier generations of industrial workers was totally alien to these new mass workers, who were known rather for their attitude of extreme egalitarianism and insubordination. In the view of veteran Italian labor activists, such a pronounced attitude of insubordination toward factory discipline among industrial workers (no doubt encouraged, to some degree, through their association with the radical student movement) signaled one of the most revolutionary elements of the mass worker's consciousness.

Vogliamo tutto

Nanni Balestrini's 1971 novel *Vogliamo tutto* (*We Want It All*), about the Hot Autumn in northern Italy during the summer and fall of 1969, describes a series of events at one of the core sites of this movement: the autoworkers' strikes and work stoppages at Fiat's huge Mirafiori plant in Turin. The novel recalls the basic mood and characteristics of mass workers during this period of intense labor unrest, which marked the beginning of the broader political program that would come to be known as *autonomia*. Balestrini is a poet and novelist whose works—apart from the 1989 translation of his novel, *The Unseen*—have not yet received widespread critical attention in the United States. He was associated with the leftist theoretical school of *operaismo* (workerism) during its formative years in the 1960s and 1970s, whose members included, among others, Mario Tronti, Sergio Bologna, and Antonio Negri.[2]

Like many of the novels we have examined in *Troublemakers*, Balestrini's narrative account of the Hot Autumn tries to represent a peculiar, and uniquely modern, kind of working-class subject: one who resists being represented on the basis of the work that he or she performs, by unions, by political parties, and even by the conventions of realist fiction. Balestrini summed up the qualities of the new generation of industrial workers he chose to be the collective subject of his novel as follows: "In the place of the specialized worker there appears a new type of worker, one who has a totally different role in the relations of production. This is the assembly-line worker: unskilled, unspecialized, mobile, interchangeable. It is the worker that belongs to the great technological advancements of the twenties and thirties, to the institution of Ford's assembly line and to Taylorism. It is the worker who has—just as he has today—a completely different relationship to the machine and to the factory.... This new type of labor power will be [known as] the 'mass' worker" (*Vogliamo tutto* 166).[3] Just as the appearance of this new kind of industrial worker had been met with fascination on the part of observers in the United States fifty years earlier, so, too, in northern Italy in the 1960s, it seemed to interested onlookers as though an entirely new species of labor power had been created by the system of mass production in large Fordist factories.

At this time, the left wing of the Italian labor movement was committed to three basic strategies for advancing the interests of the mass industrial proletariat: (1) the refusal of work, (2) the abolition of the variable wage scale (which linked wage rates to productivity), and (3) the rejection of traditional forms of representation by unions and political parties.

For its part, the effort to sever the relation between wages and productivity was an outgrowth of the first of these strategies, the "refusal of work." This strategy was theorized extensively in the writings of Mario Tronti, who observed that the "collective worker" one encounters everywhere in Italy's modern mass production industries "opposes not only the machine, insofar as it is constant capital, but also labor power itself, insofar as it is variable capital." Therefore, Tronti proposed, the mass industrial working class "must come to see the whole of capital as its enemy: including itself, then, insofar as it is a part of capital. That is, labor must view labor power—*insofar as the latter is a commodity*—as its own enemy" (55–56). C.L.R. James had argued a similar point more than twenty years earlier, asserting that "the conflict of the proletariat is between itself as object and itself as consciousness, its party" (qtd. in Nielsen 119). Taken together, then, James's and Tronti's remarks sum up a perspective that many theoreticians on the left thought they recognized in the attitude of the younger generation of non- and semiskilled mass workers (Tronti 260–261).

Because *Vogliamo tutto* sets out to represent these central tenets of the Italian workers' vigorously antirepresentational praxis, it is no surprise to discover that the novel contains a self-reflexive critique of its own representational aims and methods. Indeed, the novel questions, and in some sense refuses, its own status as a representational literary "work"; and it does this precisely in order to represent, as faithfully as possible, the refusal of work that its characters put into effect in the Fiat factory.

Balestrini tells a large portion of his story through the voice of an anonymous narrator. In the foreword he wrote for the 2003 German edition of the novel, Balestrini explains that he used this narrative device to show how "an individual's history becomes the collective history of the working class" ("Immer noch" 8; see also Balestrini 163). The nameless narrator comes from a community of rural farmers in southern Italy. Like many other young men of his generation and region, he grows up surrounded by the successes of Italy's postwar economic "miracle," which, in his eyes, holds out the promise of consumer goods such as new and stylish clothes, stereo equipment, and automobiles. Yet this same narrator has also grown up hearing tales of despair from his family and acquaintances about the world of work. The lesson he takes away from all this is that he must find and identify himself with a career of some sort, but that any work he is likely to find will be purely exploitative, with little or no opportunity for career advancement.

With a conflicted attitude toward the whole idea of work, then, he leaves his hometown to take a series of jobs in the northern industrial centers. Wherever he works in the North, he is perceived and treated as a member of a foreign and inferior (southern) race. When he finally arrives at Fiat's Mirafiori plant in Turin, he discovers that he is only one of a giant mass of migrating young southern men who have come north to find work and thus benefit from the booming economy (*Vogliamo tutto* 63).

At this point, the narrator's antiwork ethic becomes explicit, concretely illustrated through his experience at Fiat. Shortly after he begins working there, the narrator, who never accepted the ideology of the bourgeois work ethic in the first place, exclaims that the assembly-line method of production "shows you how really disgusting work is, how disgusting every kind of work is. If we [mass workers] want to improve our lot these days, then we shouldn't work anymore. We can only improve our situation by refusing to work and by fighting" (*Vogliamo tutto* 75).

Because the narrator so insistently refuses both work and the representation of work (in books or any other form), he eventually comes to demand—along with his fellow Fiat workers who are on strike—the abolition of variable wage rates. Variable wages are wages that are scaled, and thus tied, to measurable levels of productivity, just as, more generally, representations are apparently tied—or at least ideally related—to the objects they are supposed to represent. From the workers' perspective, the wage, when it functions as a representation of productivity, is simultaneously a tool of political power, which the company can use, at its discretion, to discipline its workforce. In response to this, the workers consequently refuse any sort of link between wages and productivity, demanding for themselves "a wage that isn't based on the company's production, but on [our] actual needs" (*Vogliamo tutto* 89, 92).

When wages function as representations of productivity levels—becoming instruments that the company can use to control its workforce whenever it deems this to be necessary—it follows that any struggle that aims merely to regulate or control the wage rates (much as the unions propose) is nothing but an extension of this disciplinary power of the company over its workforce. Since the task of mediating wage disputes between the company and its workers typically falls to unions, the unions, in turn, must keep their demands narrowly focused on wages alone and thus in line with the priorities of the company. However, once the whole idea of wage rates as such is rejected, the unions lose their raison d'être and must be rejected as well (*Vogliamo tutto* 92).

It is clear, then, the workers of *Vogliamo tutto* are not only interested in getting better wages. Since this is exactly what the union wants, and since it is the union's job to preserve harmony between labor and management, the workers at Fiat are out to abolish, first, the wage as a representation of the work they perform, and second, any group that tries to uphold this representational function of the wage (unions and political parties, serving as intermediaries between the company and its workforce). Throughout the novel, union officials as well as Communist Party members repeatedly try to discourage the Fiat workers from carrying out spontaneous wildcat strikes, since these are performed without the official sanction of the workers' representatives, who would mediate such disputes in the interests of both sides. However, as the striking workers in the novel explain, "Here, strikes are declared autonomously by the workers themselves, not by the union" and "The workers no longer trust any force outside themselves" (*Vogliamo tutto* 95, 108). One worker giving a speech sums up this distrust of third-party representation by proclaiming, "The workers have acquired a new consciousness and grasp of what they have to do. Even if it's just a few of them, like a vanguard, that's all that matters. *I don't speak for others*, or whatever experience they may have had" (139; emphasis added).

Once they recognize how delicately coordinated all the operations in their factory are, the workers of *Vogliamo tutto* immediately begin to exploit the fact that the main source of their workplace bargaining power—their most valuable weapon in dealing with management—is the organization of the production process itself. Demanding that "all production must be blocked," one of the strikers explains how "we've learned in this month that we possess a force of extraordinary power: all it takes is a single workshop to be shut down in order to block up production throughout the entire factory. As the level of organization in the factory grows, it connects individual workshops together and makes it possible to utilize this formidable weapon all down the line" (126). With the coordinated labor processes of mass production, where each operation depends upon the previous operations of the other workshops, a slowdown or stoppage in any single sector is liable to cripple, or at least severely limit, the output of the entire factory. Knowing and taking advantage of this fact, the workers at Fiat claim that "our struggle has given the management a strong impression of the force we possess, apart from the scanty results achieved so far. It is this force alone that we should count on to bring the company definitively to its knees" (118).

With this weapon, moreover, the workers are confident that they can outflank the union's attempts to gain control of the strike movement. For instance, at one point the narrator tells us that the workers are "responding to the election of union officials by limiting production all on their own [*l'autolimitazione della produzione*]" (*Vogliamo tutto* 108). What exactly is involved in such a limiting of production? Materials in the plant, for example, need to move constantly from one stage of production to the next. When they are prevented from leaving one workshop, or one stage of the manufacturing process, then the next shop, which totally depends upon these materials, cannot perform any of its operations, and so on throughout the entire factory. The workers at Fiat understand this simple fact, and they know how powerful each individual workshop in the plant has become as a result. Every strike, stoppage, or slowdown in production therefore has consequences that may be as crippling as they are unpredictable.[4]

From this vantage point, the basic tactical question for the workers is to find where the weak spots of the factory are, in order "to create the greatest amount of blockage by using the least amount of force" (*Vogliamo tutto* 109). Blockage, in this context, means "the interlinking of struggles [*il concatenamento delle lotte*]" in such a way that, according to the methods of the various workshops, "each individual shop, in synch with the others, strikes for two hours; and thus all the shops, by coordinating their actions, are able to block up the entire system of production in the factory" (96). To see how this happens in the case of a single workshop, take the very last stage of the manufacturing process: the moment when the finished automobiles leave the conveyor belt, to be parked and loaded onto trucks for being shipped away. Even here at this final stage, a small number of Fiat workers are able to shut down the operations of all the preceding stages of production simply because they do not use the finished cars' engines (as they normally would) to drive them off the assembly line: "Instead of driving the cars away with their own engine power, we pushed them by hand, four men per car. In this way, we clogged up the assembly line until they were forced to shut down completely. We blocked everything" (109).

Once production in the factory is blocked, and union representation of the workers' interests is blocked, and even the representational function of the wage is blocked (or temporarily suspended by the workers' critique), another question arises: How can these striking workers express their collective interests? How, or in what form, are they to represent their demands without relying to some degree upon those very same institutionalized practices of representation that they have been actively working to shut down?

In place of representation, the mass workers of *Vogliamo tutto* substitute demonstration. Instead of using language to communicate their interests and demands to Fiat's management, the workers abuse language by dispensing with the conventional protocols of linguistic exchange: "We yelled the strangest things that didn't mean a fuck. Just to be disruptive, we yelled Mao Tse Tung, Ho Chi Minh, workers' power, and other things that weren't related to anything—things we wanted to say just because we liked saying them.... Because it didn't have a fucking thing to do with Fiat, which was just fine by us" (*Vogliamo tutto* 80). A demonstration in this postwar assembly-line novel, then, looks a bit more like the disassembly, or the dismantling, of the basic elements of linguistic communication:

> Now that we've got the ball rolling, it's time for a parade. We've got to make a racket that never stops, and we should start right now by smashing the hell out of everything here. And we kicked these boxes of materials really hard just to make noise, a deep, booming, violent noise—DU-DU-DU DU-DU-DU DU-DU-DU—and this racket went on for two hours. Now and then we held meetings, sometimes on the north end of the conveyor belts, sometimes on the south end. We zigzagged back and forth through the belts, all yelling together: More money, less work! Or: We want it all! Up and down the length of the belts, yelling and holding meetings. (84)

The Fiat workers become aware of their collective power by staging demonstrations like these. They then begin to imagine how they might organize themselves into a broader movement of mass industrial workers. In addition, the anonymous narrator of the novel now ceases to figure as the story's protagonist. One of his last statements in the novel appears at the moment the collective of mass workers recognizes the potential of its socioeconomic strength beyond the gates of the Fiat factory: "And then I finally had the satisfaction to discover that everyone else was thinking the same things I've thought about for years, ever since I started working . . . that work itself is our only enemy, our only sickness" (102).

Another effect of their mass radicalization is the autoworkers' newly acquired conviction that the power they have within the Fiat factory must be extended outward to society at large, where it can be put to its greatest possible use. As they see it, the power to shut down automobile production is also—because this industry is a key component of the national economy—the power to effect broader social changes, a power to alter the living conditions in what radical Italian theorists at the time famously called the "Social Factory" (Tronti 234–252). Taking their protest beyond the gates of the factory and into the city of Turin, the Fiat workers sense that "it wasn't so much their rage that motivated them, but their joy. The joy of finally being strong. And to discover that the needs they had and the fight they were fighting were the needs and the fight of everyone" (Balestrini, *Vogliamo tutto* 155).

Recall for a moment that Balestrini chose to tell this story about the refusal of work and the refusal of representation in the form of a novel, since only the novel is capable, in his words, of showing the process whereby "an individual's history becomes the collective history of the working class" (Balestrini, "Immer noch" 8). Some of the techniques Balestrini uses to signify this process are patently conventional. For example, shortly after the strike movement grows large enough to attract the attention of Turin's (and Italy's) general population, the narrator appears in a newspaper clipping, with no indication that his actions are any more noteworthy than the actions of the other striking workers: "Thursday, May 29: A young worker from the South tried to enter the factory while carrying a picket sign. The company guards restrained him, and this caused a fight to break out" (*Vogliamo tutto* 98). Balestrini's narrative technique therefore uses a type of epic hero as a synecdoche to reflect the larger, collective struggle of mass industrial workers throughout the country—a struggle that literally absorbs this hero without, however, requiring that the novel shift its narrative focus.

Nevertheless, in spite of the novel's reliance on literary conventions, one should note that Balestrini is not simply trying to tell a straightforward story about the collective struggles of a mass industrial workforce. Instead, given that the subject of the novel (in its twofold sense: both the narrator and the strike movement of the Hot Autumn) is so acutely focused on the refusal of work, what the novel at times seems to demand of its readers is precisely that it not be read *as* a novel, namely, a literary representation that takes the form of a finished "work." Rather, Balestrini invites us to see it as a sort of machine, a fictional assembly line that manufactures a specific figure of resistance to the system of modern industrial capitalism. This figure takes the form of human excrement ("shit"), which regularly appears in the narrative as both a metaphor and a metonym for the unrest of the Italian working class.[5]

Consider one framing device in particular, an image that Balestrini highlights to imply that his story is constantly pushing against the limits of the generic category in which it is being told (that of the novel). The narrator's first job in the North is with a company called Ideal Standard that makes bathroom fixtures. On his first day there, he is put to work building toilet bowls. Consistent with his antiwork ethic, he tells us how "for every two toilet bowls that my coworkers made, I made only one" (*Vogliamo tutto* 19). When he is laid off from the job a few days later, he demands to be paid in compensation. As he tells it: "I went outside the factory to wait for the engineer to come and give me my money. But while I was waiting around I had to shit; so I went to shit, and then I missed the engineer" (24). This apparently trivial detail of the story turns out to have serious and far-reaching consequences, for it leads to a sort of miniature, one-man strike wave, a round of small-scale protest actions on the part of the narrator in his struggle to get his money. His taking a shit, then, not only defers and interrupts the process of receiving payment for his labor in the representational form of the wage but also serves as the impetus for a series of individual acts of resistance that finally culminate, a few months later, in the massive strike wave of the Hot Autumn, centered in and around the Fiat Mirafiori plant in Turin. Again, when the narrator first begins working at Fiat he notes how "a factory is really the most absurd and disgusting thing that ever existed" (58). Finally, two pages before the end of the novel, in the midst of the chaotic rioting in the streets of Turin—a riot that had begun as a workers' demonstration just outside the Fiat factory gates—the narrator makes one last appearance as an individual in order to say: "We came up to the street and saw a wide alley where there was still a lot of fighting going on. Everything was so confused, you couldn't tell who was winning. I just wanted to stand still for a minute and take a shit somewhere—I couldn't take any more of this" (144).

Balestrini's re-marking or reiteration of the image of shit, at the beginning and at the end of the novel, is not accidental but strategic. Italy's mass industrial worker, here, wants to shit because his shit is practically the only thing about him, the only thing he possesses, that cannot be turned into a commodity and sold on the open market. As the most tangible index of the worker's noncommodified humanity, this image also functions as the positive sign—indeed, as a demonstration, if not a representation—of the movement's antiwork ethic (Balestrini and Moroni 212). Yet ironically, mass production factories such as Fiat's Mirafiori plant were originally designed and used, like giant toilet bowls, to contain the mass workers' figurative "shit": to trap, sanitize, and dispose of labor unrest as efficiently as possible through Fordist methods of production. To "want it all" in this context, as the workers' chant proclaims (*Vogliamo tutto!*), is to want exactly what Fiat will never be able to take away from its workforce: their desires, their drives, and their physiological needs as human beings. Such desires and drives, because they cannot be commodified without at the same time being exploited, are figured here—or rather disfigured—as the shit that keeps coming back, the shit that will not go away but remains in circulation, even as the workers' movement appears to disintegrate in the riot that concludes the novel.

It seems that Balestrini chooses this image to represent the otherwise unrepresentable (unspeakable, unseemly, or unsightly) power of Italy's mass industrial working class. This is a power that modern capital cannot contain or dispose of because it gets produced, and even strengthened, by the only thing that would ever be able to contain it, the very same apparatus that was designed to minimize the growth of working-class power: the modern system of mass production itself.

Notes

Introduction

1. Unless otherwise noted, all translations are my own.

2. The concept of embodiment, in the sense in which it is being used here, cannot be dissociated from the representational strategies used to define, comprehend, or otherwise contain it. The physical body that bears the commodity of human labor power, in the context of the modern industrial enterprise, is both essential for and resistant toward the structural (vertical) integration of the capitalist firm. The body functions as a foundation for modern methods of mass production, including the logistical-representational modes through which mass industrial firms are organized. In doing so, however, it also comes to acquire, through its very materiality, the power effectively to dismantle the organizational and representational constructs according to which it is defined as nothing more than a material substance. That is, it acquires agency through the condition, and as the condition, of its material embodiment. The point, then, is to think of the body not as in some way anathema to, or oppositionally distinct from, representational practices but rather as that which enables—and is in turn produced by—these practices, while nevertheless allowing one to contest them at a fundamental level.

3. To be exact, the worker's intellectual and corporeal condition—and not, as Elaine Scarry would have it, a universally human will-to-create (61–62)—is the source of labor power's fictitious qualities, as well as the basis of whatever formal and aesthetic features it shares with modes of literary fiction. Elsewhere, Ernesto Laclau and Chantal Mouffe attribute the fictitious character of the commodity of human labor power to the needs of orthodox Marxist theoreticians rather than to those of a market-based economy (78, citing Bowles and Gintis).

4. This last point should be understood as a reference to, as well as an inversion of, Michael Denning's observation that "work itself resists representation." Whereas Denning claims that strikes provided working-class writers with concrete and exciting

events to narrate, to tell a story about, and that this in turn solved the problem of representing the monotonous day-to-day experience of work—in his words, "the strike novel used the interruption of work, the festival of the oppressed, as a solution" to this problem (244)—*Troublemakers* argues that the strike novel encounters its own set of unique, and more formal, problems regarding the possibility of narrative representation. Hence, its general thesis might read, "Direct action itself (and the work stoppage that results from it) resists representation."

5. The distinction being made here between iconic, symbolic, and indexical modes of representation is informed by the work of W. J. T. Mitchell (14) and Raymond Williams (266–269).

Part One / The Making of the Mass Worker

1. See Chandler, "General Introduction" 10–11, 14–15, "Introduction to Part II" 96, "General Motors' Innovations" 112–113, and *Strategy* 24–25; Edwards 78.

2. See Aitken 21, 28; Arnold, "Production" 921; Arnold, "Six Examples" 997; "Editors' Introduction" 741; "Education" 616.

3. By the 1920s, it had become possible for some firms actually to achieve this goal. In a 1929 article entitled "We Build a Plant to Run without Men," the owner of the A. O. Smith Corporation, an auto frame manufacturer in Milwaukee, Wisconsin, explained how the company had managed to eliminate most of its human workforce (Smith 137).

4. It is often overlooked that not every worker at Ford was automatically qualified to receive the five-dollar wage. The purpose behind the Ford Motor Company's creation of its Sociological Department, under the direction of John R. Lee, was to ensure that those who received the high wage were physically, mentally, and morally fit to deserve it (Chandler, "New Type" 180; Gartman 206–211). For a thorough history of Ford's Sociological Department, Lee's various reform efforts, and Ford's use of assembly-line technology as a way to "Americanize" its immigrant workforce, see Meyer.

5. For a much richer account of the introduction of continuous-flow methods of production in the automotive industry more generally, which stresses how such innovations were developed as a direct response to real or potential acts of worker resistance, see Gartman 83–101.

1 / The Powerless Worker and the Failure of Political Representation

1. Aitken's characterization of Taylor's ideal worker (a machine) implies what many other members of the works management movement—with the notable exception of Arnold and Taylor—would have typically sought to disguise behind a discourse of the supposed cultural edification and intellectual enlightenment mass workers were to gain through their daily encounters with modern machinery (see Outerbridge, "Educational Influence" and "Emancipation"; Higgins).

2. Antonio Gramsci saw in this connection between the physicality of manual labor and the presumption of the worker's low mental capacity a central principle of "Americanism"—a term he defined as the ideal of any society that organizes itself on the basis of Fordist methods of production (302).

3. Elizabeth Esch and David R. Roediger have recently shown that scientific managers inherited this specifically racial model for classifying different types of workers from the more widespread and commonly accepted "racialised labour-systems" of the

United States. The latter were rooted in antebellum U.S. managerial methods, particularly those that had been developed on southern plantations.

4. Although Ford also acquired a reputation as the only major automaker to hire considerable numbers of African Americans on fair and equitable terms, this notion has been refuted by actual Ford employees (Cruden, *End* 8).

5. While Taylor has nothing to say about the feminization of "muscle work" that the widespread application of scientific management in U.S. industrial enterprises would later require, Braverman discusses at great length the predominantly female—and racially nonwhite or ethnic—workforce in the growing U.S. service economy (cf. Kessler-Harris).

6. For an analysis of Sinclair's racist depiction of Chicago's stockyard workers, see Phelps 22 and Noon 430–432. Also in this regard, see David R. Roediger's reading of Eugene O'Neill's *The Hairy Ape* (*Colored White* 45–48).

7. Christophe Den Tandt's reading of the "people of the abyss" takes them instead to be an illustration of the mass "crowd" that Gustave Le Bon famously dreaded (154–155; Le Bon).

8. This reading of *Marching! Marching!* parallels Elaine Scarry's analysis of the linguistic strategies Thomas Hardy used to represent the experience of work from the unique perspective of the worker as an "embodied maker" (7, 57, 68). Compare this to how Roland Barthes identified the distinguishing feature of modern literary "style" with the "imagery, delivery, vocabulary [that] spring from the body and the past of the writer . . . a sub-language elaborated where flesh and external reality come together" (10–12).

9. Paula Rabinowitz offers a lengthier—and quite fascinating—reading of the novel along these lines (97–115; see especially 103–107). Barbara Foley (412–413, 438) and Walter B. Rideout (215–216) also provide analyses of the novel that focus on its "collectivist" formal features.

2 / The Empowered Worker and the Technological Representation of Capital

1. See Immanuel Kant's concept of the sublime (90–132). For an interesting study of figures of the sublime in U.S. naturalist fiction—encompassing both Kant's and Edmund Burke's sense of the term—see Den Tandt.

2. For these statistics, see Chandler, "General Introduction" 14; Cruden, *End* 7; Nevins and Hill, *Ford: Expansion* 293, 298, 515.

3. C.L.R. James argues that the extreme brutality (specifically, the fascist qualities) of Ford's labor practices explains why the notion of industrial unionism took hold most firmly in the automotive industry (40).

4. For an illuminating account of the role of metaphorical language in Sinclair's novel, where workers and animals function as "absent referents," see Adams 64–81.

5. Den Tandt's schematic but provocative analysis of the novel underscores this cannibalistic aspect of the meatpacking industry (174–175).

6. See Foley 414, 421–422; Murphy 154; Rideout 209, 213–214.

7. The exaggerated degeneracy of the bourgeoisie represented here is frequently cited as the novel's most serious flaw (Foley 437–438; cf. Rideout 219–220).

Part Two / Strategy and Structure at the Point of Production

1. See Chandler, "New Type" 179; Gramsci 309–310; Reitell 186.

2. See Silver 47; Torigian 329; cf. Arrighi and Silver 194–195.

3. Arrighi, "Marxist Century"; Arrighi and Silver 194–195; Kraus 190.

4. For an illuminating analysis of the theoretical, tactical, and personal links between the IWW and European syndicalist movements, see Salerno's *Red November*.

5. See Adamic, *My America* 408–409; Brecher 232; Edwards 121–122; Kraus 125; Torigian 335, 346.

6. Kraus 42; cf. Kraus 82–83, 91, 176; Fine 172; Torigian 346–347.

3 / The Disempowering Worker and the Aesthetic Representation of Industrial Unionism

1. Of these three authors, Ernest Poole was the most closely affiliated with the representatives and activities of the IWW (Noon 432; Poole, "Maxim Gorki" 77–78, 81).

2. For more on the Wobblies' rich tradition of songs, see the individual essays by the editors of *The Big Red Songbook* (Green, "Preface"; Roediger, "Their Horrid Gold"; Rosemont, "Lost and Found"; and Salerno, "Sizzlooks"). In addition, this volume contains numerous first-person accounts and reflections by Wobbly artists and songwriters.

3. According to the main theorist of French revolutionary syndicalism, Georges Sorel—whose writings both directly and indirectly influenced the philosophy of the IWW's founders—the struggle of mass workers to organize industrial unions would necessarily adopt a sublime character. Sorel notes how "[for] these men being engaged in a war which was bound to end in their triumph or their enslavement, the sentiment of sublimity was bound to be engendered [*le sentiment du sublime devait naître tout naturellement*] by the conditions of the struggle" (211). Sorel goes on to observe that "in a country where the conception of the general strike exists, the blows exchanged between workmen and representatives of the middle classes have an entirely different import, their consequences are far reaching and they may beget heroism [*du sublime*]" (213). For an analysis and critique of Sorel's use of the figure of the sublime, see Horowitz (146–163). See also Green, "John Neuhaus" 209–210; Kornbluh, "Lumberjacks" 251; Veblen 160–162.

4. This term refers to Richard Wagner's late-romantic notion of a "Gesamtkunstwerk," which was supposed to create an entirely new form of art by combining all the existing individual forms—such as drama, poetry, music, dance, painting, and sculpture—into one singular work. Inspired by the synthetic form of classical Greek tragedies, Wagner held that the modern "total work of art," through the balanced combination of all these traditional forms, would effectively transcend their formal, aesthetic, and semantic limitations.

5. John Reed was a journalist and political activist, as well as a poet and novelist, who is most famously associated with his chronicle of the 1917 Russian Revolution, *Ten Days That Shook the World* (1920). A bohemian intellectual in Greenwich Village during the 1910s, Reed was a frequent participant in leftist causes alongside the wealthy Mabel Dodge (Luhan), who hosted a regular series of "evenings" in her Manhattan home for the radical New York intelligentsia. Before helping to found and lead the IWW in 1905, William D. "Big Bill" Haywood had spent almost twenty years as an organizer for the Western Federation of Miners. He was a key figure in a sensational criminal trial in 1907, when he had been framed and charged as an accomplice in the murder of former Idaho governor Frank Steunenberg.

6. See Foner, *Industrial Workers* 365–366; Golin 52; Kornbluh, "Paterson" 201.

7. Steve Golin's more recent interpretation of the significance of the pageant is based entirely on the assumption that the actors and audience were indeed "fused" through the performance itself (54, 56–57, 72–74; see also Nochlin).

8. By emphasizing the spontaneity of mass industrial workers, in contrast to the supposedly rational views of their leaders, Bullard's narrator employs a familiar motif associated with the notion of an "élan vital"—an irrational living spirit or life force within all sentient beings (Adamic, *Dynamite* 167; Den Tandt 247–248). For an overview of the concept of an "élan vital" in the works of Henri Bergson and Georges Sorel, see Horowitz 39–56. On the influence of Bergson's ideas in the United States during the early years of the twentieth century, see the studies of Hanna and Pilkington.

9. Two helpful critical models for understanding how the generic conventions of nineteenth-century romance could be reinvested and redeployed in the service of a progressive political narrative are Hazel V. Carby's study of early twentieth-century African American women novelists, *Reconstructing Womanhood* (especially chs. 6 and 7, on the work of Pauline Hopkins [121–162]), and Claudia Tate's *Domestic Allegories of Political Desire*.

10. Walter B. Rideout sees in Yetta's choice to marry Isadore a renunciation of her earlier syndicalist passions (55–56). In contrast to Rideout, Den Tandt's reading of the novel argues that U.S. naturalist authors such as Bullard, Sinclair, Garland, and Teller "use the actual marriage of their protagonists as a symbol of unanimistic reconciliation" between otherwise conflicting romantic and political passions (181–185).

11. Cf. Bird and Shaffer; Conn 114; Dosch 417; Dubofsky 161; Poole, *Harbor* 336.

12. This analysis of Bill's struggle to produce a narrative of the strike is not meant to suggest that every narrative about mass industrial workers must reduce them to the figure of a single, unitary protagonist of some sort, whether individual or collective. As Barbara Foley rightly notes, by the 1930s there emerged what many critics hailed as an entirely new genre of working-class fiction, the "collective novel" (400–402; cf. ch. 11, "The Collective Novel," 398–441, passim). The other novels discussed in the present study that Foley labels "collective" include those by Weatherwax, Rollins, McKenney, and Herbst. Foley's definition of the collective novel expands on the earlier analyses of the genre by Walter B. Rideout (215–216) and Granville Hicks (Robbins 28).

13. From the perspective of Eugene O'Neill's *The Hairy Ape*, published only a few years after *The Harbor*, O'Neill's representation of brutalized coal stokers at the bottom of an ocean liner—particularly the character of Yank—can be read as a skeptical rejoinder to Joe Kramer's idealization of the mass industrial worker (O'Neill 113–118, 138, 144).

14. In contrast to Bill's form of writing, Joe's work on *War Sure* could be understood as an attempt to convert "literary" energy into "technical" energy, in Eugenio Giovannetti's sense of the term. Antonio Gramsci draws attention to this distinction in his essay "Americanism and Fordism" (306–307).

15. Jim Marsh's remarks could very well have been inspired by an actual speech, entitled "The General Strike," that William D. "Big Bill" Haywood gave in New York City on March 16, 1911 (Haywood, "General Strike" 49–50; cf. Kornbluh, "With Folded Arms" 36; "Who Is the Leader?" 204).

4 / The Powerful Worker and the Demand for Economic Representation

1. See Adamic, *Dynamite* 390; Brecher 205; Kraus 44.

2. See Chandler, "Unionizing" 195; Gramsci 309–310; Kraus 9–10; Torigian 337; Vorse 8–9.

3. See American Federation of Labor 202, 215; Chandler, "Unionizing" 195; Nevins and Hill, *Ford: Expansion* 538, 592.

4. See Chandler, "General Introduction" 19 and "Unionizing 196–198; Cruden, *End* 10–11; Fine 50; Kraus 42; Torigian 330; Wechsler 227–228.

5. See Kraus 106, 156, 266; *Monthly Labor Review* 218; Silver 47; Torigian 329.

6. See Fine 332–338; Gallico 159; Kraus 46, 96–97.

7. Michael Torigian offers a useful sketch of the basic tendencies of historians of the GM strike, who are split between those who emphasize the importance of workers' spontaneous actions and those who stress the important role played by the UAW and CIO leaders. Regarding the former group—which would include historians such as Jeremy Brecher—Torigian makes the astute observation that "purely spontaneist accounts can't explain the end of a strike, however spontaneously it might have begun, without blaming the union; but the fact that a union could have sufficient authority to end a strike only proves that it could have been a significant factor (among others) in initiating the strike" (327, 329n17).

8. See also Adamic, *My America* 407; Bernstein 501; Fine 172; Kraus 42, 82–83, 90–91; Vorse 10.

9. The wording of the NIRA's Section 7 (a) was deliberately vague, stating that employees have "the right to organize and bargain collectively through representatives of their own choosing." This phrase was then interpreted by corporations in a way that allowed them to undermine the principle of majority rule when it came to the selection of employee representatives for the purpose of collective bargaining. As a result, it became virtually impossible for any legitimate union to establish a firm presence (let alone a closed shop) among a company's workforce (Fine 30).

10. In novels such as Bell's *Out of This Furnace* and Upton Sinclair's *The Flivver King* that are so intensely focused on heralding the class-conscious ideals of industrial workers, the reality of the effects of sitdown strikes could easily be either reduced to a minor anecdote (Bell) or simply omitted altogether (Sinclair).

11. The theory of revolutionary reportage that this second group developed—most clearly articulated in Joseph North's formulations at the Writers' Congress and for the 1935 anthology *Proletarian Literature in the United States*—was meant to provide a vehicle for this new definition of writing as the instantiation of the reality of class struggle (Hart 121; Hicks et al. 211–212). Whittaker Chambers's short story "Can You Hear Their Voices? The Arkansas Farmers' Fight For Food" expressed another aspect of this embodied notion of writing, since his characters treat the creation of distinctly "proletarian" writing literally as a kind of food for their starving bodies, much as Michael Gold's *Jews without Money* (1930) and Grace Lumpkin's *To Make My Bread* (1932) identify the bodies of their characters with the concrete living conditions of their environments (New York's Lower East Side and the Appalachian hills around Gastonia, North Carolina, respectively).

12. Middle-class writers such as Meridel Le Sueur, Horace Gregory, and Tillie Olsen often felt compelled to choose between these two definitions of writing, with some opting to quit their professional careers and go to work in mines or steel mills while

others chose to identify themselves as representatives of the radical (ex-bourgeois) intelligentsia.

13. For this very reason, Conroy claimed that the fictitious factory represented in *The Land of Plenty* "did not fit into the expected pattern of intellectuals who had never worked in one" ("Robert Cantwell's *Land*" 82). Conroy is presumably referring to those leftist bourgeois intellectuals who were apt to criticize the novel's ambiguous ending.

14. Of course, this did nothing to prevent Depression-era humanist critics of the novel from accusing Cantwell of having obscured the humanity of his characters behind the representation of the mechanized environment of the industrial workplace (cf. Conroy, "Robert Cantwell's *Land*" 81–83).

15. Henry Ford shared a similar suspicion toward the inherent vagaries of conventional language: "Social conditions are not made out of words.... Propaganda, bulletins, lectures—they are nothing. It is the right act sincerely done that counts" (*My Life* 263).

16. This worker's perspective reflects an actual discourse that the UAW created to justify the sitdown strike tactic throughout the duration of the GM strike, as well as during the subsequent legal disputes that surrounded the use of the tactic (Kraus 46, 96–97).

17. Henry Kraus notes how John Thrasher, a worker at Standard Cotton (a small feeder plant for GM's Fisher Body Plant 1, whose own sitdown strike paralleled the larger GM strike), exclaimed of the strike in his plant: "Nothing that happened before the strike began seemed to register in the mind any more. It is as if time itself started with the strike" (289). The idea that sitdown strikes such as these can interrupt the smooth flow of homogeneous time is illustrated by Walter Benjamin's remarks on the significance of the concept of the "proletarian strike" in the work of Georges Sorel. See Benjamin's essay "Critique of Violence" (277–300), as well as Werner Hamacher's analysis of what he identifies in Benjamin's essay as the "afformative" force of the proletarian strike (121, 124–126).

18. See Adamic, *My America* 414; Bernstein 593; Brecher 224; Torigian 346.

Conclusion

1. Balestrini and Moroni 202 (quoting a flyer distributed among Fiat Mirafiori workers in April 1968); unless otherwise noted, all translations are my own.

2. For a fine overview of the origins and stages of development of the *autonomia* and *operaismo* movements in Italy during the 1960s and 1970s, see Steve Wright's *Storming Heaven*.

3. Unless otherwise noted, all translations are my own.

4. Tronti extrapolated from this the notion that every strike that occurs in a modern, highly integrated factory (which is the basis of every mass production industry) carries with it the potential to dismantle relations of production throughout the entire economy. This is because, in Tronti's view, every strike that takes place under such conditions, no matter how short-lived or seemingly ineffectual, "is the cessation of activity on the side of living labor, its reduction from living to dead labor, and thus *a refusal of labor to be labor*. The strike is therefore the collapse of the distinction, the separation, the counterbalance between labor and capital—hence, the most terrifying threat that can be made to the very life, as such, of capitalist society" (218; emphasis added).

5. I am grateful to David R. Roediger for drawing my attention to the various ways in which psychoanalytic theories of anality and anal-erotism have been used to lend support to—or to figure in negative terms—a critique of capitalist accumulation (see in particular Fenichel 89–108; Ferenczi 269–279; Freud 27–33; Jones 664–688; Kovel 87–135; Roediger, *Colored White* 27–43, 252n36).

Works Cited

Aaron, Daniel. *Writers on the Left: Episodes in American Literary Communism.* 1961. New York: Columbia UP, 1992.
Adamic, Louis. *Dynamite: The Story of Class Violence in America.* New York: Viking, 1934.
———. *My America, 1928–1938.* New York: Harper and Brothers, 1938.
Adams, Carol J. *The Sexual Politics of Meat: A Feminist-Vegetarian Critical Theory.* 20th anniversary ed. New York: Continuum, 2010.
Aitken, Hugh G. J. *Taylorism at Watertown Arsenal: Scientific Management in Action, 1908–1915.* Cambridge, MA: Harvard UP, 1960.
American Federation of Labor. *Proceedings of the Annual Convention of the American Federation of Labor (1935).* Chandler, *Giant Enterprise* 199–213.
Arnold, Horace L. "Modern Machine-Shop Economics." *Engineering Magazine* Apr.–Sept. 1896: 59–66, 263–298, 469–477, 673–695, 883–904, 1089–1096.
———. "Production Up to the Power Limit." *Engineering Magazine* Aug. 1895: 916–924.
———. [Henry Roland, pseud.]. "Six Examples of Successful Shop Management." *Engineering Magazine* Oct. 1896–Mar. 1897: 69–85, 270–285, 395–412, 831–837, 994–1000; Apr. 1897: 10–19.
Arnold, Horace L., and Fay L. Faurote. *Ford Methods and the Ford Shops.* 1915. New York: Elibron, 2005.
Arrighi, Giovanni. "A Crisis of Hegemony." *Dynamics of Global Crisis.* Ed. Samir Amin, Giovanni Arrighi, Andre Gunder Frank, and Immanuel Wallerstein. New York: Monthly Review, 1982. 55–108.
———. "Marxist Century, American Century: The Making and Remaking of the World Labor Movement." *New Left Review* 179 (Jan.–Feb. 1990): 29–63.

Arrighi, Giovanni, and Beverly Silver. "Labor Movements and Capital Migration: The United States and Western Europe in World-Historical Perspective." *Labor in the Capitalist World-Economy*. Ed. Charles Bergquist. Beverly Hills, CA: Sage, 1984. 183–216.

Attaway, William. *Blood on the Forge*. 1941. Introd. Darryl Pinckney. New York: New York Review of Books, 2005.

Balestrini, Nanni. "Immer noch und immer wieder: Wir wollen alles." Afterword to *Wir wollen alles: Roman der Fiatkämpfe* [*We Want Everything: A Novel of the Fiat Struggles*]. Trans. Peter Chotjewitz. Berlin: Assoziation A, 2003.

———. *Vogliamo tutto* [*We Want Everything*]. Rev. ed. 1971. Rome: DeriveApprodi, 2004.

Balestrini, Nanni, and Primo Moroni. *Die goldene Horde: Arbeiterautonomie, Jugendrevolte und bewaffneter Kampf in Italien* [*The Golden Horde: Workers' Autonomy, Youth Revolt, and Armed Struggle in Italy*]. 1988. Trans. Christel Fröhlich. Berlin: Assoziation A, 2002.

Barthes, Roland. *Writing Degree Zero*. 1953. Trans. Annette Lavers and Colin Smith. New York: Noonday, 1968.

Bell, Thomas. *Out of This Furnace*. 1941. Pittsburgh: U of Pittsburgh P, 1976.

Benjamin, Walter. "Critique of Violence." *Reflections: Essays, Aphorisms, Autobiographical Writings*. Ed. Peter Demetz. Trans. Edmund Jephcott. New York: Schocken, 1986. 277–300.

Bernstein, Irving. *Turbulent Years: A History of the American Worker, 1933–1941*. Boston: Houghton Mifflin, 1970.

Bird, Stewart, Dan Georgakas, and Deborah Shaffer. *Solidarity Forever: An Oral History of the IWW*. Chicago: Lake View, 1985.

Bird, Stewart, and Deborah Shaffer. *The Wobblies*. 1979. New York: New Video Group, 2006.

Bonosky, Phillip. *Burning Valley*. 1953. Introd. Alan Wald. Urbana: U of Illinois P, 1998.

Bowles, Sam, and Herbert Gintis. "Structure and Practice in the Labour Theory of Value." *Review of Radical Political Economics* 12.4 (1981): 1–26.

Braverman, Harry. *Labor and Monopoly Capital: The Degradation of Work in the Twentieth Century*. New York: Monthly Review, 1974.

Brecher, Jeremy. *Strike!* 1972. Rev. ed. Boston: South End, 1997.

Brissenden, Paul F. *The I.W.W.: A Study of American Syndicalism*. 2nd ed. New York: Columbia UP, 1920.

Bullard, Arthur [Albert Edwards, pseud.]. *Comrade Yetta*. New York: Macmillan, 1913.

Burgum, Edwin Berry. "The Proletarian Novel." *Partisan Review* 2.7 (1935): 11.

Cantwell, Robert. *The Land of Plenty*. 1934. Carbondale: Southern Illinois UP, 1971.

Carby, Hazel V. *Reconstructing Womanhood: The Emergence of the Afro-American Woman Novelist*. New York: Oxford UP, 1987.

Chambers, Whittaker. *Can You Hear Their Voices? A Short Story.* 1931. International Pamphlet 26. New York: International Pamphlets, 1932.
Chandler, Alfred D., Jr., ed. *Giant Enterprise: Ford, General Motors, and the Automobile Industry. Sources and Readings.* New York: Harcourt, Brace and World, 1964.
———. "Ford—Expansion through Mass Production." Chandler, *Giant Enterprise* 25–27.
———. "Ford Sticks to Tested Strategies." Chandler, *Giant Enterprise* 97–99.
———. "A General Introduction to the Readings." Chandler, *Giant Enterprise* 9–20.
———. "General Motors' Innovations in Management." Chandler, *Giant Enterprise* 112–114.
———. "Introduction" to Part II, "The Strategy of Competition." Chandler, *Giant Enterprise* 95–96.
———. "A New Type of Labor Force and Its Challenges." Chandler, *Giant Enterprise* 179–181.
———. *Strategy and Structure: Chapters in the History of the Industrial Enterprise.* Cambridge, MA: MIT P, 1962.
———. "The Unionizing of the Industry." Chandler, *Giant Enterprise* 194–198.
Coiner, Constance. *Better Red: The Writing and Resistance of Tillie Olsen and Meridel Le Sueur.* 1995. Urbana: U of Illinois P, 1998.
Conn, Peter. *The Divided Mind: Ideology and Imagination in America, 1898–1917.* Cambridge: Cambridge UP, 1983.
Conrad, Lawrence H. *Temper.* 1924. New York: AMS, 1976.
Conroy, Jack. "Robert Cantwell's *Land of Plenty.*" *Proletarian Writers of the Thirties.* Ed. David Madden. Carbondale: Southern Illinois UP, 1968. 74–84.
———. "The Worker as Writer." Hart 83–86.
Crouch, Colin, and Alessandro Pizzorno, eds. *The Resurgence of Class Conflict in Western Europe since 1968.* 2 vols. New York: Holmes and Meier, 1978.
Cruden, Robert L. [James Steele, pseud.]. *Conveyor.* New York: International Publishers, 1935.
———. *The End of the Ford Myth.* International Pamphlet 24. New York: International Publishers, 1932.
De Caux, Len. *The Living Spirit of the Wobblies.* New York: International Publishers, 1978.
Den Tandt, Christophe. *The Urban Sublime in American Literary Naturalism.* Urbana: U of Illinois P, 1998.
Denning, Michael. *The Cultural Front: The Laboring of American Culture in the Twentieth Century.* London: Verso, 1996.
Dosch, Arno. "What the IWW Is." *World's Work* 26 (Aug. 1913): 417.
Dos Passos, John. "The Writer as Technician." Hart 78–82.
Dubofsky, Melvyn. *We Shall Be All: A History of the Industrial Workers of the World.* Chicago: Quadrangle, 1969.

Dubois, Pierre. "New Forms of Industrial Conflict, 1960–1974." Crouch and Pizzorno 2:1–34.
Dunn, Robert W. *Labor and Automobiles*. New York: International Publishers, 1929.
"Editorial Comment." *Engineering Magazine* Oct. 1899: 113–114.
"Editorial Comment." *Engineering Magazine* Dec. 1900: 433–434.
Editors' Introduction to "Repetitive Shop Processes and Interchangeable Machine Parts," by Barton Cruikshank. *Engineering Magazine* 21, no. 5 (August 1901): 741.
"The Education of Machinists." *Engineering Magazine* Jan. 1900: 616.
Edwards, Richard. *Contested Terrain: The Transformation of the Workplace in the Twentieth Century*. New York: Basic Books, 1979.
Ehrenreich, Barbara, and Annette Fuentes. "Life on the Global Assembly Line." *Ms.* Spring 1981: 47.
Esch, Elizabeth, and David Roediger. "One Symptom of Originality: Management of Labour in the History of the United States." *Historical Materialism* 17 (2009): 1–41.
Federal Trade Commission. *Report on the Motor Vehicle Industry (1939)*. Chandler, *Giant Enterprise* 27–34, 53–59, 170–175.
Fenichel, Otto. "The Drive to Amass Wealth." *The Collected Papers of Otto Fenichel: Second Series*. New York: Norton, 1954. 89–108.
Ferenczi, Sandor. "The Ontogenesis of the Interest in Money." *Sex in Psycho-Analysis (Contributions to Psycho-Analysis)*. Trans. Ernest Jones. New York: Dover, 1956. 269–279.
Fine, Sidney. *Sit-Down: The General Motors Strike of 1936–1937*. Ann Arbor: U of Michigan P, 1969.
Flynn, Elizabeth Gurley. "The Truth about the Paterson Strike." Kornbluh, *Rebel Voices* 214–226.
Foley, Barbara. *Radical Representations: Politics and Form in U.S. Proletarian Fiction, 1929–1941*. Durham, NC: Duke UP, 1993.
Foner, Philip S. *The Industrial Workers of the World, 1905–1917*. Vol. 4 of *History of the Labor Movement in the United States*. New York: International Publishers, 1965.
———. *The Policies and Practices of the American Federation of Labor, 1900–1909*. Vol. 3 of *History of the Labor Movement in the United States*. New York: International Publishers, 1964.
Ford, Henry. *My Life and Work*. With Samuel Crowther. Garden City, NY: Doubleday, Page, 1922.
———. *My Philosophy of Industry: An Authorized Interview by Fay Leone Faurote*. New York: Coward-McCann, 1929.
Freud, Sigmund. "Character and Anal Erotism." *Character and Culture*. Ed. Philip Rieff. New York: Collier, 1963.
Gallico, Paul. "Sit-Down Strike." *Cosmopolitan* Apr. 1938: 155–180.

Gartman, David. *Auto Slavery: The Labor Process in the American Automobile Industry, 1897–1950*. New Brunswick: Rutgers UP, 1986.

Giedion, Siegfried. *Mechanization Takes Command: A Contribution to Anonymous History*. New York: Oxford UP, 1948.

Gold, Michael. "Go Left, Young Writers!" *New Masses* Jan. 1929. *Mike Gold: A Literary Anthology*. Ed. Michael Folsom. New York: International Publishers, 1972. 186–189.

———. *Jews without Money*. 1930. New York: Carroll and Graf, 1996.

———. "John Reed and the Real Thing." *New Masses* Nov. 1927. *Mike Gold: A Literary Anthology*. Ed. Michael Folsom. New York: International Publishers, 1972. 152–156.

Golin, Steve. "The Paterson Pageant: Success or Failure?" *Socialist Review* 69 (May–June 1983): 45–78.

Gramsci, Antonio. "Americanism and Fordism." *Selections from the Prison Notebooks of Antonio Gramsci*. Ed. and trans. Quintin Hoare and Geoffrey Nowell Smith. New York: International Publishers, 1971. 279–318.

Green, Archie. "John Neuhaus: Wobbly Folklorist." *Journal of American Folklore* 73.289 (1960): 189–217.

———. Preface. Green et al. 1–12.

Green, Archie, David Roediger, Franklin Rosemont, and Salvatore Salerno, eds. *The Big Red Songbook*. Chicago: Charles H. Kerr, 2007.

Hallgren, Mauritz A. *Seeds of Revolt: A Study of American Life and the Temper of the American People during the Depression*. New York: Knopf, 1933.

Hamacher, Werner. "Afformative, Strike: Benjamin's 'Critique of Violence.'" Trans. Dana Hollander. *Walter Benjamin's Philosophy: Destruction and Experience*. Ed. Andrew Benjamin and Peter Osborne. London: Routledge, 1994. 110–138.

Hanna, Thomas, ed. *The Bergsonian Heritage*. New York: Columbia UP, 1962.

Hapke, Laura. *Labor's Text: The Worker in American Fiction*. New Brunswick: Rutgers UP, 2001.

Hart, Henry, ed. *American Writers' Congress*. New York: International Publishers, 1935.

Haywood, William D. "The General Strike." Kornbluh, *Rebel Voices* 44–50.

———. "The Rip in the Silk Industry." Kornbluh, *Rebel Voices* 205–208.

Herbst, Josephine. *Rope of Gold: A Novel of the Thirties*. 1939. Old Westbury, NY: Feminist Press, 1984.

Hicks, Granville, et al., eds. *Proletarian Literature in the United States: An Anthology*. New York: International Publishers, 1935.

Higgins, Milton P. "Intensified Production and Its Influence upon the Worker." *Engineering Magazine* Jan. 1901: 568–576.

Hoagland, Tony. "Dialectical Materialism." *Unincorporated Persons in the Late Honda Dynasty*. Minneapolis: Graywolf, 2010. 39–41.

Horowitz, Irving Louis. *Radicalism and the Revolt against Reason: The Social Theories of Georges Sorel*. Carbondale: Southern Illinois UP, 1961.
Industrial Workers of the World. "Manifesto." Kornbluh, *Rebel Voices* 7–10.
———. "Preamble (1905)." Kornbluh, *Rebel Voices* 12.
James, C.L.R. *State Capitalism and World Revolution*. 1950. Chicago: Kerr, 1986.
Jenks, Leland H. "Early Phases of the Management Movement." *Administrative Science Quarterly* 5.3 (1960): 421–447.
Jones, Ernest. "Anal-Erotic Character Traits." *Papers on Psycho-Analysis*. 5th ed. Baltimore: Williams and Wilkins, 1948. 664–688.
Kant, Immanuel. *The Critique of Judgment*. Trans. James Creed Meredith. Oxford: Clarendon, 1991.
Kessler-Harris, Alice. *Out to Work: A History of Wage-Earning Women in the United States*. Oxford: Oxford UP, 1982.
Kornbluh, Joyce L. "Lumberjacks: North and South." Kornbluh, *Rebel Voices* 251–256.
———. "Paterson: 1913." Kornbluh, *Rebel Voices* 197–203.
———, ed. *Rebel Voices: An IWW Anthology*. New and enl. ed. Chicago: Kerr, 1998.
———. "With Folded Arms: The Tactics of Direct Action." Kornbluh, *Rebel Voices* 35–39.
Kovel, Joel. *White Racism: A Psychohistory*. New York: Random House, 1970.
Kraus, Henry. *The Many and the Few: A Chronicle of the Dynamic Auto Workers*. 2nd ed. Urbana: U of Illinois P, 1985.
Kraut, Alan M. *The Huddled Masses: The Immigrant in American Society, 1880–1921*. Arlington Heights, IL: Harlan Davidson, 1982.
Laclau, Ernesto, and Chantal Mouffe. *Hegemony and Socialist Strategy: Towards a Radical Democratic Politics*. London: Verso, 1985.
Le Bon, Gustave. *The Crowd: A Study of the Popular Mind*. 1896. Mineola, NY: Dover, 2002.
Lee, John R. "The So-Called Profit Sharing System in the Ford Plant." 1916. Chandler, *Giant Enterprise* 189–194.
Levinson, Edward. "Labor on the March." 1937. Chandler, *Giant Enterprise* 222–224.
London, Jack. *The Iron Heel*. 1907. London: Journeyman, 1974.
Luhan, Mabel Dodge. *Movers and Shakers*. Vol. 3 of *Intimate Memories*. New York: Harcourt, Brace, 1936.
Lukács, Georg. *History and Class Consciousness: Studies in Marxist Dialectics*. Trans. Rodney Livingstone. Cambridge, MA: MIT P, 1971.
Lumpkin, Grace. *To Make My Bread*. 1932. Urbana: U of Illinois P, 1995.
Luxemburg, Rosa. *Selected Political Writings of Rosa Luxemburg*. Ed. Dick Howard. New York: Monthly Review, 1971.
Marx, Karl. *Capital: A Critique of Political Economy*. Vol. 1. Introd. Ernest Mandel. Trans. Ben Fowkes. London: Penguin, 1976.

McKenney, Ruth. *Industrial Valley*. 1939. Ithaca, NY: ILR, 1992.
Meyer, Stephen, III. *The Five Dollar Day: Labor Management and Social Control in the Ford Motor Company, 1908–1921*. Albany: State U of New York P, 1981.
Mitchell, W.J.T. "Representation." *Critical Terms for Literary Study*. 2nd ed. Ed. Frank Lentricchia and Thomas McLaughlin. Chicago: U of Chicago P, 1995. 11–22.
Monthly Labor Review. "The General Motors Corporation Strike." March 1937. Chandler, *Giant Enterprise* 218–222.
Murphy, James F. *The Proletarian Moment: The Controversy over Leftism in Literature*. Urbana: U of Illinois P, 1991.
Nevins, Allan, and Frank Ernest Hill. *Ford: Expansion and Challenge, 1915–1933*. New York: Scribner's, 1957.
———. *Ford: The Times, the Man, the Company*. New York: Scribner's, 1954.
Nielsen, Aldon Lynn. *C.L.R. James: A Critical Introduction*. Jackson: UP of Mississippi, 1997.
Nochlin, Linda. "The Paterson Strike Pageant of 1913." *Art in America* 52 (May–June 1974): 67.
Noon, Mark. "'It Ain't Your Color, It's Your Scabbing': Literary Representations of African American Strikebreakers." *African American Review* 38.3 (2004): 429–439.
Norwood, Edwin P. *Ford Men and Methods*. Garden City, NY: Doubleday, Doran, 1931.
O'Neill, Eugene. *Selected Plays of Eugene O'Neill*. New York: Random House, 1967.
Osborne, James D. "Paterson: Immigrant Strikers and the War of 1913." *At the Point of Production: The Local History of the I.W.W.* Ed. Joseph R. Conlin. Westport, CT: Greenwood, 1981. 61–78.
Outerbridge, Alexander E., Jr. "Educational Influence of Machinery." *Engineering Magazine* May 1895: 225–231.
———. "The Emancipation of Labor by Machinery." *Engineering Magazine* Sept. 1895: 1012–1020.
"The Pageant as a Form of Propaganda." Rev. of *The Pageant of the Paterson Strike*. *Current Opinion and Survey* June 1913. Kornbluh, *Rebel Voices* 212–214.
"The Pageant of the Paterson Strike." Program. Kornbluh, *Rebel Voices* 210–212.
Phelps, Christopher. "Introduction: Upton Sinclair and the Social Novel." Upton Sinclair, *The Jungle*. Ed. Christopher Phelps. Boston: Bedford, 2005. 1–39.
Pilkington, Anthony Edward. *Bergson and His Influence*. New York: Cambridge UP, 1976.
Polanyi, Karl. *The Great Transformation*. 1944. Boston: Beacon, 1957.
Poole, Ernest. *The Harbor*. New York: Macmillan, 1915.
———. "Maxim Gorki in New York." *Slavonic and East European Review (American Series)* 3.1 (1944): 77–83.

Rabinowitz, Paula. *Labor and Desire: Women's Revolutionary Fiction in Depression America*. Chapel Hill: U of North Carolina P, 1991.

Regalia, Ida, Marino Regini, and Emilio Reyneri. "Labour Conflicts and Industrial Relations in Italy." Crouch and Pizzorno 1:101–158.

Reitell, Charles. "Machinery and Its Effect upon the Workers in the Automobile Industry." 1924. Chandler, *Giant Enterprise* 181–188.

Rideout, Walter B. *The Radical Novel in the United States, 1900–1954: Some Interrelations of Literature and Society*. 1956. New York: Columbia UP, 1992.

Robbins, Jack Alan, ed. *Granville Hicks in the New Masses*. Port Washington, NY: Kennikat, 1974.

Roediger, David R. *Colored White: Transcending the Racial Past*. Berkeley: U of California P, 2002.

———. "'Their Horrid Gold': John Handcox and the Uncopyrighted Red Songbook." Green et al. 23–28.

Rollins, William, Jr. *The Shadow Before*. New York: McBride, 1934.

Rosemont, Franklin. "Lost and Found: Other IWW Songs and Poems." Green et al. 13–22.

———. "A Short Treatise on Wobbly Cartoons." 1987. Kornbluh, *Rebel Voices* 425–443.

Salerno, Salvatore. *Red November, Black November: Culture and Community in the Industrial Workers of the World*. Albany: State U of New York P, 1989.

———. "Sizzlooks, Scissorbills, Sabcats and Songs: Language and Image in Wobbly Expressive Art Forms." Green et al. 29–34.

Scarry, Elaine. *Resisting Representation*. New York: Oxford UP, 1994.

Scott, Leroy. *The Walking Delegate*. New York: Doubleday, Page, 1905.

Seaver, Edwin. "The Proletarian Novel." Hart 98–103.

———. "What Is a Proletarian Novel? Notes toward a Definition." *Partisan Review* 2.7 (1935): 6.

Silver, Beverly J. *Forces of Labor: Workers' Movements and Globalization since 1870*. Cambridge: Cambridge UP, 2003.

Sinclair, Upton. *The Flivver King: A Story of Ford-America*. 1937. Chicago: Kerr, 2006.

———. *The Jungle: The Uncensored Original Edition*. 1906. Tucson, AZ: See Sharp, 2003.

Smith, L. R. "We Build a Plant to Run without Men." *Magazine of Business* Feb. 1929: 135–139.

Sorel, Georges. *Reflections on Violence*. Trans. T. E. Hulme and J. Roth. 1906. Mineola, NY: Dover, 2004.

Tate, Claudia. *Domestic Allegories of Political Desire: The Black Heroine's Text at the Turn of the Century*. New York: Oxford UP, 1992.

Taylor, Frederick W. *The Principles of Scientific Management*. 1911. New York: Norton, 1967.

Thompson, Sanford E. "The Taylor Differential Piece-Rate System." *Engineering Magazine* Jan. 1901: 617–630.
Torigian, Michael. "The Occupation of the Factories: Paris 1936, Flint 1937." *Comparative Studies in Society and History* 41.2 (1999): 324–347.
Tronti, Mario. *Operai e capitale* [*Workers and Capital*]. Turin: Einaudi, 1973.
Trumbo, Dalton. *Johnny Got His Gun*. 1939. New York: Bantam, 1982.
Veblen, Thorstein. *The Theory of Business Enterprise*. 1904. New York: Mentor, 1958.
Vorse, Mary Heaton. *Labor's New Millions*. 1938. New York: Arno and New York Times, 1969.
Wald, Alan M. *Writing from the Left: New Essays on Radical Culture and Politics*. New York: Verso, 1994.
Weatherwax, Clara. *Marching! Marching!* New York: Day, 1935.
Wechsler, James A. "River Rouge Revolt." 1941. Chandler, *Giant Enterprise* 226–227.
"Who Is the Leader?" 1913. Kornbluh, *Rebel Voices* 204.
Williams, Albert, Jr. "Racial Traits in Machine Designing." *Engineering Magazine* Oct. 1895: 92–98.
Williams, Raymond. *Keywords: A Vocabulary of Culture and Society*. Rev. ed. New York: Oxford UP, 1983.
Wixson, Douglas. *Worker-Writer in America: Jack Conroy and the Tradition of Midwestern Literary Radicalism, 1898–1990*. Urbana: U of Illinois P, 1994.
Wright, Erik Olin. "Working-Class Power, Capitalist-Class Interests, and Class Compromise." *American Journal of Sociology* 105.4 (2000): 957–1002.
Wright, Steve. *Storming Heaven: Class Composition and Struggle in Italian Autonomist Marxism*. London: Pluto, 2002.
Zandy, Janet. *Hands: Physical Labor, Class, and Cultural Work*. New Brunswick: Rutgers UP, 2004.

Index

Adamic, Louis, 119, 181, 188
adaptation of mass workers, 8, 23–24, 69–71, 98, 103, 104–105
aesthetic representation: defined, 15–17; and industrial unionism, 121–122, 141; of mass workers, 18–19, 124–140, 144–146. *See also* journalistic representation
AFL (American Federation of Labor): and the Amalgamated, 193–197; and craft unionism, 113–115, 117, 227; in literature, 153, 216–239; and NIRA, 186–187; rejection of, 123; William Green, 220, 227. *See also* UAW (United Auto Workers Union)
African Americans, 47, 261n4
agency of mass workers, 2–3, 31, 171–172, 175–177, 222–223, 298n2
Aitken, Hugh, 37
Amalgamated Association of Iron, Steel and Tin Workers (The Amalgamated), 193–197
American Federation of Labor. *See* AFL (American Federation of Labor)
Americanism, 26on2 (chap. 1)
American Tragedy, An (Dreiser), 88
antiwork ethic, 251–252, 257
Arnold, Horace, 27, 36–37, 42, 62–63
Arrighi, Giovanni, 111–112
articulated strikes, 243–244, 246, 254–255
assembly lines. *See* continuous-flow assembly

associational power, 10–12, 118. *See also* industrial unionism; trade unions
Attaway, William, *Blood on the Forge*, 62
automobile industry: globalization of, 239–240, 242–243; and industrial unionism, 9–11, 261n3 (chap. 2); in Italy, 243–258; in literature, 78–85, 88, 229–231, 239–240, 250–258; management of, 74–76, 79–83, 109, 261n3 (chap. 2); and mass production, 28, 67, 69–77; strikes, 187–192, 229–231, 238. *See also* Fiat Mirafiori plant; Ford Motor Company; GM (General Motors)

Balestrini, Nanni, *Vogliamo tutto*, 239–240, 250–258
bargaining power, 11–12, 111–113, 189, 193–197, 207–208, 216, 232, 253
Barthes, Roland, 6, 261n8
"Bartleby, the Scrivener" (Melville), 127
Bell, Thomas, 67, 184; *Out of This Furnace*, 20, 34, 43–47, 62, 65–66, 87–88, 98, 192–201, 264n10
Benjamin, Walter, 265n17
Bennett, Harry, 75
Blood on the Forge (Attaway), 62
Bologna, Sergio, 250
Bonosky, Phillip, *Burning Valley*, 62
Brecher, Jeremy, 13, 191, 242, 264n7
Brissenden, Paul, 123

Bullard, Arthur, *Comrade Yetta*, 122, 140–141, 152–167, 172, 177–180, 184
Burck, Jacob, 77
Burgum, Edwin Berry, 103
Burning Valley (Bonosky), 62

Cantwell, Robert, 237; *The Land of Plenty*, 185, 204–216, 237, 265nn13–14
"Can You Hear Their Voices?" (Chambers), 264n11
capital, representations of, 65–68, 125. *See also* technological representation
capitalism, 113, 201–204, 213
Carby, Hazel, 263n9
cartoons (IWW), 116, 124–129, 131
Chambers, Whittaker, 264n11
Chandler, Alfred, 76
Chaplin, Charlie, 63
Chaplin, Ralph, 116, 124, 126
checkerboard strikes, 245–246
Chrysler, 187–189
CIO (Congress of Industrial Organizations): and critique of the AFL, 113–115, 117, 227; and direct democracy, 221–222; economic representation of mass workers, 19; as enforcer of labor contracts, 236–237; founding of, 181–182; in literature, 4, 87, 200; and sitdown strikes, 187–192. *See also* industrial unionism
class consciousness: development of, 19, 264n10; in Italy, 249–250; in literature, 48, 158–163, 169, 214–215; and mass workers as physical mass, 217–219; and *The Pageant of the Paterson Strike*, 138
Coiner, Constance, 5
collective novel, 263n12
Columbia Chemical strike (Barberton, OH), 217
commodification of mass workers: degradation through, 104; fictitious representation of human labor power, 6–9, 237–238, 259n3; in literature, 88, 146–148, 174; resistance to, 14–15
commodities that speak (Marx's figure of), 174
communication by mass workers, 54–58, 60–62, 146–147, 205–206, 208–210, 220–221
Communist Party in Italy, 253

Communist Party of the United States, 58, 78, 201–204, 213, 219, 228–229
company spies, 75, 186–187
Comrade Yetta (Bullard), 122, 152–167, 172, 177–180, 184
Congress of Industrial Organizations. *See* CIO
Conn, Peter, 178
Conrad, Lawrence H., *Temper*, 66, 67, 88–98
Conroy, Jack, 202–205, 210–211, 265n13; *A World to Win*, 205
continuous-flow assembly, 29, 36–37, 67–69, 73–74, 79–86, 109–110, 224–225
Conveyor (Cruden), 66–67, 77–83, 85, 87–88, 98, 210
conveyor belts. *See* continuous-flow assembly
craft unionism, 113–115, 117, 227
creeping May (Italy 1968-1969), 245
Cruden, Robert, 184; *Conveyor*, 66–67, 77–83, 85, 87–88, 98, 210

Debs, Eugene V., 48
decommodification of mass workers, 9, 18–19, 104, 121–123, 258
degradation of mass workers, 45–50, 58–62, 64, 67, 69, 88, 92–98, 104
democracy: direct democracy, 115–117, 221–222; self-representation, 122, 125, 129, 164, 169–175; of sitdown strikes, 190; of unions, 123, 141–150, 163–165
Denning, Michael, 5, 259–260n4
deskilling of mass workers, 2, 43–46, 111, 160
Deventer, John H., 72
direct action, 115–120, 171–174, 204–216, 243–246, 254–258. *See also* spontaneity of strikes
"Direct Action Makes Capitalism See Stars," 128
direct democracy, 115–117, 221–222
Disinherited, The (Conroy), 205
Dodge (Luhan), Mabel, 131, 133–134, 136, 140
Dos Passos, John, 202–203
Dreiser, Theodore, 88
Dubofsky, Melvin, 162
Dunlap, John R., 25
Dunn, Robert W., 76

Ebert, Justus, 115
economic representation: and commodification of mass workers, 237–238; defined, 16–17; and industrial unionism, 141; in literature, 144–146; and the silk workers' strike, 133, 139–141
Edwards, Richard, 8, 30, 36
efficiency, labor. *See* works management movement
élan vital (Bergson), 263n8
embodiment, 259n2. *See also* "living tools" or machines, mass workers as
Employee Representation Plans. *See* ERPs (Employee Representation Plans)
"Engineer as Economist, The," 25
Engineering Magazine, 25
ennobling of mass workers, 3, 14, 17–18, 65–68, 82–83, 87–105, 184, 210. *See also* class consciousness; solidarity
epic hero, 256. *See also* ennobling of mass workers
ERPs (Employee Representation Plans), 186, 192–200, 217
Esch, Elizabeth, 260–261n3 (chap.1)
ethnic stereotyping, 41–44, 46–47, 58–59

Farrell, James T., 203
"Father Hagerty's Wheel of Fortune" (Hagerty), 114
Faurote, Fay L., 37, 62–63
female workforce, 261n5
Fiat Mirafiori plant (Turin, Italy), 243, 246–249, 250–258
fictional characters: *Comrade Yetta*: Isadore, 161, 163; Jake Goldfogle, 154–155, 162; Mrs. Weinstein, 155; Walter Longman, 153, 161, 163, 165, 179; Yetta Rayefsky, 152–167, 172, 177–180; *Conveyor*: Jim Brogan, 78–83, 85, 98, 210; Marie Brogan, 82; *The Flivver King*: Tom Shutt, 237; *The Hairy Ape*: Yank, 67–68, 263n13; *The Harbor*: Bill, 168–181; Jim Marsh, 169, 173–175, 263n15; Joe Kramer, 168–173, 177–179, 263n14; *Industrial Valley*: Alex Eigenmacht, 222, 228; Jim Keller, 229; Mr. Claherty, 220; *The Iron Heel*: Avis Everhard, 52–54; Ernest Everhard, 51; *Johnny Got his Gun*: Joe Bonham, 54–57; *The Jungle*: Billy Hinds, 50; Jurgis Rudkos, 47–49, 84–85; *The Land of Plenty*: Carl, 208–212; Dwyer, 214; Hagen, 206, 210, 214; Johnny, 206, 208; Vin Garl, 214–215; Winters, 211–212, 214; *Marching! Marching!*: Mario, 61; Pete, 61; Tim, 59–60; *Out of This Furnace*: Burke, 195–199; Dobie Dobrejcak, 87–88, 98, 192–193, 195, 197–201; Flack, 195–196; Gralji, 193–194; Mike Dobrejcak, 44–45, 47, 87; Mike Tighe, 194; Mr. Forbes, 195–199; Walsh, 193–195; *Rope of Gold*: Ed Thompson, 230; *The Shadow Before*: Doucet, 99; Marvin, 101–102; Micky, 98–99, 101–102; Thayer, 100; *Sit-Down Strike*: Alan, 233; Appleby, 232; *Temper*: Cameron, 93; Paul Rinelli, 88–98; Smith, 89; *The Walking Delegate*: Buck Foley, 141–151, 159; Mr. Baxter, 146–148; Ruth Arnold, 148–149, 151–152, 177; Tom Keating, 141–152, 159
fictional representation, 6, 13, 15, 96–97, 121, 127, 152, 163. *See also* "living tools" or machines, mass workers as; writing and writers
figurative language, 16, 85–87, 92, 99, 121, 163–165, 176–177, 180, 258. *See also* continuous-flow assembly; "living tools" or machines, mass workers as
Fine, Sidney, 191, 231
Firestone truck tire plant (Akron, OH), 223–227
Flivver King: A Story of Ford-America, The (Sinclair), 69, 237, 264n10
Flynn, Elizabeth Gurley, 135, 137–140
Foley, Barbara, 5, 261n9, 263n12
Foner, Philip S., 124, 131
Ford, Henry, 28–30, 42, 73, 75, 83–86, 265n15
Fordism, 24, 71, 213, 239–240. *See also* Fordist-Taylorist factory system
Fordist-Taylorist factory system (Torigian), 5, 10–14. *See also* scientific management; works management movement
Ford Motor Company: company spies, 187; and continuous-flow assembly, 63, 68–69, 73–74; Highland Park plant, 29, 37, 42, 62, 73, 75, 107–108; in literature,

77–78; management, 74–76, 109, 261n3 (chap. 2); and mass production, 28–31, 37; and racial-ethnic stereotyping, 42, 261n4; River Rouge plant, 69, 71–77; Sociological Department of, 260n4; and the UAW, 140, 187; and vertical integration, 71, 73
foreign workers, 41–44

Gallico, Paul, *Sit-Down Strike*, 185, 231–234, 237
Gannt, Henry L., 27
garment workers, 152–167
Gartman, David, 110
gender stereotyping, 43
"General Strike, The" (Haywood speech), 263n15
"General Strike, The" (photomontage by Sam), 125
General Tire and Rubber Company (Akron, OH), 218, 221
Gesamtkunstwerk, 131, 262n4 (chap. 3)
Giovannitti, Arturo, 105
globalization of the automobile industry, 239–240, 242–243
GM (General Motors), 187–192, 230, 242, 264n7, 265n16
Gold, Michael, 201–204, 205; "Go Left, Young Writers!", 203; *Jews without Money*, 264n11
"Go Left, Young Writers!" (Gold), 203
Goodyear strike (Akron, OH), 218, 227–229
Gramsci, Antonio, 64, 95, 109, 213, 260n2 (chap. 1)
Great Depression, 181, 183–184, 191–192
Green, William, 220, 227
Gregory, Horace, 264–265n12

Hagerty, Thomas, 114
Hairy Ape, The (O'Neill), 67–68, 263n13
Halsey, Frederick A., 27
Hamacher, Werner, 265n17
"Hand That Will Rule the World, The" (R. Chaplin), 124
Hapke, Laura, 5, 88
Harbor, The (Poole), 121–122, 140–141, 167–181, 184, 263n14
Haywood, William D. "Big Bill," 131, 133–135, 138, 140, 169, 262n5 (chap. 3)

Herbst, Josephine, 190, 203, 229; *Rope of Gold*, 185, 230–231, 237
heroic characters. *See* ennobling of mass workers
Highland Park plant (Ford Motor Company), 29, 37, 42, 62, 73, 75, 107–108
homogenization of mass workers, 24, 100, 172
Hormel Packing Corporation strike (MN), 117
Hot Autumn of 1969 (in Italy), 243–258

iconic mode of representation, 16–17
identification (with mass workers), 165–166, 177–179
indexical mode of representation, 16–17
industrial unionism: and the automobile industry, 9–11, 261n3 (chap. 2); democracy of, 123, 141–150, 163–165; development of, 113–117; and direct action, 119; and division of working classes, 242; and forms of representation, 121–122, 141, 227–228; and individualism, 221; as IWW's sublime experience, 19, 133, 144, 165–166, 262n3 (chap. 3); in literature, 4, 141–167, 180–181
Industrial Valley (McKenney), 3, 20, 184–185, 216–239, 232
Industrial Workers of the World. *See* IWW
Iron Heel, The (London), 34, 50–54
ironworkers (in *The Walking Delegate*), 141–152
Italy, 239–240, 243–258
IWW (Industrial Workers of the World): artwork, 125, 129–131; cartoons, 124, 126–128; and the CIO, 181–182; and decommodification of mass workers, 18–19; formation of, 114–117; and forms of representation, 19, 124–140, 129; goals of, 123–126, 160–163; and individualism, 221; in literature, 4, 58, 123, 153, 156–157, 163–181; "Little Red Songbook" (IWW), 129, 134; and Poole, 262n1; and the Socialist Party, 124, 162–163; and Sorel, 262n3 (chap. 3); and the Spirit of Revolt, 156, 163–164; suppression of, 181. *See also* industrial unionism

I.W.W. in Theory and Practice, The (Ebert), 115

James, C.L.R., 6, 69, 213, 236–237, 251
Jenks, Leland, 26
Jewish workers, 42, 152–167
Jews without Money (Gold), 264n11
Johnny Got His Gun (Trumbo), 20, 34, 54–57
journalistic representation, 152, 158, 164–165, 172, 231–232, 264n11
Jungle, The (Sinclair), 3, 34, 46–50, 62, 83–86

Kant, Immanuel, 202, 261n1 (chap. 2)
Klann, William C., 75
knowledge: and bargaining power, 193–197, 207–208; of mass workers, 118, 222–227, 254–256; and power, 215
Kraus, Henry, 190

Labor and Automobiles (Dunn), 76
labor contracts, 125, 191, 228–229, 235–237
labor unions: and control of mass workers, 228–229, 247; corporate bureaucracy of, 193–194; declining strength of, 112; and enforcement of labor contracts, 191, 235–237; in Italy, 244–247, 253–258; in literature, 87, 100–102; recognition of, 87, 183, 193, 195–197, 234–237, 264n9. *See also* industrial unionism
labor unrest, 241–242, 243, 247–250. *See also* sitdown strikes; strikes
Land of Plenty, The (Cantwell), 185, 204–216, 237, 265nn13–14
Lang, Fritz, 62–63
language, inadequacy of, 59, 208–210, 255, 265n15
Le Bon, Gustave, 261n7
Lee, John R., 260n4
Lenin and Leninism, 201–204, 213
Le Sueur, Meridel, 264–265n12
Lewis, John L., 187–189, 200, 221, 230
Lewis, J. Slater, 26
literary techniques: anonymous narrator, 252; élan vital, 263n8; embodiment, 261n8; epic hero as synecdoche, 256; figurative language, 86; novel as assembly line, 257; syntax of speakers, 59–60; typographic mimesis, 98–100

"Little Red Songbook" (IWW), 129, 134
"living tools" or machines, mass workers as, 27, 36–40, 58–64, 80–83, 87–88, 90–100, 208, 216, 265n14
London, Jack, *The Iron Heel*, 34, 50–54, 56
Lotta Continua, 244, 246
lumber mill workers, 57–62, 204–216
Lumpkin, Grace, 264n11

"Machinery and Its Effect upon the Workers in the Automobile Industry" (Reitell), 69
management: and the automobile industry, 74–76, 79–83, 109, 261n3 (chap. 2); disruption and ignorance of, 209–210; and mass production, 25–26; and representation in the workplace, 192–200; surprise and fear of, 230–232; of textile mills, 100
Marching! Marching! (Weatherwax), 34–35, 57–62
marketplace bargaining power, 11, 111–113
marriage plots, 161–164, 263n10
Marx, 6, 82, 174
Marxism, 111–112, 201
massification, 1–2, 249–250
mass production, 28–31, 62–63, 71, 86, 220. *See also* continuous-flow assembly; Fordist-Taylorist factory system
mass workers: associational power of, 10–12, 118; bargaining power of, 11–12, 111–113, 189, 193–197, 207–208, 216, 232, 253; docility of, 36–37; fictitious representation of power, 6–9, 237–238, 259n3; mechanization, 98; power arising from mechanization, 98, 101, 207–208, 216, 224–225; powerlessness of, 17, 85; as speakers, 54–57; and structural power, 10–12, 144–146, 171, 244
McKenney, Ruth, 219; *Industrial Valley*, 3, 20, 184–185, 216–239, 232
meatpacking industry, 33, 46–50, 83–86
mechanization, and mass workers' power arising from, 98, 101, 207–208, 216, 224–225
media and strikes, 231–232
Melville, Herman "Bartleby, the Scrivener," 127
Metropolis (Lang), 63

mimesis, typographic, 98–100
Mirafiori plant (Turin, Italy), 243, 246–249, 250–258
Modern Times (Chaplin), 63
Modestino, Valentino, 135
moving assembly lines. *See* continuous-flow assembly; Fordist-Taylorist factory system
Murray, Philip, 200

narrator, anonymous, 252
National Industrial Recovery Act. *See* NIRA (National Industrial Recovery Act)
Nelson, W. Allen, 74
New Deal, 186
"New Model - 1932" (cartoon), 77
newspapers. *See* journalistic representation; media and strikes
NIRA (National Industrial Recovery Act), 186–187, 192–200, 216–239, 264n9
North, Joseph, 203
Norwood, Edwin P., 72
"Now He Understands the Game" (R. Chaplin), 126

Ohio Insulator plant (Barberton, OH), 218
Olsen, Tillie (Lerner), 264–265n12
One Big Union (as ideal), 19, 123–124, 164–165
O'Neill, Eugene, *The Hairy Ape*, 67–68, 263n13
operaismo (workerism), 250
"Organize on the Job Where You Are Robbed" (Machia and Reeder), 127
Out of This Furnace (Bell), 20, 34, 43–47, 62, 65–66, 87–88, 98, 192–201, 264n10

pace setters, 80–81, 91, 154
Pageant of the Paterson Strike, The, 122, 131–140, 170–171
personification (of strikes), 174–177
physicality (of mass of workers), 217–219, 225–226
physical stereotyping, 58–59
piece-rate systems, 27
Pinkertons, 187
Pirelli Settimo plant strike (Italy), 245
Polanyi, Karl, 7–8, 146–148
political representation: declining strength of, 112; defined, 15–17; direct democracy, 115–117; and the IWW, 123, 126–127, 162–163; in literature, 169; loss of faith in, 45–46; and self-representation, 122; and the Socialist Party, 3, 48–51, 56, 162–163
Poole, Ernest, 140–141, 262n1; *The Harbor*, 121–122, 140–141, 167–181, 184; *The Pageant of the Paterson Strike*, 134
Potere Operaio, 246
Potter, Grace, 135
Pouget, Emile, 115
productivism, 210–213
proletarian literature, 185, 201–204. *See also* Bell, Thomas; Cantwell, Robert; Conroy, Jack; Cruden, Robert; Gallico, Paul; Gold, Michael; Herbst, Josephine; Lumpkin, Grace; McKenney, Ruth; Rollins, William, Jr.; Weatherwax, Clara
psychological dissatisfaction (of mass workers), 108–109

Rabinowitz, Paula, 5, 59
racial stereotyping, 41–44, 46–47, 58–59, 260–261n3 (chap.1)
railroad construction, 24
Reed, John, 131, 133–134, 204, 262n5 (chap. 3)
refusal of work strategy, 251
Reitell, Charles, 9, 63–64, 69–71
representation. *See* aesthetic representation; economic representation; ERPs (Employee Representation Plans); journalistic representation; labor unions; political representation; self-representation; technological representation; theatrical representation
resistance, collective acts of. *See* sitdown strikes; strikes
revolutionary reportage, theory of, 264n11
Rideout, Walter B., 77, 261n9, 263n10, 263n12
River Rouge plant (Ford Motor Co.), 69, 71–77
Roediger, David R., 260–261n3 (chap.1), 265n5
Rollins, William, Jr., 184; *The Shadow Before*, 67, 98–103
Rope of Gold (Herbst), 185, 230–231, 237
Rosemont, Franklin, 128

Roth, Henry, 203
rubber worker strike (Akron, OH), 117, 184, 216–239
Russell, Phillips, 136

sabotage, 32, 104–105, 115–116, 172–173, 181, 228, 235. *See also* sitdown strikes
Salerno, Salvatore, 131, 166
Scarry, Elaine, 258n3, 261n8
scientific management, 23, 248–249. *See also* Fordist-Taylorist factory system
Scott, Leroy, 140–141; *The Walking Delegate*, 20, 122, 140–152, 159, 177
Seaver, Edwin, 202
self-representation, 122, 125, 129, 164, 169–175
Shadow Before, The (Rollins), 67, 98–103
"Silent Agitator" (IWW stickers), 130
silent communication, 58, 62
silk workers' strike (Paterson, NJ), 131–140, 162
Silver, Beverly, 6, 10–11, 112, 242–243
Sinclair, Upton, 33, 67, 69, 84; *The Flivver King*, 69, 237, 264n10; *The Jungle*, 3, 34, 46–50, 62, 83–86; *The Pageant of the Paterson Strike*, 134
Sit-Down Strike (Gallico), 185, 231–234, 237
sitdown strikes: in the automobile industry, 184, 187–192, 222–231; in literature, 184, 222–229; as revolutionary force, 220, 233–234; vs organized union structure, 191, 237; wave of during Great Depression, 191–192. *See also* direct action
skilled laborers, 2, 160
socialism, 46–51, 156–157, 165–166, 177, 213
Socialist Party (U.S.), 3, 45–51, 112, 124, 137, 152–153, 162–163
solidarity, 156–158, 160–163, 217–219, 225–226. *See also* class consciousness
Sorel, Georges, 153, 262n3 (chap. 3), 263n8, 265n17
Sorensen, Charles E., 74
Soviet Union, 213
speakers, mass workers as, 54–57
speedups: and Akron rubber workers, 219; during Great Depression, 181; as key principle of mass production, 219; in literature, 80–83, 91, 97, 211–212; in meatpacking industry, 85–86; post World War I, 181; at the River Rouge plant, 75–77

Spender, J. A., 72
Spirit of Revolt, 156, 163–164
spontaneity of strikes, 111, 153–156, 160–163, 217, 220, 238, 263n8
Standard Cotton strike, 265n17
Statuo dei Lavoratori, 247
Steele, James. *See* Cruden, Robert
steelworkers, 43–46, 87, 192–200
Steel Workers Organizing Committee (SWOC), 200
strikes: articulated, 243–246, 254–255; as direct action, 115–120; as direct democracy, 221–222; and economic and political struggle, 13; Italian tactics, 243–246; post World War II, 241–242; and productivism, 210–213; as result of mechanization, 98, 101; spontaneous, 111, 153–156, 160–163, 217, 220, 238, 263n8; wildcat, 219–222, 235; and workplace bargaining power, 12; during World War II, 140. *See also* sitdown strikes; specific strikes
striking on the job. *See* direct action; sitdown strikes
structural power, 10–12, 144–146, 171, 244. *See also* associational power
student-worker coalitions in Italy, 244–245
sublime experience: and the IWW's vision of industrial unionism, 19, 133, 144, 165–166, 262n3 (chap. 3); mass workers as, 177–181, 261n1 (chap. 2); of modern factories, 63, 71–72, 84
SWOC (Steel Workers Organizing Committee), 200
symbolic mode of representation, 16–17
syndicalists. *See* IWW (Industrial Workers of the World)
syntax of speakers, 59–60

Tandt, Christophe Den, 178
Tate, Claudia, 263n9
Taylor, Frederick Winslow, 10, 23, 26–27, 35–41, 63
Taylorism, 23, 88, 213. *See also* Fordist-Taylorist factory system
technological representation: defined, 16–17; and degradation of mass workers, 64; in literature, 97–98. *See also* capital, representations of
Temper (Conrad), 66, 67, 88–98
textile workers, 98–103

theatrical representation, 122, 144–150, 158–159, 190
Thrasher, John, 265n17
To Make My Bread (Lumpkin), 264n11
Torigian, Michael, 5
Towne, Henry R., 25, 27
trade unions, 3. *See also specific unions*
Tronti, Mario, 1, 6, 20, 248–251, 365n4
Trumbo, Dalton, 184; *Johnny Got His Gun*, 20, 34, 54–57

UAW (United Auto Workers Union), 78, 140, 187–192, 236–237, 265n16

vanguardism, 246
variable wage rates, 251–253
Veblen, Thorstein, 8, 64, 103
vertical integration: defined, 24; and the Ford Motor Company, 71, 73; in literature, 205; and the meatpacking industry, 84; of production in Italy, 243; vulnerability of, 31, 107–110, 253–254; and wartime production, 241
Vogliamo tutto (We Want It All) (Balestrini), 239–240, 250–258
voice. *See* communication by mass workers
Vorse, Mary Heaton, 139, 190

wage incentive systems, 20, 37, 251–253

Wagner, Richard, 262n4 (chap. 3)
Wald, Alan, 5
Walking Delegate, The (Scott), 20, 122, 140–152, 159, 177
wartime powers, 241
"We are Coming Home, John Farmer..." (R. Chaplin cartoon), 116
Weatherwax, Clara, 184; *Marching! Marching!*, 34–35, 57–62
"We Build a Plant to Run without Men" (Smith), 260n3
"Why Manufacturers Dislike College Students" (Taylor), 36
wildcat strikes, 219–222, 235
Wobblies. *See* IWW (Industrial Workers of the World)
workplace bargaining power, 11–12, 111–113, 189, 208, 216, 232, 253
works management movement, 25–26, 29, 35, 42, 58, 71, 260n1 (chap. 1). *See also* Fordist-Taylorist factory system; scientific management
World to Win, A (Conroy), 205
Wright, Erik Olin, 10, 242
writing and writers: in novels, 151–181; role of, 149, 169–172, 201–204, 240, 251. *See also* journalistic representation

Zandy, Janet, 5

About the Author

William Scott is an Associate Professor in the Department of English at the University of Pittsburgh. His essays have appeared in *American Literature, Callaloo, CR: The New Centennial Review, MLN, ADFL Bulletin,* and *German Quarterly.*